AMERICAN CRISIS

"I am honored to be asked to write a few comments about this new book. I found *American Crisis: The Collapse of Christian Culture* to be well written, insightful, well researched, and enlightening."

REVEREND PAUL PAPAS

www.narrowpathministries.org

"America has long been something special among the nations. What a precious light to go out, and what a loss to the world if it should.

"Yet the values that made the American experiment not only the greatest wealth-building enterprise in history, but also the unique proponent of a previously unheard of freedom, are by no means vanquished. They existed prior to the state. And there are those who continue to carry them forward, handing the light to their children.

"In a time of deepening darkness in America, how do you find 'true north'?

"William D. Howard provides a stunningly detailed guide to what went wrong, where it's all headed, and how to navigate truth in a culture that increasingly perpetuates falsity.

"Beautifully researched, accessibly presented. I highly recommend *American Crisis*."

DOUGLAS KRUGER

author of *Poverty Proof* and *Political Correctness Does More Harm Than Good*

"In *American Crisis*, the author provides remarkable insight on politics, religions, and world cultures. This book will definitely raise your awareness of the key problems facing American society and the world."

E. J. MCKNIGHT

director of Together As One
a charitable non-profit, providing assistance
to the poorest of the poor in the Philippines

AMERICAN CRISIS

THE COLLAPSE OF CHRISTIAN CULTURE

WILLIAM D. HOWARD

Ambassador International

GREENVILLE, SOUTH CAROLINA & BELFAST, NORTHERN IRELAND

www.ambassador-international.com

American Crisis

The Collapse of Christian Culture
©2024 by William D. Howard
All rights reserved

ISBN: 978-1-64960-501-6, hardcover
ISBN: 978-1-64960-588-7, paperback
eISBN: 978-1-64960-545-0
Library of Congress Control Number: 2024931639

Cover Design by Hannah Linder Designs
Interior Typesetting by Dentelle Design
Edited by Katie Cruice Smith

Scripture taken from the King James Version of the Bible. Public Domain.

Ambassador International titles may be purchased in bulk for education, business, fundraising, or sales promotional use. For information, please email sales@emeraldhouse.com.

AMBASSADOR INTERNATIONAL
Emerald House
411 University Ridge, Suite B14
Greenville, SC 29601
United States
www.ambassador-international.com

AMBASSADOR BOOKS
The Mount
2 Woodstock Link
Belfast, BT6 8DD
Northern Ireland, United Kingdom
www.ambassadormedia.co.uk

The colophon is a trademark of Ambassador, a Christian publishing company.

This book is dedicated to the memory of the two finest people I have ever known,

Emily and Charles Howard.

Without their love and moral example, this book and my faith in God would have been impossible.

"A great civilization is not conquered from without until it has destroyed itself from within."

—Will Durant

TABLE OF CONTENTS

PREFACE

MY GENERATION, THE "BABY BOOMERS," and certainly my parents' "The Greatest Generation" lived their lives in two different cultures. The former was inherited from our colonial ancestors and the founding fathers of our nation. This culture is called Judeo-Christian. It put God, family, and country as the top priority. It was a culture where sexual modesty was respected and vulgarity, profanity, and obscenity were socially censured. It was a culture that insisted on the sanctity of human life and promoted charity and compassion in human relationships.

The second half of our lives have been lived in a different culture—a culture created for us by people who do not share the values or spiritual outlook of the first more traditional American culture. This new culture is a strange hybrid: part secular-humanist and part neo-pagan. America is now experiencing a cultural crisis based upon the conflicting values and aims of these two cultures. This culture war has been developing over the last sixty years of American history but has now reached a decisive turning point.

When I retired after a long career as an educator of history, philosophy, and world religions, I decided to write a book that would explain this cultural crisis: its causes, social effects, and what the probable long-term outcome would be in America. After eight years of research and writing, *American Crisis* is the result.

My personal history is also the product of these two cultures. I was raised in a loving Christian household and accepted Jesus Christ at an early age as my personal Lord and Savior. But like many young people who reached adulthood in the 1960s and 70s, I followed the road of the Prodigal Son. I left home to seek adventure and pleasure. On one occasion, I backpacked through Europe and slept in a cave on the island of Crete. I thank God my core values never changed. The loving, morally upright example of my parents and the early Christian teaching I never stopped believing in were irresistible magnets drawing me back to God and truth. *American Crisis* is my tribute to the life-saving qualities of Judeo-Christian culture and a warning of outer darkness which our nation is entering into by abandoning it.

—William D. Howard

ACKNOWLEDGMENTS

MY THANKS TO THE EDITORS and publisher of AmericanThinker.com for being the first national website to publish (as separate essays) the first four chapters of this book. From that small beginning, *American Crisis* began to take its first breaths of life and grow into what it is now. I must also express special thanks to my friend and colleague, Martin Doherty. He patiently read each chapter of the book, and based upon his intelligent insight and skillful pre-editing, *American Crisis* was born. I must also thank Donald Isaac and Wyne Karnath for their technical assistance taming the computer beast. Finally, I must not forget to thank some of my oldest friends, Jim Stehr and R.G. Edwards, who consistently encouraged me to not give up the good fight of writing.

—William D. Howard

INTRODUCTION

IN 1945, AMERICA ACHIEVED THE status of the greatest country on earth. It had already, for some time, been the greatest economic power on the planet. After four years of world war, we were recognized as the leader of the free world and the most admired country on earth. Our military, with the help of our allies, had both saved Old Europe from Nazi hegemony in the West and Japanese imperialism in the East. America was the only nation capable of resisting and containing the new enemy of global freedom: communism. But as great as these military and economic achievements were, America was also known for our "soft power"—love of freedom, insistence on the rule of law, and compassion for the weak and the poor.

To borrow Winston Churchill's famous phrase, "This was our finest hour." Since 1945, the United States of America has continued to scale new heights in military power, cultural influence, and economic growth. We are now the only nation to carry the label of Super Power.

Civilizations are never static. Like all life forms, they are constantly changing. They grow stronger or weaker. They are born, then age, then die. They may last over a thousand years, like ancient Rome or Egypt, but they all experience an eventual day of reckoning. The great American republic is no exception to this rule of world history. American civilization has never been in its past what it is today.

If one seeks a symbolic date for the fall of Judeo-Christian culture in America, it would be the official announcement made by President Obama on May 9, 2012. On that date, Obama proclaimed that he was in favor of homosexual marriage. The then-leader of America cited the thoughts of his pre-teen children as the conclusive masterstroke of reason that brought him to his new social and moral position. His open support for homosexual marriage was in opposition to a moral touchstone that had existed for thousands of years and was agreed upon by all the great religions of the world. A marriage that was upheld as a covenant between only one man and one woman was suddenly discarded based upon the whim of children who lacked both life experience and knowledge of the subject. Obama's use of his children was a perverse adaptation of Jesus' famous quote in Matthew 19:14: "But Jesus said, Suffer little children, and forbid them not, to come unto me: for of such is the kingdom of heaven."

If we seek an actual legal date for the fall of Judeo-Christian culture in America, it was June 26, 2015, the day the Supreme Court ruled that homosexual marriage was a constitutionally protected right. But cultural values are not replaced by a single act or statement. Long before the Supreme Court ruling on this issue, thirty-six states had already established the same right.

The great American historian Will Durant, nearing the end of his eleven-volume history of the world, *The Story of Civilization*, questioned "whether a moral code unsupported by religion could maintain social order." Durant's answer was we still "live in that critical experiment."[1] Over two hundred years before Durant struggled to answer that question, the European philosopher Joseph de Maistre wrote, "Nations have never been civilized except by religion . . . Religion accompanied the birth of all civilizations, and the absence of religion heralds their death."[2]

Durant was an agnostic, but he was an honest agnostic. His book *The Story of Civilization: Vol. 9* contains numerous statements extolling the positive influences of religious faith. Writing of religion, he states, "It

---

1   Will and Ariel Durant, *The Age of Voltaire, Vol. 9. The Story of Civilization*, Vol. 9 (New York: Simon and Schuster, 1975), 336.
2   Ibid, 4.

arises spontaneously and repeatedly from the needs and hopes of men . . . to moderate the barbarous impulses of men . . . the disruptive egoism and natural anarchism of men."[3] He was also wise enough to realize that science can never be an adequate replacement for religious faith, stating, "Science gives man ever greater powers but ever less significance; it improves his tools and neglects his purposes; it is silent on ultimate origins, values, and aims; it gives life and history no meaning or worth that is not canceled by death."[4]

The two main ways our present culture has departed from our past tradition are in its increasing disrespect for human life and its low level of sexual morality. If a poll were taken today of the world's population, America would be known for its rap music, increasingly violent and sexually explicit movies, hate-filled politics, and the different types of violence which permeate our society. The Judeo-Christian cultural foundation of America, which was established by our colonial ancestors and Founding Fathers, is no longer shared by most of our educational institutions, our cultural elites, and certainly not the mecca of movie-making Hollywood. We still have laws based upon our former culture, and we still have the Constitution, but they are standing naked against a freezing wind of secular humanism and the gleeful acceptance of neo-pagan values that increasingly fascinate America's public.

If the history of the world proves anything about the reason why civilizations self-destruct, it is their loss of morally disciplined family structures. Without these structures, peace and order soon begin to unravel. History provides many examples of what I call "cultural self-genocide." The process is always the same: honored values and religious beliefs that define a civilization for centuries suddenly become the topic of social and cultural ridicule. Other values or beliefs are accepted with little scrutiny and even turned into a culturally fashionable campaign. A wise, old Greek said thousands of years ago that "custom is king." Morals, traditions, and religious

---

3   Ibid.
4   Ibid.

beliefs are the real foundation of a civilization; and if that template is broken, violence and chaos will soon follow.

Americans are shocked by the terrible mass murders happening all too often, but we should not be surprised by why they are happening. Beginning in the 1960s, we began to give up our parental rights to those who create and control our mass-popular culture. Movies, TV, video games, and music are now the surrogate parents of our young.

Americans have mostly given up on traditional Judeo-Christian sexual morality. The results of this moral abdication are a steady increase in premarital sex, out-of-wedlock births, divorce, and single-parent families; but one thing that didn't rise was the percentage of religiously affiliated Americans who regularly attended religious services. The highpoint of religious practice in America was reached in the 1950s and since then has been in steady decline, but most alarming is the fact young adults make up the largest group of those who call themselves "non-religious."

Following these social and cultural trends, there has been an almost-steady increase in all types of violence. Mass murders are getting the big headlines, but there are many other types of violence that are exponentially greater. Violent crime quadrupled between 1960 and 1991.[5] The rate of suicide increased 33 percent between 1999 and 2017.[6] In America, there have been over sixty-one million abortions (and counting) since 1973, and human trafficking is growing in every state. Should we be surprised that the proportion of young people who are committing mass murder is increasing? Should we be surprised that the majority of these young people come from broken homes, and 85 percent of shooters are religiously non-practicing?[7] The elements

---

5   "The Worst Decades for Crime," World Atlas online, Accessed July 9, 2017, https://www.worldatlas.com/articles/which-decade-had-the-most-crime.html.

6   Holly Hedegaard, Sally Curtin, and Margaret Warner, "Suicide Mortality in the United States, 1999-2017," NCHS Data Brief, No. 330 (Hyattsville: National Center for Health Statistics, 2018), https://www.cdc.gov/nchs/products/databriefs/db330.htm.

7   Ken Lambert, "The Link Between Atheists, Agnostics and Mass Shooters," Catholic Business Journal online, 2018, https://www.catholicbusinessjournal.com/voices/contributors/ken-lambert/the-link-between-atheists-agnostics-and-mass-shooters/.

of national self-destruction are now in place. There seems to be a general foreboding among people of faith that America is a doomed civilization. The main questions are how did we get here, and is there anything that can change this self-destructive trajectory? There were earlier warnings. In the preface to his book, *The Story of the Christian Church*, first published in 1918, Dr. Lyman Hurlbut wrote:

> Never in all recorded history has there been a greater need for religion . . . Enlightened by knowledge gained through science— benefited by the strides in technocracy, modern man stands bewildered that good will on earth has never been further from accomplishment . . . Spiritual values have been torn up and cast about as if they were weeds preventing the growth of progress. The result is chaos.[8]

This book was published at the end of World War I, at that time the most destructive war in human history. For Dr. Hurlbut, it must have seemed that we were close to the biblical Apocalypse, the climatic stage in the downward spiral of world culture. But his book would be republished many times before that final stage would be reached. The world chaos he described was accurate, but there would be even greater benchmarks of human depravity yet to come, through Hitler, Stalin, Mao, Pol Pot, and many others.

Closer to our own time in history, Jean-Francois Revel observed and reported on the societal changes taking place in America during the 1960s to 1970s:

> The Revolution of the twentieth century will take place in the United States. It is only there that it can happen. And it has already begun. Whether or not that revolution spreads to the rest of the world depends on whether or not it succeeds first in America . . . Earth Day . . . in America was one huge pantheistic

---

8   Jesse Lyman Hurlbut, "Preface," in *The Story of the Christian Church* (Grand Rapids: Zondervan, 1970).

feast . . . The young men and women . . . in California walked naked through the forests, singing and playing guitars . . . We can therefore conclude that a counterculture . . . has already sprung up . . . a demand for absolute individual and cultural freedom, without moral censorship.[9]

Revel, a French Socialist, both welcomed these changes and was puzzled by the strange, cultural mix of Left-leaning politics and neo-pagan religious views. He was critical of the hippies for what he called "their nebulous ideology, which is a mixture of confused Orientalism and adulterated primitivism."[10]

What Ravel was witnessing in America was odd but not totally without precedent. The Roaring Twenties witnessed the same kind of outburst of youthful enthusiasm and rebellion. The 1920s and '30s were a period when American thinkers and writers flirted with Left-wing politics and countercultural themes. This period of American history combined many of the same sociological and ideological traits: a generational gap between young and old; a rejection of traditional Judeo-Christian sexual morality; and a radical change in the style of music, clothing, and hair. What Revel observed, if taken in the larger context of the history of Western civilization, was even less singular. It was just the newest in a long line of rehearsals before the collapse of Judeo-Christian culture.

Currently, the dominant culture in America and Europe is primarily pagan. The most recent Pew Research confirms a steady decline in Judeo-Christian religious affiliation and a steady increase in agnostic, atheist, and neo-pagan belief, especially among young adults.[11] America is not raising glorious new temples to pagan gods or engaging in the bloody sacrifice of millions of animals (or people). Still, the underlying values of our dominant popular culture are the same: pleasure, fame, power, and riches.

9   Jean-François Revel and J. F. Bernard. *Without Marx or Jesus: The New American Revolution Has Begun* (Garden City: Doubleday, 1971), 356.
10   Ibid, 354.
11   "Religions," Pew Research online, Accessed December 29, 2022, https://www.pewresearch.org/religion/religious-landscape-study/.

Except for the most recent period of modern history, Judeo-Christian culture had been in an ascending pattern of growth and had been the most significant and most positive influence on world civilization. Its age-old struggle for survival and development has always been against its two greatest enemies of secular humanism and paganism. Now the world must see what will come from this new, strange hybrid culture based upon the mutually contradictory beliefs of secular humanism and neo-paganism. The one thing we know they have in common is their deep hatred of Judeo-Christian beliefs.

Based upon a deep dive into world history and having examined both the destructive influence of secular humanism and paganism, it is my contention that the fall of Judeo-Christian culture will result in a catastrophe more destructive than any in human history—a catastrophe more significant than the rise of national socialism in Germany or communism in Russia. As disastrous as those past events were, we still had a strong Judeo-Christian civilization to thank for their defeat.

In like manner, the fall of the ancient Roman Empire opened the gates to barbarian savagery, which resulted in a Dark Age of lawlessness, ignorance, and economic poverty that lasted over five hundred years. It was the Christian church that provided the seed ground for the creation of a new Western civilization. This civilization would eventually promote an age of European discovery, the Scientific Revolution, capitalism, representative democracy, and the rule of law.

Whenever America (or Western civilization) has failed, it has always been when they have deviated from their core Judeo-Christian values and beliefs. These have been our template—our conscience. With the fall of Judeo-Christian culture in Western civilization, we will soon begin to witness another "Dark Age" in human morality greater than that which happened after the fall of Rome. It will be a greater social/moral collapse because, without Judeo-Christian culture, the source of civilized recovery will be lacking.

The salvation of the world will never be found in secular humanism or neo-paganism, which are, after all, the sources of the world's problems. Both individuals and civilizations require a moral/spiritual standard to live by, but not just any standard. It must be consistent with universal truth. It must be a standard which has withstood the test of time for thousands of years and has been proven effective within any cultural/racial/geographical context. Judeo-Christianity is that truth.

In this book, we will examine both the reasons why secular humanism and paganism have failed and the reasons why the Judeo-Christian culture has proven itself successful.

PART ONE
THE FALL OF JUDEO-CHRISTIAN CULTURE

CHAPTER ONE

THE STRANGE ALLIANCE: SECULAR HUMANISM AND NEO-PAGANISM

BEGINNING IN THE 1700S IN Europe, a strange and mutually contradictory alliance of intellectuals, artists, and writers made up what we now call the Enlightenment. Broadly speaking, the Enlightenment was a much-needed antitoxin against religious fanaticism, senseless wars, and the social/political injustices of that period. But as all social movements carry within them the seeds of ideological extremes, so did the Enlightenment. Secular humanism was one of these extremes and neo-paganism the other.

Instead of seeking to reform the Judeo-Christian religion and returning it to its original, humane beginning (as taught by the Gospel of Jesus Christ), the secular humanists of this period opted for the total elimination of religious faith. They saw religion as having a regressive influence on society.

On the other side of this ideological divide were the neo-pagans who wanted to return society to the worship of nature. The secular humanists were the dominant voices in this clash of theories, but the neo-pagans could claim the most famous writer of this period—Jean-Jacques Rousseau.

Rousseau began the modern cult of nature worship and promoted a view of morality based upon the standard of one's personal feelings. Rousseau's tremendous influence on both the French Revolution and the next cultural/ social movement known as Romanticism is well established by historians.

The eighteenth century used Rousseau's philosophy as the basis for its art, music, novels, and plays. He is considered the "godfather of Romanticism."

The debates we see in modern American culture today are the same that existed during the Enlightenment. We have the secular humanists who want to eliminate religious belief and another group of writers and thinkers who are promoting a "New Age" of nature worship. In one sense, they are natural enemies, but they each hold the Judeo-Christian tradition as the greater enemy. They share the main objective of ending what has been, until recently, the prevailing influence of Judeo-Christian culture.

Another thing they have in common is the tendency to reduce truth and goodness to human-sized standards. In the world they are working to bring about, each individual person is his own oracle, or as the once-prominent radical of the 1960s, Jerry Rubin, told us, "If it feels good do it."[12]

Rubin is an excellent example of the strange hybrid mix of pagan values, nature worship, and Marxist ideology. Based upon his own immature understanding of life and history and following the pagan credo of "feelings first," Rubin made wild statements that excited an ignorant youth culture of that day. This is why young voters today are carried away by the socialist rhetoric of Bernie Sanders, Elizabeth Warren, and Alexandria Ocasio-Cortez. Without an understanding of the lessons of history and without core values that have withstood the test of time, all people are subject to the sway of demagoguery.

Secular-humanists believe that a society can be highly moral and prosperous without people having religious faith, but a study of history has proven that it takes the inspiration of religious belief to maintain a high moral standard over a long period of time. The other great enemy of Judeo-Christian culture, the neo-pagans, talk a good game of peace, love, and healing-the-planet but continuously contradict this by attempting to undo the linkage between sexual morality and the sacredness of human life. Religious studies author Michael

12   Jerry Rubin, *Do It: Scenarios of the Revolution* (New York: Simon & Schuster, 1970).

F. Strmiska wrote, "In pagan magazines, websites, and internet discussion . . . Christianity is frequently denounced as an antinatural, antifemale, sexually and culturally repressive, guilt-ridden . . . authoritarian religion that has fostered intolerance, hypocrisy, and persecution throughout the world."[13]

Unfortunately for neo-pagans and secular-humanists, a statistical study of the world's different cultural regions proves that those parts of the world which have been most impacted and influenced by the Judeo-Christian tradition are the same areas of the world that are most prosperous and have the best record of human rights and democracy. In modern history, they also have experienced the least number of wars and genocides. Those who object to this view and point to the wars and genocides in Europe before 1945 must face the historical fact that Hitler's Nazi-German empire was based upon pagan values. Western civilization rejected those values and paid a high cost to defeat Hitler's racist empire.

The same is also true of secular-humanists who would promote a socialist or so-called "progressive" agenda; they must face the facts that the wars and mass-murder perpetrated by Communist Russia and China were the product of a violent off-shoot of secular humanism. The theory of Marxism was not an accident. It came out of the malevolent human mind of Karl Marx. He was a totally egotistical man who thought he knew more than all the religious teachers and moral philosophers who had ever lived. When you take God or Divine revelation out of the equation, you are only left with human philosophies; and some are more hate-filled and dangerous than others.

If one overlays a series of maps showing those regions of the world that today have the least degree of freedoms, have the most human rights violations, are the poorest, and have produced the most wars and refugees, one sees another common connection: they are the same regions of the world which historically have had the most enduring pagan cultures. Where there

---

13   Michael F. Strmiska, ed., *Modern Paganism in World Cultures: Comparative Perspectives* (Oxford: ABC-Clio, 2005).

are exceptions to this rule (e.g., Japan or South Korea), it can be explained by the fact that they have been highly influenced and reformed by the value system of Western civilization.

Despite the overwhelming historical evidence in favor of the positive influence of the Judeo-Christian tradition, secular-humanists and neo-pagans continue their tireless efforts to undermine and replace our American heritage with a new pagan foundation. Opinion polls on questions about sexuality prove that they have largely succeeded. In a piece published by the University of Chicago in 2013, Tom W. Smith stated the bottom line: "There has been an increase in sexually-permissive attitudes over the last four decades . . . with more approval of premarital sex, same-gender sex, gay marriage . . . and the legal access to pornography."[14]

These changes are not accidental. They are the by-product of the intentional efforts of a committed community of believers who are now in control of our mass-popular culture. President Obama's endorsement of homosexual marriage and the Supreme Court's narrow ruling in its favor were only the cherries on top, a white flag surrendering America's Christian values.

The American Psychological Association reported as early as 2001 that "68 percent of television shows during the 1999-2000 season contained sexual content."[15] A Kaiser Family Foundation report from 2011 found that between 1998 to 2005, the number of sex scenes on American television had doubled.[16] Another recent study showed that in the 1970s, there were only five homosexual characters presented on American television, but by the 2000s, there were 390.[17] The Atlantic reported that in 2011, "92% of Top Billboard

---

14   Tom Smith, "Attitudes Towards Sexual Permissiveness: Trends, Correlates, and Behavioral Connections," University of Chicago, January 1994, https://www.researchgate.net/publication/237440754.

15   R. Ballie, "Study Shows a Significant Increase in Sexual Content on TV." *American Psychological Association* 32, No. 5 (May 2001), 16. https://www.apa.org/monitor/may01/sexualtv.

16   "Number of Sex Scenes on TV Nearly Double Since 1998," Kaiser Family Foundation online, October 30, 2005. https://www.kff.org/other/event/sex-on-tv-4.

17   "List of Dramatic Television Series with LGBT Characters: 1960s-2000s," Wikipedia Foundation, last edited December 25, 2022, https://en.wikipedia.org/wiki/List_of_dramatic_television_series_with_LGBT_characters:_1960s%E2%80%932000s.

songs are about sex."[18] Chrysalis L. Wright, Ph.D. wrote in *Media Psychology Review* that "young adults listen to music between two and four hours each day . . . more than 1/3 of popular songs contain explicit sexual content and 2/3 of these references are degrading."[19]

The latest homosexual propaganda that has recently appeared on TV is an ad entitled "Beyond I Do." It presents two silent lesbians holding several small children and looking very content. The message is clear: gay marriage is not the end of the homosexual rights campaign but its beginning. The gay rights campaign is exactly that: a military-style campaign with both short-term and long-term objectives.

Homosexual marriage, once celebrated by Progressives as the capstone of gay rights, is now viewed by the same people as the cornerstone on which to build America's pagan future. Starting in the 2020 school year, the state of Illinois required its public schools to include LGBTQ history in their curriculum. Christians and Jews have, of course, been here before; and just as it was when in ancient Rome, they refuse to celebrate human carnage as sports entertainment or refuse to commit collective adultery and honor it by calling it "love-making," we must now refuse to accept the politically correct "new speak" of, "One Love."

The great author of *Animal Farm* and *1984* would, if he were alive today, easily recognize the language used by liberals as a form of propaganda. The words "gay" and "homophobia" are both insidious. Gay is a euphemism for a lifestyle that is anything but benign, and homophobia is especially insidious because its use transfers the sting of the abnormal to the normal. In an upside-down world of morality, the deviant becomes the normal.

---

18 Dino Grandoni, "92% Of Top Ten Billboard Songs Are about Sex," Atlantic Media Company, September 30, 2011, https://www.theatlantic.com/culture/archive/2011/09/92-top-ten-billboard-songs-are-about-sex/337242.
19 Chrysalis L. Wright and M. Craske, "Music's Influence on Risky Sexual Behavior: Examining the Cultivation Theory," *Media Psychology Review* 9, No. 1 (2015), https://mprcenter.org/review/musics-influence-on-risky-sexual-behaviors-examining-the-cultivation-theory.

Like America's culture today, ancient Rome set a very low bar for sexual morality. In ancient Rome, Jews and Christians faced the same type of smear campaign. Jews and Christians who lived morally correct lives were labeled "anti-social," even "lovers of death." In the end, they suffered for their beliefs, but it was pagan Rome that eventually collapsed under the weight of its own perversion. Pagan Rome promoted a harsh double standard in the treatment of women. With few exceptions, it licensed male promiscuity and allowed pederasty and rape of women and children who were enslaved.

Judaism raised the standard to a much higher level. It strongly condemned adultery, homosexuality, a husband forcing himself on his wife, and sex outside of marriage. Judaism produced the healthiest and most wholesome family life in the ancient world. Jesus, a Jew, raised the standard to an even higher level. His view was encapsulated in His statement, "Whosoever looketh on a woman to lust after her hath committed adultery with her already in his heart" (Matt. 5:28).

His statements, in general, implicitly condemned polygamy and easy divorce and made the only acceptable standard for human relationships, love. All of this raised the value of life and improved the treatment of women. Most importantly, Jesus' teachings linked the sacredness of human life with his teaching on sexual purity. By linking these two principles of Judeo-Christianity, it became impossible to pretend that rape, pedophilia, adultery, prostitution, and permissive sexuality were compatible with respect for life, either slave or free.

CHAPTER TWO

AMERICAN EXCEPTIONALISM UNDER ATTACK

FROM OUR BEGINNING AS A nation, our leaders took note of the symbiotic relationship between religious faith and stable government. American leaders such as James Madison, Ben Franklin, Thomas Jefferson, George Washington, and John Adams supported the inculcation of Judeo-Christian values through education. In 1789, the day after the establishment of the Bill of Rights, Congress passed a resolution calling for a day of national prayer. From the historical evidence, it is clear that Jefferson's "Wall of separation between Church and State" had a number of openings through which Judeo-Christian moral instruction was allowed to pass. Historian Paul Johnson stated, "The Founding Fathers saw education and religion going hand in hand."[20]

The Northwest Ordinance, which promoted the settlement of the frontier West, stated, "Religion, morality and knowledge, being necessary to good government . . . and the happiness of mankind . . . the means of education shall forever be encouraged."[21] Throughout most of American history, those means included moral training based upon Judeo-Christian sources. Washington wrote, "Of all the dispositions and habits which led to political prosperity, Religion and Morality are indispensable supports."[22]

---

20   Paul Johnson, *A History of the American People* (New York: HarperCollins, 1997), 209.
21   Ibid.
22   Ibid, 229.

A democratic society depends on a highly moral citizenry, but even more significant than that was the acceptance of the grander theme of American exceptionalism. This belief was fundamental to how Americans viewed their country from the beginning. It was the belief that America's role in the world is unique, idealistic, and constructive for the greater world's good. American exceptionalism implies a purposeful Creator.

The earliest examples of this American exceptionalism come from colonial times. John Winthrop's use of biblical language promoting "a city on a hill"[23] provided an enlightened example for the world, as did William Penn's "Holy experiment"[24] in religious toleration acted out in Pennsylvania. America's second president, John Adams, linked the two beliefs together, writing, "One of the great advantages of the Christian religion is that it brings the great principles of the law of nature and nations, love your neighbor as yourself, and do to others as you would that others should do to you."[25] Even America's most famous skeptic, Thomas Jefferson, said America was "the world's best hope." And during a very dark period of the American Civil War, Lincoln used similar language, saying that America was "the last best hope of the earth." Modern presidents like JFK and Ronald Reagan also promoted American exceptionalism.

Paul Johnson writes, "America had been founded primarily for religious purposes . . . There is no question that the Declaration of Independence was, to those who signed it, a religious as well as secular act . . . "[26] All of the following American historical documents declared faith in God and many specifically included a faith in Jesus Christ:

- The Declaration of Independence
- The Articles of Confederation
- The Mecklenburg Declaration

---

23   Ibid, 33.
24   Ibid, 64.
25   Ibid, 208.
26   Ibid, 204.

- Washington's First Inaugural Address
- Washington's Farewell Address
- The United States Constitution
- The First Charter of Virginia
- The Fundamental Orders of Connecticut
- Lincoln's First Inaugural Address
- The Emancipation Proclamation
- Lincoln's Gettysburg Address
- The Federalist Papers
- The Proclamation of Amnesty 1863

Beginning in the 1960s, an ongoing attack began from Progressives. They began to undermine the confidence of the American people in our great nation. They didn't believe the U.S. had a role to play in the world beyond a material or secular function. During the 1960s and '70s, America transitioned from the most admired country in the world to the most repudiated. The disaster of the Vietnam War served to fuel an angry counterculture led by Left-wing radicals. These new radicals were hybrids: half-Marxist and half-hippie. These were the "Greta Thunbergs" of the '60s and '70s, whose utopian visions were boosted by LSD.

Those who lived through this period can well remember the popularity of large wall posters featuring Marx, Mao, Castro, and Che Guevara. The ideological pedigree of the Left-wing movements of this period is even more certain. The Black Panthers were Marxist-Leninists; the Weathermen followed the teachings of Leon Trotsky; and the Free Speech movement found its inspiration in Chairman Mao, the communist leader of China. (Antifa and the reverse-racist movement known as Black Lives Matter are modern examples of Left-wing activism.)

Progressives scoff at the notion of America as a Christian nation. In one sense, they are correct. Faith, especially the Christian faith, is a matter of free choice. The great Protestant reformer Martin Luther said it best over five hundred years ago: "As a man must die by himself, he must believe by himself."[27] Part of the belief in American exceptionalism means promoting religious toleration as well as all the other basic human rights in which Americans believe. Christians are not a nation of believers. They are believers that inhabit many nations, but what is historically certain is the claim that Judeo-Christian moral/spiritual values have been America's dominant culture from the beginning.

For atheists, agnostics, and secular humanists, all religions are created equal. They believe that they are equally mythological (a product of human imagination). Secular humanists can accept universal truths in any field of knowledge except morals or religion. For them, if someone promotes an absolute, universal, and timeless concept of religion, they see it as an act of bigotry and small-mindedness.

In their attack on America today, the Progressives (like all Leftists) emphasize a materialist agenda with big government as the preferred agent of change. Their point of view is agnostic at best and atheistic at worst. Like the atheist scientist Carl Sagon, who marveled at the fact that there are "billions upon billions of stars," Progressives reduce the importance of mankind when compared to a vast universe. They have no place for God in that vast universe.

American exceptionalism implies a purposeful Creator, and secular humanists flee from the thought of Divine purpose. The problem with downsizing America's purpose and our Judeo-Christian values is that it leaves little motivation for our nation to resist hateful ideologies and authoritarian governments in our future. The leadership of totalitarian governments are full of implacable men who believe in implacable ideologies. Marxism and Nazism had no problem motivating millions of people to die for their evil causes. Today, ISIS and the Taliban have no problem motivating suicide attacks.

---

27   "Martin Luther Quotes," BrainyQuote online, Accessed November 16, 2022, https://www.brainyquote.com/authors/martin-luther-quotes.

The English philosopher Bertrand Russell wrote, "Rationalism and anti-rationalism have existed side by side since the beginning of Greek civilization."[28] What this means for the future of the world is that there will always be wars and conflicts, always challenges and revolts against the humane, civilized conduct of human life. A civilization, like individual people, needs to have something to believe in beyond the mundane.

The Progressives are busy chipping away at the confidence of our great nation to play a meaningful role in the future of the world, and by undermining the belief in American exceptionalism, they are leaving us with a superficial value system that can neither protect us or improve the life of the world.

---

28   Bertrand Russell, *In Praise of Idleness and Other Essays* (London: Allen and Unwin, 1976), 68.

CHAPTER THREE

THE FUTURE OF AMERICA: PEERING INTO THE LOOKING GLASS OF EUROPE

WHEN NOTRE DAME CATHEDRAL BURNED in 2019, it was symbolic of a greater European-wide collapse of religious faith which had already taken place. That great cathedral, like most of the others in Europe, had long since passed from being a vibrant community of active worshippers to an architectural showpiece attracting millions of tourists taking photographs.

If America wants to know its grim future, it only needs to consult the facts of present-day European society. What must be understood are the characteristics of this new post-Judeo-Christian Europe. What does the sociological data tell us is happening there?

Sociologists, psychologists, and historians agree on one point: the family unit is the basis of all societies. The present European family is in a state of crisis. As much as we lament America's high divorce rate of 53 percent, Europe's is higher, in some countries reaching 60 percent. But worse than the high divorce rates are the high out-of-wedlock birth rates and the vast increase in single-parent families.[29]

The *Max Planck Society* published the following in 2016: "The significance of marriage slowly started to decline as early as 1970, a process linked to the advance of secularization in many countries . . . By 1990, the share of unmarried

---

29   "Families Unmarried." Max-Planck-Gesellschaft online, April 21, 2016, https://www.mpg.de/10451277/unmarried-families.

births had already increased fourfold . . . In many parts of northern and western Europe, there are already more births out of wedlock than births within marriage."[30] The exact process is taking place in America. We are moving in the same direction as Europe but at a slower pace. The difference is that America's religious attendance was much higher than Europe's when the process started.

The process which has brought about the death of Judeo-Christian culture in Europe is now being replicated in America. If we begin with a comparison of religious practice, the surveys of American society show a number between 37 percent and 22 percent of Americans who attend weekly services.[31] The average of these numbers is below 30 percent—the lowest in modern American history. But if you are a person of faith in Europe, you would be celebrating this as the sign of a "great religious revival." The average church attendance for the countries of Northern Europe is 4 percent. There are only three countries in Europe where more than 10 percent of young people attend religious services on a weekly basis.[32]

French philosopher Alexis de Tocqueville, who visited America in the 1800s, took note of America's highly religious, national character as compared to European society. He knew the horrors into which French society was plunged as a result of extreme, anti-religious sentiment. From the earliest days of American history, religion played an outsized role. Even during the 1700s, when it was intellectually fashionable for some of our leaders, like Thomas Jefferson, to scoff at supernaturalism and prefer deism to theism, they still held tightly to the moral and spiritual truths expressed in the Holy Bible.

Some of our early political leaders could do without a belief in miracles in general but not the necessary miracle of a Creator God Who had established

---

30   Ibid.
31   "Why Americans Go (and Don't Go) to Religious Services," Pew Research Center's Religion & Public Life Project. Pew Research Center, August 1, 2018, https://www.pewresearch.org.
32   Jonathan Evans and Chris Baronavski, "How Do European Countries Differ in Religious Commitment? Use Our Interactive Map to Find Out," Pew Research Center, December 5, 2018, https://www.pewresearch.org/fact-tank/2018/12/05/how-do-european-countries-differ-in-religious-commitment.

an unchanging moral order. The history of the world is littered with failed revolutions that promised to remake their societies in a better image. The American Revolution is among the few that have succeeded. The bad news is that we are no longer on the same path. We have opted for the European social model. The last sixty years of American history reveal that we are on a new path. It is a path that leads away from freedom and individual responsibility. It is a path that mistakes vice for freedom and socialism for progress, and because European societies began this journey before us, we can now see our future in their present.

The fact that European societies are still relatively prosperous and orderly, despite their social demographic changes, is proof of the lasting influence of religious faith. No society will collapse immediately. In Europe these social changes are now showing themselves in a variety of dark statistics.

The crisis in the European family is rapidly becoming a mental health crisis. The most recent large-scale study of 514 million Europeans found that mental illness had increased to 38 percent.[33] And based on World Health Organization statistics, Europeans commit suicide more often than the people of any other region of the world. Russia has the highest rate, followed by other eastern European nations—all of which were, until recent years, ruled by communist governments that viewed religion as taboo. Following these Eastern European nations, the most secular parts of Western and Northern Europe have the next highest rates of suicide. The more traditional and culturally conservative parts of Europe have the lowest rates of suicide.[34] America is lagging behind Europe but making great strides to catch up. The CDC reported in 2018 that America now has the highest rate of suicide in fifty years.[35]

In Europe, this is not just a problem of highly depressed people wanting to end their lives. There is a concerted effort on the part of medical

---

33 Kate Kelland, "Nearly 40 per Cent of Europeans Suffer Mental Illness," Thomson Reuters, September 6, 2011, https://www.reuters.com/article/uk-europe-mental-illness-idUKTRE7832KL20110905.

34 "Suicide Worldwide in 2019," World Health Organization, June 16, 2021, https://www.who.int/publications-detail-redirect/9789240026643.

35 "Facts about Suicide," Centers for Disease Control and Prevention, last revised October 24, 2022, https://www.cdc.gov/suicide/facts/index.html.

professionals to assist others in doing so. Belgium now carries the label of "world's euthanasia capital," even allowing suicide by lethal injection for children.[36] Following the same guiding principle of utility, Europe is now number four on the list of continents that carry out the most abortions. The fact that the primary victim of an abortion is an unborn child without a voice makes the problem easier to ignore.

Much harder to ignore is the explosion in human trafficking taking place in Europe. The Department of Homeland Security has described the problem of human trafficking as a "modern day form of slavery . . . among the world's fastest growing criminal industries."[37] *BusinessLine* reported in 2019 that "children now account for 30 per cent[sic] of those being trafficked . . . Trafficking for sexual exploitation is the most prevalent form in European countries."[38]

Three of the top ten countries where sex tourism takes place are located in Europe, and all the others are located in poor, less-developed regions of the world. In America, the same thing is now happening. Feminists, pro-homosexual rights advocates, and cultural celebrities are using terms like "pansexual," "gender fluidity," and "One Love" to begin the major re-education of American society.

The Europeans have both imagined and are realizing this "brave, new world" and the "new morality" look a lot like the "old immorality." The imagined-utopian welfare state of Europe is now being realized for what it is: a dystopian society where the soul of humanity dies and selfish appetites reign. In America, we are faithfully re-tracing the European steps, which include the death of faith, the death of the family, and the dehumanization of mankind.

---

36   Cecilia Rodriguez, "Euthanasia Tourism: Is the E.U. Encouraging Its Growth?" Forbes online, March 17, 2019. https://www.forbes.com/sites/ceciliarodriguez/2019/03/17/euthanasia-tourism-is-the-e-u-encouraging-its-growth/.

37   PTI, "Human Trafficking Takes 'Horrific Dimensions' in Europe: UN." The Hindu BusinessLine online, January 8, 2019, https://www.thehindubusinessline.com/news/variety/human-trafficking-takes-horrific-dimensions-in-europe-un/article25942442.ece.

38   Ibid.

PART TWO
THE DESTRUCTIVE POWER OF MYTH

CHAPTER FOUR

FEAR EXALTED

WHEN MYTH IS SEEN FROM the Age of Science as imaginative literature, it is fascinating. But for thousands of years, myth was not viewed as a charming story. For the pagan world, it was an explanation of reality.

Most human beings who lived during prehistoric, ancient, and medieval times suffered under its cruel dictates. Pagan systems of thought favored the group-over-individual free thought. Where these mythological systems were dominant, they suffocated rational discovery, invention, and science. They decided on the issues of war and peace. They controlled not only the moral/spiritual realm of behavior but also the political, social, economic, and cultural aspects of human life. They propped up and perpetuated systems of injustice and promoted a general state of mental illness characterized by acute anxiety, paranoia, and panic. Overall, they can be described as a straitjacket on the development of humanity. Beliefs such as universal morality, objective truth, social/political progress, and the belief in free will were an abomination to those in power.

Today, when people use terms like superstition, magic, or mythology, they do so without the fear of the context in which these beliefs were once believed and practiced. To the modern mind, these terms have been neutered of their toxic essence; conjuring up mythological ideas seems exciting and harmless. Mythology today is called "quaint" or "charming" and is seen as lacking the power to cause harm. But pagan belief systems still harm the lives of millions, if not billions, of people today in Africa, Asia, Latin America, and the Pacific Islands.

Current statistics on religious belief show that pagan mythology is making a significant comeback in both Europe and America. The two most prevalent mythological systems of the twentieth century—Nazism and communism—were responsible for more than one hundred million deaths.

Wikipedia describes paganism as "a term used in the fourth century by early Christians for people . . . who practiced polytheism . . . modern pagan religions . . . express a world view that is pantheistic, polytheistic, or animistic."[39] Under the title of the *History of Modern Paganism*, the BBC states:

> Paganism has grown in popularity greatly during the last hundred years. The growth coincides with a decline in Christianity in Europe . . . It was not until 1951 that the first practitioners of modern-day witchcraft became known . . . The 1960s and 1970s were times of radical social change . . . the hippie trail led people to become interested in Eastern religions . . . Paganism found an ally in the ecological and feminists movements of the 1960s.[40]

Beliefs that had been discredited by science for over five hundred years are now making a major comeback. The growing shoots of a new culture are beginning to reveal what is hidden beneath the soil in both Europe and America. Paganism clusters around a variety of names: neo-paganism, occultism, Wiccan, and esotericism. All these beliefs are part of a worldwide movement. Its nomenclature dazzles with a considerable number of nonsensical permutations, but its core beliefs remain the same.

What links all these diverse belief systems are their fundamental tenets: worship of nature, moral relativism, truth as subjective, and a magical world in which magic is used to fulfill one's needs and desires. The prophetic

---

39 "Paganism," Wikipedia Foundation, last modified December 25, 2022, https://en.wikipedia.org/wiki/Paganism.

40 History of Modern Paganism," BBC online, last updated October 2, 2002. https://www.bbc.co.uk/religion/religions/paganism/history/modern_1.shtml.

gardeners of this new culture are making many false claims to a gullible world raised on *Harry Potter, Outlander,* and *Twilight*. Like the gnostic charlatans that lived during first century Christianity, they are promising ever-expanding personal powers and special, mystical insights to their true believers.

A major flaw in these new versions of paganism is their false belief that because primitive/pagan peoples worshipped nature, they must have necessarily lived in a more harmonious relationship with it. The problem with this hypothesis is that the thousands of taboos that regulated their lives were all based upon fear. The level of irrational fear which characterized primitive/pagan thought can only be viewed as pathological.

The wisest and most advanced thinkers in the ancient world knew this. People like Plato, Socrates, Aristotle, Confucius, and Buddha stand out as examples of enlightened minds which promoted the use of reason and logic to attack either directly or indirectly the fear-causing and morally confusing mythologies of their cultures. The ancient Roman poet/philosopher Lucretius summed up the issue when he wrote, "Fear was the mother of the gods . . . to so many evils religion has persuaded men."[41] The Greek word for superstition literally meant "fear of the gods." It was impossible for people's relationship with nature to be harmonious because the nature they knew through mythology was thought to be teeming with a multitude of unpredictable, capricious, malicious gods, goddesses, demons, or lesser spirits that cared little or nothing about their welfare. Any interruption in the usual nature pattern was viewed as a spirit-directed terrorist attack. The Greek poet Homer expressed the common view of the gods when he wrote, "We men are wretched things, the gods, who have no care themselves, have woven sorrow into the pattern of our lives."[42]

What is called "worship of nature" was really the worship of imaginary, supernatural personalities that pagans believed controlled nature. Because

---

41 "Lucretius," Quoteslyfe, Accessed October 26, 2022, https://www.quoteslyfe.com/quote/Fear-is-the-mother-of-all-gods-830238.

42 Homer, "Book 24," in *The Iliad*, translated by Barry B. Powell (New York: Oxford University Press, 2014).

of their personalized view of nature, people's attitudes about it were highly variable. Throughout all primitive/pagan cultures, there are many examples of inanimate objects or simple life forms that were viewed as evil or dangerous— things like mountains, forests, rivers, caves, winds, animals, plants, and rocks. Entire regions of the earth, like northern Europe, and celestial bodies such as the moon, Saturn, and Mars were viewed by some cultures as evil.[43] What complicated this world of fear was their belief that spirits could shapeshift to take on different bodily forms, metamorphizing from plant to animal, from animal to animal, and from animal to man. In their world, there was no such thing as inanimate objects. Everything that existed was alive and had a personality and a spirit. They even gave their weapons and tools personal names.

This was a tricky world in which to live, with many snares and pitfalls to navigate. In paganism, there was no distinction between the objective and subjective world. Interestingly, this distinction is what makes science possible; rational, modern minds fear the destructive power of earthquakes, tornados, and forest fires, but we don't hate them as if they are alive and spiritual. We don't believe they are personally out to get us, have a malicious intent, or act to harm us based upon premeditation.

Far from having peace of mind, the priests of ancient Egypt performed magical rites each day to ensure that the sun would rise.[44] The Aztecs carried the same fear to a hysterical level and sacrificed hundreds of thousands of people annually to the sun god to prevent the end of the world.[45] In many less bloody cultures, people feared being born on unlucky days, months, or years, all of which could result in being put to death. Common were the beliefs that there were "water spirits" that caused storms at sea, "underground spirits" that caused earthquakes, and "spirits in the air" that caused storms on land. All the horrific acts of human sacrifice, bodily mutilation, and cannibalism

---

43   Cavendish, 80, 82, 126-7.

44   James George Frazer, *The Golden Bough: A Study in Magic and Religion* (London: Penguin Books, 1996), 94.

45   Michael Harner, "The Enigma of Aztec Sacrifice," *Natural History* 86, No. 4, April, 1977, 46-51, https://www.latinamericanstudies.org/aztecs/sacrifice.htm.

were required to rebalance their relationship with nature or the spirits they believed controlled nature.

Writing of the great variety of fears that plagued the pagan world, Richard Cavendish states in his book *The Powers of Evil*, "The times of maximum vulnerability are when you start to do something and when you finish it . . . evil gathers around the childbed and the deathbed . . . around wedding . . . around ploughing and harvesting . . . The threshold of a house . . . midday and midnight."[46] A common practice found in many primitive/pagan cultures was the attempt to expel the demons that they believed infested their lands. In his book *The Golden Bough*, James G. Frazer provides these examples: "The people of Bali . . . have periodic expulsions of devils upon a great scale . . . the priest issues orders to expel them by force, lest the whole of Bali should be rendered uninhabitable."[47] He also writes, "Annual expulsions of demons, witches or evil influences appear to have been common among the heathen of Europe."[48] On the Gold Coast of West Africa, "When an epidemic is raging . . . people will sometimes turn out armed with clubs and torches, to drive the evil spirits away."[49]

Upon this fundamental layer of irrational fears can be added all the normal fears pagan cultures associated with old age, pain, and death. They had a belief in an afterlife, but it provided little comfort. For most pagan cultures, the afterlife was viewed as a place of continual suffering: a miserable place where both the good people and the bad experienced the same types of torments. Those who were still alive had to protect themselves from both unknown, evil spirits and the spirits of their deceased family and tribal members. Burial or cremation was not so much about respect or care for the dead but a way to prevent their souls from returning to this life. Richard Cavendish writes, "Anyone who was not buried could not enter the underworld and stayed in this world as a menace to the living, and those who were buried but subsequently

---

46   Cavendish, 232.
47   Frazer, 357-671.
48   Ibid.
49   Ibid.

neglected would become famished with hunger and might return to this world and roam the streets . . . attacking people."[50]

Their great fear of the dead grew over time and was expressed in large social festivals. In ancient Athens, this was called Anthesteria, a time when the ghosts of the dead crowded the city. In ancient Rome, it was the festival of the Compitalia; in other parts of Europe, it was Hallowe'en or All Souls Day. Trick-or-treating was not originally about fun and games but a time when angry souls roamed the earth seeking to revenge themselves on their negligent descendants.[51]

The fears which plagued these people's minds were not just personal problems but also bled into the fabric of society and produced social conflict. Their belief in magic contributed to general paranoia and suspicion of others. Their belief in a magical world whose outcomes could be controlled by magical means caused tribes and civilizations to employ it to harm others. Fear and suspicion led to a perceived need for retaliation or even a preemptive strike against others who might use magic against them.

Based upon these fears, pagans were very careful with the disposal of their hair cuttings or the parings of their fingernails. If someone else got ahold of things like these, they believed they could be used in a magical way to harm them. Frazer gives an example of this when he writes, "The Tahitians buried the cuttings of their hair at the temples."[52] A person's spittle, teeth, and footprints were also used in magical rites to harm or kill. In many pagan cultures, a person had both a common name and a secret name. Their constant fear was that someone would learn their secret name and use it against them.

With the development of civilization, this climate of fear did not change. The general, pervasive fear that pagan religions promoted led to larger wars, conquests, and enslavements. The building and support of their ever-larger

---

50   Cavendish, 36-38.
51   Ibid, 50, 116.
52   Frazer, 281-84.

temple complexes required an increasing labor force. Growing ranks of priests and priestesses had to be maintained, and increasing wealth was necessary for the sacrificial gifts that were offered to their greedy, selfish gods.

Pagan religious leaders had no problem with sanctifying or promoting the conquest and enslavement of other people. They were, after all, the prime beneficiaries of the spoils of war. The population of ancient Rome's slaves was between twenty-five to forty percent. In ancient Athens, it was forty percent. These were the types of urban communities which had the most extensive temple complexes. In Ancient Egypt, the following pharaohs left recorded statements that proudly announced contributions of slaves who had built various temple complexes: Thotmose III, Amenhotep III, Rameses II, and Seti I. Pharaoh Rameses III himself provided 113,000 slaves.[53] A partial list of the offerings of Pharaoh Rameses III included the following:

> 228,380 jars of wine . . . 1,075,635 amulets . . . 355,084 bricks . . . 285,385 cakes . . . 1,933,766 jars of incense . . . 6,272,421 loaves . . . 20,602 oxen . . . 50,877 robes . . . 1,663 golden vases . . . 113,433 slaves . . . 493,386 head of cattle . . . 5,279,652 sacks of corn . . . 353,719 geese . . . 331,702 jars of incense, honey, and oil . . . 2,382,605 fruits . . . 466,303 jugs of beer . . . 494,000 fish . . . 19,130,032 bouquets of flowers.[54]

In Egypt, as well as all the other pagan civilizations, there was no single, morally perfect, benevolent God Who was believed to be the Father of the entire human race. There was no pagan god that required all people to be treated with respect and love. Pagan gods and goddesses were competitive, selfish, dishonest, lustful, and cruel. They were bigger-than-life but not better than the people who imagined them, and above all, they were vengeful and demanded human blood.

Essentially, truth matters, and false beliefs have consequences in every field of knowledge, including religion. People living today generally associate

---

53   Adolf Erman, *Life in Ancient Egypt* (New York: Dover Publications, 1971), 299.
54   Ibid.

religions with moral instruction or acts of charity, but for thousands of years before Judeo-Christianity, it promoted immorality and aggression toward others.

CHAPTER FIVE

THE CHEAPNESS OF LIFE

IN WESTERN CIVILIZATION AND OTHER parts of the world that have been reformed and influenced by its culture, there is still, generally, a pro-life tendency. This is not true in the case of protecting the unborn; but after babies are born, at minimum, they are viewed as having some rights as a human being. Any search in an old-fashioned phone book or the modern internet will reveal a plethora of secular or religious public service and charitable institutions offering help to those in need. It is common to find services offering to help the blind, the mentally ill, the suicidal, the hungry, and the disabled, as well as help for abused women and children. Internationally, there are many organizations that campaign in favor of human rights, against torture, capital punishment, and to end poverty. This is primarily a by-product of the influence of Judeo-Christian culture.

In the pagan world, none of this existed. Poverty was a general fact of life. They viewed it as a condition decreed by the gods. In like manner, the blind or disabled were viewed as being punished by the gods for their sins or their parents' sins. Often, they were disposed of at birth or left to beg to support their continued existence. The mentally ill were in a different category. They were either viewed as having a "special gift from the gods" or being possessed by an evil spirit, for which they would be put to death.

The pagan world cared little about the rights of women or children. They could be abused, raped, sold into slavery, and even put to death based upon the whim of their fathers or husbands. Far from a moral and pro-life culture, paganism was pro-death. Until the triumph of Judeo-Christian culture, suicide was even valued as one of the few rights which all people had.

The pagan world was a world where life was cheap. There were no international organizations promoting the common interests of all humanity. These couldn't exist because there was no universal standard used to judge right and wrong. The criteria the pagan world used were unique to each culture and based upon the mythologies and gods of those cultures. If fear was the primary characteristic of paganism, its primary result was the cheapening of human life. In an essay entitled "Priests," published in the famous *French Encyclopédie* of the 1700s, Baron von Holbach describes both how power shifted to a pagan priesthood and its results: "Superstition having multiplied the ceremonies . . . persons conducting the ceremonies soon formed a separate order . . . the priests depicted the gods as cruel, vindictive, implacable . . . human blood flowed in great streams over the altars; the people, cowed with fear . . . thought no price too high to pay for the good will of the gods."[55]

What Baron von Holbach described was both accurate and universal. This was the only cultural pattern that existed in the world before it was challenged by the Judeo-Christian tradition. Judaism was the first to *literally* raise a prophetic voice against it. It was out of this Jewish culture and sharing the same enlightened ideas that a rapidly spreading Christianity would maximize this prophetic voice and, in time, overturn the dominance of pagan culture in the later period of the Roman Empire. Buddhism and Confucianism were ethical systems of philosophy that also challenged these pagan values, but they were, within a short period of time, absorbed or co-opted into a mainstream culture that remains, even today, largely pagan. The founders of Buddhism and Confucianism never claimed to be gods, nor did they intend that people would worship them.

---

55   Baron von Holbach, "Priest," in *Good Sense Without God* (London: W. Stewart & Co, 1772).

As late as the sixteenth century, in another part of the world—
Mesoamerica—ultimate acts of ritual, human sacrifices were still taking
place. In A.D. 1487, the Aztecs dedicated a new temple in their capital city
of Tenochtitlan, and up to eighty thousand people were sacrificed over
a four-day period. The Aztecs believed their rain god required the tears of
children to make rain. Based upon this belief, they tortured and sacrificed
large numbers of children. When they planted their cornfields, they offered
infants and sprinkled their blood on the ground. Anthropologist Michael
Harner estimated that during the fifteenth century, the Aztecs sacrificed
250,000 people per year.[56]

The old liberal view, which new research has now debunked, held that
the Aztecs were an aberrant, *sui generis* culture, meaning that their beliefs
and practices were unique in Mesoamerica. In terms of the scale of human
sacrifice, this is true, but in terms of the practice of human sacrifice in general,
it is not.

In 2018, *National Geographic* reported on the most significant single site
containing the remains of sacrificed children in Peru.[57] The Phoenicians,
a much older Middle Eastern culture, were also notorious for sacrificing
children. At one of their sites, archaeologists have found the remains of
twenty thousand children.[58] From Chile in the South to Canada in the North,
the general pattern of Native American life included continual intertribal
warfare, torture, enslavement, and at least some human sacrifice. Child
sacrifice was a widespread practice of many American tribes: the Natchez,
Timucua, Creeks, Potomacs, Dakota, Pawnee, Pueblo—to name a few.[59]

---

56   Harner, ibid.
57   Kristin Romey, "Exclusive: Ancient Mass Child Sacrifice in Peru May Be World's
     Largest," National Geographic online, April 26, 2018, https://www.nationalgeographic.
     com/science/article/mass-child-human-animal-sacrifice-peru-chimu-science.
58   Katelyn DiBenedetto, "Analyzing Tophets: Did the Phoenicians Practice Child
     Sacrifice?" Honors Thesis, (University at Albany, 2012). https://scholarsarchive.library.
     albany.edu/honorscollege_anthro/5/.
59   William Christie, "Child Sacrifice in North America, With a Note on Suttee," *The
     Journal de la société des américanistes* 23, No. 1 (Société des Américanistes, 1931), 127-38,
     https://www.jstor.org/stable/24601335.

Almost every primitive culture or pagan civilization that we know of carried out ritualistic human sacrifice. Like the wars and enslavement which feed it, human sacrifice was one of many ways in which pagan culture minimized the value of human life. Long before the Aztecs achieved their status of being the supreme ritual/serial killers in human history, another highly advanced civilization was perfecting mass murder through single and group combat.

Like so many of their achievements, the Romans borrowed their gladiator games from the earlier civilization of the Etruscans and then increased their use on a large scale. The Circus Maximus could provide space for 180,000 spectators, and the deadly events that took place there could last several days. Sometimes, as many as ten thousand combatants took part. The Romans applauded, cheered, and eagerly anticipated the next exhibition of human and animal slaughter.[60] These were mega events in which Roman culture celebrated its dominance over other cultures. Like all pagans, they honored their gods the only way they understood that their gods could be honored: with food, drink, and violent entertainment. There were, of course, exceptions among the pagan Romans themselves.

The stoic philosopher and statesman Seneca wrote, "I come home more greedy [sic], more cruel and inhuman because I have been among human beings . . . where man a sacred thing . . . is killed for sport and merriment."[61] Seneca, like the Buddha in India and Confucius in China, was a sharp critic of the paganism of his day and the immorality that it fostered in daily life. The ancient Christian writers, St. Augustine and Tertullian, both admired Seneca and thought of him as a "pre-Christian" Christian.

Seneca's answer to Rome's problem of cultural degeneracy was to spread Stoicism, a philosophy that viewed all people as equally human and deserving of respect. The problem with this strategy is that philosophy only affects the lives of a few highly educated intellectuals; most common people

---

60   Will Durant, *Caesar and Christ*, Vol. 3, *The Story of Civilization* (New York: Simon & Schuster, 1972), 360.
61   Ibid, 387.

would remain untouched. The philosophy of Stoicism was in advance of its time, but, unlike the Judeo-Christian tradition, it could not bring about a deep, heartfelt, and personal transformation that could affect the majority of ordinary people. It could not overthrow the cruel dictates of paganism and become the basis of a new civilization.

Over time, most of the world's civilizations began to wean themselves from the practice of large-scale human sacrifice. Mostly, where it continued, it was limited to periodic responses to crisis situations: war, disease, and starvation. The large-scale sacrifice of animals became the new norm. In primitive cultures and in civilizations that were more isolated from other societies, it continued on a large-scale—Mesoamerica, Africa, South America, and the remoter parts of Asia and the Pacific Islands. The ancient Greeks and Romans would eventually sneer at the practice of human sacrifice as brutal, but as a whole, their civilizations did not become kinder or gentler.

The "glory that was Greece and the grandeur that was Rome" that Edgar Allen Poe wrote about was primarily the product of the conquest and enslavement of others. Their pagan value system would remain selfish and narrowly ethnocentric until successfully challenged by the growing influence of Christianity. Athenian society can be admired for its creativity and diversity of thought but not for its humanitarianism.

Historian Will Durant writes of their lack of compassion: "They are seldom altruistic to any but their children; conscience rarely troubles them, and they never dream of loving their neighbors as themselves . . . law and public opinion accept infanticide . . . The children of slaves are seldom allowed to live."[62] Romans not only exhibited the same callousness toward the suffering of others, they also seemed to have delighted in finding new ways of turning the suffering of others into entertainment. They maintained unique markets which sold a great variety of disabled people that could be purchased for amusement.

---

62 Durant, *Vol 2*, 293-94.

The ethnocentric view that the Greeks and Romans held was not the exception but the rule of world history. This cruelty and selfishness were a universal feature of both pagan civilizations as well as primitive societies. Long before the early civilizations were conquering and enslaving each other, primitive tribes were practicing these same patterns of behavior. The primitive tribes were the first ethnocentric people. Some Native Americans referred to themselves as "the Only Men," others as "Men of Men," or "We alone are people.[63]

On the other side of the world, the ancient Japanese were being told, based upon their creation mythology, that they were a special people who had descended from their sun goddess, Amaterasu. One of their famed teachers stated the difference between the Japanese and other people this way: "The gods who created all countries . . . were all born in Japan . . . Foreign countries were . . . not . . . which is the cause of their inferiority."[64] These myths, which were the basis of their religion Shintoism, were used by the Japanese to justify their conquest of the other parts of Asia during World War II.

Thousands of years before World War II, the Chinese had drawn a map of the world and had labeled it "the Middle Kingdom." In their view, China was located in the center of the world. All of the other people of the earth constituted a peripheral outer ring of lesser beings. Like all pagan cultures that lacked a concept of universal morality, and they spent little time worrying about the needs of others. This is, of course, most true of China's present, single-party, communist dictatorship. It allows no questions of universal morality to curb its appetite for expansion or total political power.

In ancient India, the creation mythology of the Vedas was used in the same way to justify their discriminatory caste system. Millions upon millions of people were labeled "Untouchable." The caste system, in general, produced what became a social, political, and economic straight-jacket on India's

---

63   Will Durant, *The Ancient World*, Vol. 1, *The Story of Civilization* (New York: Simon and Schuster, 1976), 54.
64   Ibid.

development. The Brahman caste were the Hindu priests who invented this mythology and, not surprisingly, placed themselves at the top of this rigid social system.

Throughout the long period of primitive societies and pagan civilizations, those whose lives were most devalued were women and children. In Japan, China, Africa, India, Egypt, and pagan Europe (e.g., Vikings), if a man died, his wife was expected to follow him to the grave. If that husband was also a king, many hundreds and even thousands of others were expected to make the same dark, sacrificial journey.

In China, male children were valued higher than females because their religion said that only sons could offer the necessary sacrifice to honor their ancestors. The value of a female child was expressed in one of their ancient songs: "How sad it is to be a woman! Nothing on earth is held so cheap . . . No one is glad when a girl is born . . . When she grows up she hides in her room, Afraid to look a man in the face.[65]

In many cultures, mythology has been used to justify the cruel dominance of one group over another. In the final analysis, each religious belief system can only be judged based upon what it teaches and the practical effects of that religion when practiced. Jesus warned His followers to "Beware of false prophets, which come to you in sheep's clothing" (Matt. 7:15).

After almost two thousand years, we have an excellent sample with which to judge Judeo-Christianity, and with five thousand years of pagan belief and practice, we have more than enough to judge paganism. The modern enemies of Judeo-Christian culture and Western civilization are constantly carping about America's historical sins, ethnocentric mindset, and exclusivity. But the truth is that Western civilization is the most multicultural civilization in the world. Its dynamic capitalism and global trade, beginning with fifteenth-century exploration, opened it up to the influences of the wider world. Based upon this increased knowledge of a bigger world, Western civilization also

---

65   Fu Hsuan "Woman Song," Third Century China, Public Domain.

started to think in universal terms. Unlike the isolated cultures of Africa, Asia, and the pre-Columbian Americas, Western civilization produced a truly outward-looking civilization in terms of geography, culture, astronomy, economics, philosophy, and religious belief.

The sins and atrocities of Western civilization deserve criticism, but they must be viewed within the context of a dynamic, evolving society that has lasted fifteen hundred years and has proven to be both self-critical and reform-minded. Judeo-Christianity provided Western civilization with a conscience—a moral compass—with which to judge its performance. Often that conscience was troubled; but it was still there to nag on ethical, social, economic, and political reform. What did not exist among primitive societies or pagan civilizations until much later in history was any concept of individual human rights. There were no 911 or community hotlines to report the abuse of women or children. Before the influence of Judeo-Christianity, these primitive societies or pagan civilizations did not demonstrate a progressive, self-critical, reform-minded, humanitarian culture.

It is not surprising that in Africa, Asia, and the Pacific Islands, it was Western civilization's influence that ended the slave trade and human sacrifice.[66] The modern European and American practices of slavery were short-term crosscurrents that had many critics even during its highpoint. Slavery was a crosscurrent that ran counter to Western civilization's main historical course. If there had been no exploration and colonialization in the Americas by Europe, there would not have been a catalyst to bring about a more progressive, humanitarian direction in that region of the world. A strong, unified, and free United States of America in the future would never have existed. There would have been no USA to provide a tremendous economic and military counterweight, to prevent Hitler's racist Nazi empire, Stalin's

---

66   John Oldfield, "Abolition of the slave trade and slavery in Britain," British Library online, February 4, 2021, https://www.bl.uk/restoration-18th-century-literature/articles/abolition-of-the-slave-trade-and-slavery-in-britain#:~:text=This%20occurred%20first%20through%20the,trade%20once%20and%20for%20all.

Soviet-Communist empire, or Japan's "Empire of the Rising Sun" from taking over the earth in the 1940s and '50s.

If we start with the big topic of modern genocide, thirteen out of the top fifteen countries listed are located in Asia, Africa, Latin America, or the Middle East. The exceptions to this rule were Hitler's Holocaust and Stalin's genocide against the Ukrainians. As previously stated, Nazism was based upon neo-pagan values, which glorified war and the dominance of others. Stalin's genocide was based upon atheistic Marxism. Both philosophies rejected the moral/spiritual values of Western civilization, and both were defeated by a combination of countries that shared Judeo-Christian values.

In an article published in *BusinessInsider.com*, Will Martin writes that the "28 most dangerous countries in the world . . . are concentrated in Africa and the Middle East."[67] Confirming Martin's analysis, the International Crisis Group reported in 2018 that "there were at least 77 worldwide out-breaks of crisis concentrated mainly in North and Central Africa and the Middle East and Asia."[68] Clans and castes are sociological holdovers from pagan culture.

Tribalism is the natural enemy of the belief in universal truth, values, and humanity. It is a vestige of the pagan belief in multiple gods or spirits unique to each tribe. In an article published by Penn State in 2017, Barbara Mcginnis explains that "tribalism is considered the curse of . . . Africa . . . Tribalism is the cause for the failed attempts at ethnic cleansing, authoritarian regimes, and political corruption."[69] As stated before, it is women and their children who have suffered the most under pagan culture. Any summary of the effects of the devaluing of human life must include the increasing amount of sexual assault and child abuse, which is most prevalent in these same regions of the

---

67   Will Martin "The 28 Most Dangerous Countries in the World," Business Insider online, June 29, 2018, https://www.businessinsider.com/most-dangerous-countries-in-the-world-global-peace-index-2018-6.

68   Robert Malley, "15 Years of Tracking Conflict Worldwide," International Crisis Group, September 3, 2018, https://www.crisisgroup.org/content/15-years-tracking-conflict-worldwide.

69   Barbara Callie Mcginnus, "African Tribalism," Penn State University, April 19, 2017, https://sites.psu.edu/global/2017/04/19/african-tribalism.

world. In the Rwandan genocide alone, it resulted in up to one million dead and up to five hundred thousand women raped.

In 2018, *The Straits Times* reported a list of the ten most dangerous countries in the world for women in order of rank:

1. India
2. Afghanistan
3. Syria
4. Somalia
5. Saudi Arabia
6. Pakistan
7. Congo
8. Yemen
9. Nigeria
10. U.S.[70]

Because many of these countries are in active war zones, one would expect all types of violence against women and children to be high. Other studies excluding war zones have found "Latin America is the world's most violent region for women."[71] The World Health Organization reported that the three regions of the world with the most intimate partner violence against women were Southeast Asia, the Middle East, and Africa.[72]

The growing criminal activity we call human trafficking (a.k.a. modern slavery) plays a significant role in the abuse of women and children. According

70   Martin, ibid.
71   "Home, the Most Dangerous Place for Women, with Majority of Female Homicide Victims Worldwide Killed by Partners or Family, UNODC Study Says," United Nations: Office on Drugs and Crime, Accessed October 27, 2022, https://www.unodc.org/unodc/en/press/releases/2018/November/home--the-most-dangerous-place-for-women--with-majority-of-female-homicide-victims-worldwide-killed-by-partners-or-family--unodc-study-says.html.
72   "Violence against Women," World Health Organization, Accessed August 31, 2022, https://www.who.int/news-room/fact-sheets/detail/violence-against-women.

to an article published in *worldatlas.com* by John Misachi, those countries most involved in human trafficking were: Equatorial Guinea, Eritrea, Iran, Afghanistan, Turkey, Iraq, Pakistan, United Arabs Emirates, North Korea, Central African Republic, Mauritania, Saudi Arabia, Syria, Algeria, Papua New Guinea, Russia, Venezuela, Kuwait, Libya, Sudan, Yemen, Zimbabwe, Belize, Burundi, Cuba, Haiti, and Laos.[73] In 2017, the International Labor Organization estimated the number of victims to be almost twenty-five million and more than half of these victims were sex slaves.[74]

As previously discussed in chapter two, if one overlays a series of maps showing those regions of the world today which have the most human rights violations, have produced the most wars and refugees, and are responsible for the most sexual assault and human trafficking, one sees a shared connection. They are the same regions of the world that historically have had the most enduring pagan cultures.

---

73   John Misachi, "Worst Countries for Human Trafficking Today," World Atlas online, January 17, 2019, https://www.worldatlas.com/articles/worst-countries-for-human-trafficking-today.html.
74   "Global Estimates of Modern Slavery: Forced Labour and Forced Marriage," International Labour Organization, September 19, 2017, https://www.ilo.org/global/publications/books/WCMS_575479/lang--en/index.htm.

CHAPTER SIX

RELIGION AS MADNESS AND VICE AS VIRTUE

THE CLEVELAND CLINIC DEFINES A delusional disorder as "a type of serious mental illness in which a person cannot tell what is real from what is imagined."[75] Primitive societies and pagan civilizations developed into what are prime examples of mass delusion. Not only were they unaware of the laws of nature, they also substituted, for natural laws, a system of mythological fantasy. Because almost all the people in specific cultures shared the same delusional beliefs, their abnormality was seen as normal by the majority.

As we saw in chapter five, pagan people suffered greatly from chronic anxiety caused by irrational fears. It is now an established medical fact that anxiety can trigger delusional thoughts, and delusional thoughts can, in turn, produce anxiety. Research has shown that one of the side-effects of both anxiety and delusional thought is an increase in hallucinations. Today, in regions where pagan belief still holds sway, psychological research shows this correlation.

In an article published by Oxford University Press entitled "Culture and Hallucinations," authors Laroi, Luhrmann, and Woods state, "Euro-American cultures dampen the rate of hallucinations because the . . . culture strives to clarify and distinguish whether a given experience is real or imaginary . . . In contrast many non-western societies do not make such a rigid distinction

---

75 "Delusional Disorder: Causes, Symptoms, Types & Treatment," Cleveland Clinic online, Accessed October 18, 2022, https://my.clevelandclinic.org/health/diseases/9599-delusional-disorder.

between reality and fantasy . . . studies have found that non-western cultures experience more hallucinations.[76]

Anthropological literature provides many examples of what they call "Culture-Specific Disorders." They list bizarre forms of mental illness associated with primitive societies such as Amok, Latah, Imu, Koro, Tromba, Piblokto, and Witiko. To use only one example, Witiko "takes the form of a homicidal spree during which the individual may kill and eat members of his family. He believes that he is possessed by a spirit . . . the "Witiko."[77]

Less specific are several general ways in which pagan cultures have contributed to mental illness. The three that stand out are child-rearing practices, the use of social sanctions, and the high level of stress related to the fear and violence which permeated these cultures. In cultures where brutalizing children and women were normative and where harsh social sanctions against women still exist for menstruation or not being able to produce children, widespread mental disorders are inevitable. A report by the Center of Mental Health and the NIH stated that "cultural and social context weigh more heavily in causation of depression . . . the evidence points to social and cultural factors, including . . . violence playing a greater role in the onset of major depression . . . PTSD is a mental disorder caused by exposure to severe traumas such as genocide, war . . . torture or extreme threat of death or serious injury."[78] This is precisely the cultural context in which the primitives and pagans lived.

English philosopher Bertrand Russell said, "The attempt to escape from pain drives men . . . to self-deception, to the invention of vast collective

76   Carla Moleiro, "Culture and Psychopathology: New Perspectives on Research, Practice and Clinical Training in a Globalized World," *Frontiers in Psychiatry* 10, No. 9, (2018), https://www.frontiersin.org/articles/10.3389/fpsyt.2018.00366/full.

77   Carina Coulacoglou and Donald H. Saflofske, "Advances in Theoretical, Developmental, and Cross-Culture Perspectives of Psychopathology," *Psychometrics and Psychological Assessment* (Cambridge: Academic Press, 2018).

78   "Chapter 2: Culture Counts: The Influence of Culture and Society on Mental Health," in *Mental Health: Culture, Race, and Ethnicity: A Supplement to Mental Health: A Report of the Surgeon General* (Rockville: Substance Abuse and Mental Health Services Administration, 2001), https://www.ncbi.nlm.nih.gov/books/NBK44249/.

myths."[79] What Russell didn't say is that this attempt was a complete failure. Where primitive or pagan culture existed, the threshold of pain and mental confusion increased. Much of this confusion was related to their identity.

The earliest mythologies attempted to explain their existence based upon the belief in totemism. Britannica.com defines totemism as a "belief in which humans are said to have kinship . . . with a spirit being, such as an animal or plant.[80] The tribe believed that their primordial ancestor was some type of animal or plant which they looked to for protection and spiritual guidance. It is a common belief found among many primitive cultures and, in time, was incorporated into the religious thinking of the early pagan civilizations.

Writing about the religion of ancient Egypt, Adolf Erman explains that each town had its own god/goddess which "were supposed to show themselves to their worshippers in the form of some object . . . The form chosen was generally that of some animal."[81] In ancient Rome, the founding of the city was linked to the myth of Romulus and Remus, who were saved by being suckled by a she-wolf.

In India today, there are Hindu-built temples for snakes, rats, and crocodiles. Their fundamental belief in reincarnation is not only that a man or woman at death would be reborn into another human form but potentially into another animal form. Anthropologist James Frazer explained this difference in thought between the modern and the primitive: "the sharp line of demarcation which we draw between mankind and the lower animals does not exist . . . many other animals appear as his equal or even his superior."[82] Some of the tribes of Madagascar trace their descent from crocodiles and consider them brothers. The American Cherokee Indians did everything in their power to avoid killing the rattlesnake. The Iroquois traced their heritage from the first women who had mated with bears or wolfs. Some of the tribes

---

79   Russell, *In Praise*, 37.
80   *Encyclopedia Britannica*, s.v. "Totemism," accessed October 18, 2022, https://www.britannica.com/topic/totemism-religion.
81   Erman, 299.
82   Frazer, *The Golden Bough*, 638.

in the Pacific Islands said they were the offspring of eels, wild pigs, serpents, turtles, or dogs.

None of these beliefs were prompted by a benign love of nature, animals, or plants. Their hyper-reverence was born out of deep fear and confusion about the natural world. They paid a heavy price for the protection and wise counsel they thought their totems would provide. If we use the law of the Cherokee as one example, it stated that "all human disease were imposed by animals in revenge for killing and each species had invented a disease with which to plague man."[83] According to Frazer, "The primitive hunter who slays an animal believes himself exposed to the vengeance either of its disembodied spirit or of all the other animals of the same species."[84]

Totemic belief encouraged a strong sense of guilt and fear. The neo-pagan or the radical environmentalist would most likely applaud these pantheistic beliefs as being scrupulously eco-friendly, but in reality, these are the actions of deeply neurotic individuals. Modern psychiatry attempts to relieve individuals from irrational guilt complexes, but pagan mythology encouraged them.

The belief in totemism was an impediment to humanity's moral development. Instead of engaging in rational self-examination that all moral philosophy and healthy religion promotes, totemism led man down a blind alley of nonsense and magic. On the metaphysical level, rocks, trees, and snakes were valued as much as human life. This pantheistic belief system swallowed up any attempt at moral improvement or personal responsibility. If all of nature is alive and filled with souls, from the smallest insect to the largest whale, the significance of human life is diminished. The sacred cat or cow is equivalent to or greater than Abraham Lincoln, Socrates, Buddha, and even Jesus Christ. In that kind of world, all the noble deeds that any human being had ever done would be diluted in an ocean of un-differentiated beings.

---

83   John Reid, *The Law of Blood: The Primitive Law of the Cherokee Nation* (Northern Illinois University Press, 2006).
84   Frazer, ibid.

With animals as mankind's moral guides, there are only a few lessons that could be learned. First is a fierce will to survive, and last is loyalty to their group. Beyond these basic instincts, humanity needed other role models to help them progress to a higher stage of morality and spiritual thought. No matter how long man studied the movement of foxes, the flights of birds, or the crawling of a spider, a higher truth would be unattainable. Unfortunately, the religions of the first civilizations did little to improve the moral understanding of humankind.

Their creation mythologies, almost without exception, provided gods and goddesses that were as flawed as those who imagined them.

As was written earlier in this book, the wisest philosophers and religious thinkers of antiquity knew that paganism was a dead system of evil thought. Writing toward the end of the fourth century A.D., the great philosopher and churchman St. Augustine described the subtle linkage between the destructive power of pagan myth and the moral confusion that it was causing in ancient Rome:

> Woe is thee, thou torrent of human custom! Who shall stand against thee? . . . How long roll the sons of Eve into that huge and hideous ocean . . . Did not I read . . . of Jove the thunderer and the adulterer? . . . These were Homer's fictions, transferring things human to the gods . . . attributing a divine nature to wicked men, that crimes might be no longer crimes, and whoso commits them might seem to imitate . . . the celestial gods.[85]

What Augustine calls the torrent of human custom is what we today call "mass-popular culture" and includes movies, TV, music, novels, and plays. Drip by drip, day by day, year after year, generation after generation, we have replaced Judeo-Christian culture with neo-paganism. Our history is reversing the trend that started in the ancient pagan world when Christianity

---

85   St. Augustine, *Confessions* (New York: Everyman's, 1975) 15-16.

overcame paganism and founded a new culture and civilization based upon its values and beliefs.

The early identity confusion promoted by totemism was magnified even more in the elaborate mythologies developed by the first civilizations. Everywhere we study the evidence (Asia, Africa, Europe, and the Americas), the gods and goddesses were consistently inconsistent when it came to moral or humane behavior. According to Hesiod's *Theogony*, which explained the origin of the Greek gods, the gods were mostly a product of a series of crimes: "Earth gave birth to Uranus, the starry sky, to be her mate and by him had children . . . Uranus hated his children and prevented them from being born . . . In pain and resentment Earth . . . incited her sons to attack their father . . . The older brothers were afraid, but Cronus . . . castrated Uranus . . . triumphant Cronus had children by his sister, Rhea and these were the Olympian gods."[86]

In pagan mythology, creation is often the by-product of some unintended action, confusion, or sin. In Egyptian mythology, the sun god Ra is deceived by his unfaithful wife Nut; and as a result, Osiris, the god of the Nile, is born. Osiris is tricked into having sexual relations by one of his sisters. Horus, the son of Osiris, cuts off his mother's head; and Set, the god of the west wind, murders his brother Osiris. The Babylonian creator-god Apsu is murdered by his children.

In the same way, the mythologies which explain the existence of the human race are often the product of chance, mistakes, cruelty, and selfishness on the part of the gods. Greek mythology tells us that the king of the gods, Zeus, destroyed the Titans with a thunderbolt and from their ashes made man.[87] In Aztec creation mythology, one sees their early attempt to justify their obsession with human sacrifice. Their god Quetzalcoatl throws his son into a fire to create the sun. Their god, Taloc, does the same thing to create

---

86   Hesiod, *The Homeric Hymns and Homerica*, Vol. 57, Trans. by Hugh G. Evelyn-White (London: William Heinermann, 1914).

87   Hesiod, *Theogony*, translated by Martin L. West (Oxford: Clarendon Press, 1966).

the moon.[88] Hindu creation myth explains the human race as the by-product of the incestuous mating of the god Brahma and his daughter.

Far from providing mankind with moral clarity or a guiding light of truth, ancient mythologies unsettled the human mind with unnecessary fears, magical hopes, and inconsistent or confusing examples of morality. The philosopher Plato criticized the religious practice of his day, writing, "Prophets go to rich men's doors and persuade them that they have a power committed to them of making atonement for their sins or those of their fathers by sacrifices or charms . . . and persuade not only individuals but whole cities."[89]

The primary function of pagan priests was not to teach or promote moral behavior but provide magical solutions to life's problems. The famous Egyptian *Book of the Dead* contained magical rites that could be used to deceive the gods into thinking a person had lived a better life than they had. This was essentially the same purpose that Plato had described. What we call vice today in the pagan world was acceptable or, worse, viewed as an act of virtue.

From the earliest civilizations of Egypt, Sumer, Phoenicia, and Greece, antiquity temple prostitution was a common feature. Aphrodite, the Greek goddess of love and motherhood, was worshipped in conflicting forms. She was viewed as both sacred and profane. In Athens, she was honored by prostitutes who gave the money they earned to the temple priests. In Egypt, where the most popular gods took animal form, women were sometimes offered to animals as mates.[90] In his book *Crete & Pre-Hellenic*, Donald Mackenzie states that in Babylonia, "the oldest deities are indistinguishable from demons."[91]

We can add to this schizophrenic view of the gods a hefty dose of confusion related to their sexual identity. Isis, Ishtar, Adonis, Baal, Shiva, Mithra, Nannar, and Zeus are examples of gods and goddesses being

---

88   Anothony S. Mercatante, *Good and Evil: Mythology and Folklore* (New York: Barnes & Noble, 1978), 164.
89   Donald A. Mackenzie, *Crete & Pre-Hellenic* (London: Random House, 1996), 48.
90   Erman, 260.
91   Mackenzie, ibid.

double-sexed. This general confusion about morality caused pagan cultures to believe that evil was eternally necessary. This belief produced a fatalistic attitude about sin and life in general. The Egyptian priests even had a name for this belief; they called it "the secret of the two partners."[92]

We see this hopelessness expressed in many pagan cultures. In Viking mythology, the entire world is waiting on its destruction. Their gods were as hopeless as the people who worshipped them. They believed there would be one last battle, evil would triumph over all their gods, and the world would be destroyed. Aztec and Hindu mythology foretold recurring cycles of destruction and recreation. In Sophocles' famous Greek play *Oedipus at Colonus*, the message was that we would be better off never being born or at least dying young.[93]

Major offenses that we view with horror today (e.g. murder, rape, kidnapping, incest) were once considered venial and, in many cultures, praised as acts of courage and daring. The Japanese Samurai warrior had to follow a strict code of conduct, but if he felt disrespected by any member of the lower class, he could kill them on the spot. One of the best examples of morality turned upside-down is found among the pagan Vikings. In their culture, heroic violence and savage cruelty eclipse all other virtues. The reward of a pleasurable afterlife only belonged to the most violent and cruel. The main prize, which they imagined for those who would enjoy an afterlife, was the continuation of violence. In Viking myth, those who were judged as "insufficiently violent" were the ones punished and who spent the afterlife in a freezing environment ruled over by the goddess Hel.[94]

Periodically, in both primitive societies and pagan civilizations, immoral group activities were promoted as acts of worship. These "festivals of license" sanctioned sexual promiscuity and acts of violence. In ancient Rome, this

---

92   Mercatante, 19.
93   Cavendish, 68.
94   "Hel (The Underworld)," Daniel McCoy, https://norse-mythology.org/cosmology/the-nine-worlds/helheim/.

holiday was called the "Saturnalia," and in Greece, the "Aphrodisia." In primitive societies and some civilizations, human sacrifice was also part of this activity.

Even within this general context of immorality and confusion, there were still some cults that stood out for their degree of mania or mental derangement. Among the Greeks, the most socially disruptive was the cult of Dionysus. Dedicated to the wine god, it consisted of group drunkenness, and at its high point, violence was directed against either an animal or a person. Will Durant describes it this way: "The . . . center of their ceremony was to seize upon a goat, a bull, sometimes a man . . . tear the live victim to pieces . . . then drink the blood and eat the flesh . . . they thought, the god would enter them and possess their souls."[95]

Richard Cavendish explains, "There are clear parallels between [the rites of Dionysus] and those which medieval witches were believed to celebrate. Central to both is the belief that the divine is achieved through the letting loose of the ravening animal in human nature and the consequent reversal of conventional standards."[96] Both are examples of religion as mania and irrational activity unleashed by powerful emotions. In the cult of Dionysus, the emotions raised to a fever pitch are directed toward the homicide of an innocent victim. In other cults, the hysteria aroused resulted in an attack upon the self.

There were several pagan mystery cults that promoted self-mutilation and were popular in the ancient Roman Empire. One of these was the worship of Cybele, a goddess of fertility, and Attis, her consort. James Frazer described the highpoint of this worship: "the twenty-fourth of March, was known as the Day of Blood: the high-priest drew blood from his arms . . . the inferior clergy whirled about in dance . . . into a frenzy of excitement

---

95 Will Durant, *The Life of Greece*, Vol. 2, *The Story of Civilization* (New York: Simon and Schuster, 1939), 190.

96 Cavendish, ibid.

. . . they gashed their bodies . . . on the same Day of Blood . . . the novices sacrificed their virility."[97]

In another example, he describes the worship of the Syrian fertility goddess Astarte as follows: "While the flutes played, the drums beat, and the eunuch priests slashed themselves with knives, the religious excitement gradually spread like a wave among the crowd of onlookers . . . man after man . . . flung his garments from him, leaped forth and shout, and seizing one of the swords . . . castrated himself on the spot."[98]

In psychiatric language, this type of religious mania is known as "hyper-religiosity" and is sometimes found in people who suffer from schizophrenia and bipolar disorder. It is safe to say that when the emotional highpoint of religion is expressed in either homicide or self-mutilation, there is clearly something wrong with that religious belief system.

Geoffrey Abbot sums up some of the purposes behind these acts of self- mutilation: "In antiquity and prehistoric cultures ceremonial whippings were performed in rites of initiation, purification, and fertility . . . Floggings and mutilations were sometimes self-inflicted. Beatings inflicted by masked impersonators of gods or ancestors figured in many Native American initiations."[99]

Other forms of pagan self-torture, which are making a popular return to Western civilization and can be traced back over five thousand years, are scarification and tattooing. Kenneth Michael Felsenstein writes of the practice of scarification, "Scarification draws its roots from tribal primitivism . . . Perhaps the most obvious examples of this are . . . tribes of Africa and the western Pacific . . . It has been seen in many tribes as a cathartic purging of bad spirits from the body and a medium for connecting to higher beings."[100]

---

97 Frazer, 420.
98 Ibid.
99 Geoffrey Abbott, *Encyclopedia Britannica*, s.v. "Flagellation," accessed October 18, 2022, https://www.britannica.com/topic/flagellation.
100 Kenneth Michael Felsenstein, "Scarification harmful cultural practice or vehicle to higher being?" *Hektoen International Journal*, February 28, 2017, https://hekint. org/2017/01/27/scarification-harmful-cultural-practice-or-vehicle-to-higher-being/.

Tattooing is a more colorful and elaborate form of scarification. The original purpose behind tattooing was to provide magical protection against evil spirits. It was a common practice in the Indo-Pacific region of the world and was associated with headhunting. In ancient Rome and China, it was a form of punishment for criminals and enslaved people. Its rapid spread in today's modern culture is the perfect symbol for the fall of Judeo-Christian civilization and the rise of neo-paganism.

For multiple millennia, human beings have lived, suffered, and died believing in irrational mythologies. In the next chapter, we will examine the empowered systems of mind control that prevented the development of human rights in the ancient, pagan world and yet still delay its development in a large portion of the earth today.

CHAPTER SEVEN
MIND CONTROL AND ANTI-HUMAN RIGHTS

IN OUR CURRENT HIGHLY PARTISAN age of politics when states are color-coded red or blue and news is labeled fake, spun, or complete lies and propaganda, we are all too familiar with the danger of mass-public opinion being manipulated. This sense of danger is heightened by our awareness of historical examples of mind-control practiced by Nazi Germany and Communist Russia and the ongoing attempts of modern totalitarian states like North Korea, Iran, China, and Cuba.

For thousands of years, pagan theocracies exercised a stranglehold on free thought and, as a consequence, prevented the development of individual human rights. In Edith Hamilton's classic study of ancient Greece, *The Greek Way*, she explains why the ancient Athenian Greeks developed a political democracy while the other early civilizations didn't. She concluded that all other pagan societies, unlike the Greeks, were ruled by theocracies and were under the tight control of a powerful caste of priests backed up by the absolute authority of a pharaoh or priest-king who was considered at least part god.[101]

In the mythology of the first river valley civilizations (Egypt, Babylon, India, and China), gods and goddesses were born and ruled in a constantly shifting state of intrigue and conflict, but on earth, their human servants and regents spoke with one unified voice of absolute control. The majority

---

101   Edith Hamilton, *The Greek Way* (New York: Discus/Avon, 1973), 13-18.

of Greeks were just as superstitious and foolish in their thinking as other pagan cultures, but they did not have god-kings or armies of meddling priests to determine their everyday actions or politics. This left their best minds some space for free thought; and out of this free thought came philosophy, literature, and science for which they are now famous. But we should not over-estimate their degree of freedom or human rights. Socrates, who was required to drink poison in 399 B.C., provides the perfect example of the limits of Athenian freedom. His accusers claimed that his philosophy was an act of "refusing to recognize the gods recognized by the state."[102]

The direct democracy developed by the Athenians was unique in the ancient world but very limited in who possessed these human rights. Only a few Athenian Greeks took part in their democracy, and their entire society rested upon the backs of a large class of enslaved people. Before most adult humans could exercise fundamental human rights, the world had to experience a moral/spiritual revolution more extraordinary than any before or since in human history. This revolution would be based upon the belief in the equal sacredness of all human life. It was Judaism which provided that understanding, and Christianity was responsible for its rapid spread. Until this historical change took place, there were pagan parents who were willing to sacrifice their children's lives to satisfy a monstrous concept of God.

One example of this was the Incan prayer uttered before such a sacrifice: "Oh Lord, we offer thee this child, in order that thou wilt maintain us in comfort, and give us victory in war."[103] Such sacrifice was not the random act of a crazed individual or small cult; it was a required act mandated by those who ruled over these societies.

Most of these pagan civilizations were theocracies ruled by powerful priests and a monarch who claimed personal divinity. The distinguished professor of history, Herbert J. Muller wrote of this oppressive system

---

102 Bertrand Russell, *History of Western Philosophy* (Chicago: Touchstone, 1972), 87.
103 Victor Wolfgang von Hagen, *Encyclopedia Britannica*, s.v. "Inca Religion," accessed October 18, 2022, https://www.britannica.com/topic/Inca-religion.

of government, "Everywhere men were governed by an absolute monarch, who was an agent of the gods, when not himself a god, and who was supported by the priesthood . . . the ruling principle . . . was absolute obedience . . . as a divinely ordained institution, it was immune to searching inquiry or criticism."[104]

Durant agreed with Muller, stating, "The individual was hardly recognized as a separate entity."[105] In the scholar Isaiah Berlin's essay on "Liberty," he supports the same view: "there seems to be scarcely any discussion of individual liberty as a conscious political ideal . . . in the ancient world."[106] The great theologian Reinhold Niebuhr explains, "An irrational society accepts injustice because it does not analyze the pretensions made by the powerful and privileged groups of society."[107]

Contrary to the often-romanticized view of primitive societies being freer than civilizations, Durant writes, "In general the individual has fewer 'rights' in natural society . . . The primitive individual moves always within a web of regulation . . . a thousand taboos restrict his action, a thousand terrors limit his will."[108]

According to Muller, in ancient India, there was not even a word for "freedom" nor in ancient China a word for "rights."[109] Ancient Egypt lasted thousands of years without major cultural change. The same can be said of ancient China and India. The leaders of each of these pagan civilizations claimed their social order was established by the gods. The rulers of Egypt called this social order "Maat." The ancient Hindus called it "Dharma," and

---

104 Herbert J. Muller, "Freedom and Justice in History," in *Freedom: Its History, Nature, and Varieties* by James A. Gould and Robert E. Dewey (London: MacMillan, 1970), 17.
105 Durant, Vol. 1, 29.
106 Isaiah Berlin, "Two Concepts of Liberty," in *Freedom: Its History, Nature, and Varieties* by James A. Gould and Robert E. Dewey (London: MacMillian,1970), 89.
107 Reinhold Niebuhr, *Moral Man and Immoral Society* (New York: Charles Scribner's sons, 1960), 31.
108 Durant, ibid.
109 Muller, 21.

in China, it was referred to as "Dao." In all these civilizations, the pagan priesthoods jealously guarded their monopoly control of religious belief.

In ancient India, the common man and all women were strictly denied any personal access to the mythological sources of Hinduism, the Vedas. For most Hindus, hearing, reciting, or reading the Vedic scriptures was illegal. The Braham priests of Hinduism composed and rigidly enforced the regulations that governed the lives of each of India's three thousand separate castes.

The widespread belief and practice of fortune-telling, which included astrology and consulting oracles, provides abundant evidence that people in the ancient and medieval world believed their futures were predetermined. Instead of acting by a belief in free will, these pagan cultures spent a significant amount of time delving into what they thought had already been decided. Theirs was a retroactive, rather than proactive, style of living and precluded the belief in free will and historical progress.

Modern philosopher and Christian theologian Paul Tillich identified several types of non-historical belief systems which dominated thought during the ancient world and impeded human progress. Taoism (Daoism) in China and Hinduism in India were two of the main ones. On the social effect of Taoism in China, Tillich writes, "The past is glorified . . . ancestor determine life more than those who are living."[110] In India, where Hinduism teaches that time and space are only illusions, Tillich says, "It deprives all things in time and space . . . of their ultimate reality and meaning . . . Consequently, no events in time can have ultimate significance."[111] Hinduism teaches that the world developed in four ages, starting with the best and ending with the worst, and then the process starts over again. In this worldview, any positive change in the world would be cancelled out in the future.

Even in Greek philosophy, Tillich says, "There is no expectation of a more perfect future."[112] Only with the advent of Judeo-Christian thought is

---

110   Paul Tillich, *The Protestant Era* (Chicago: The University of Chicago Press, 1966), 17.
111   Ibid, 17-18.
112   Ibid.

historical change viewed as important and progress as possible. Far worse than the pagan belief that life on earth was meaningless was their belief that it was an intractable form of punishment. Tillich describes the Greek concept of fate as having "demonic qualities. It was a holy and destructive power. It entangled man in an objective guilt that was working out its baleful consequences . . . avenging his guilt by dire punishment even though the guilt was not a matter of freedom."[113]

In Hinduism, the problems of guilt and punishment are even worse because their belief in reincarnation means that people would have to suffer multiple lifetimes. For Tillich, Judeo-Christianity offers human beings an escape from these depressing, antiquated paradigms of pagan thought. Judeo-Christianity teaches that the world we live in is real, not a dream. Judeo-Christianity provides a more positive, hopeful view of the future. It teaches that history is real and that in the present world, our actions and thoughts matter in determining the future. Jews and Christians teach that the creation of the world was a one-time event, and based upon this fundamental belief, the concept of progress is possible for both individuals and societies. For Christians and Orthodox Jews, the creation of the world gives them a starting point, and the belief in a final judgment of the world gives them a goalpost in life by which to measure their present thoughts and actions.

One of the great anti-Christian myths perpetrated by ancient pagans and now being repeated by neo-pagans is the myth that Judeo-Christianity promotes an other-worldly attitude that deprives them of a concern to improve or reform the present world. Nothing could be further from historical truth. Judeo-Christianity has been the greatest catalyst for more positive change in the world than any other belief system.

The destructive power of myth was challenged in the fifth and sixth centuries B.C. by great minds like Confucius, Socrates, Gautama (the Buddha), and, of course, the Jewish prophets. They all emphasized morality and

---

113 Ibid, 5.

reason over immorality and magic. They offered advanced criticism of pagan immorality but no one system of belief that could unify and motivate the entire world to follow their example. Confucianism was an ethical/political philosophy directed at the leadership of China. Buddhism was an ethical philosophy which promoted detachment from the concerns and desires of the physical world.

Judaism was a complete religious system superior to every other belief system in the ancient world, but what Judaism needed was presentation of Judaism, which was detached from the cultural minutiae. Burdensome regulations impeded its acceptance by the larger audience of universal humanity—this is the change that Jesus the Messiah accomplished.

The genius of Judaism is not just the belief in one God but the fact that this God is a composite of all possible perfections: He is all-powerful, all-knowing, all-wise, and all-good. If anyone removes any of these God-traits from the total mix, the whole system of belief falls apart. No one would want a God Who is all-powerful if He is not all-good. Nor would anyone want a God Who is all-good if He is not all-wise. Judaism, unlike paganism, provided the world a concept of God that was rational but also showed He loved His creation and was ever-present in His attempts to guide and promote human happiness.

A fundamental misunderstanding that neo-pagans have today is that paganism is a more progressive belief system when it comes to women's rights. Many feminists, and especially homosexual feminists, are drawn to a faith system which includes goddesses. They believe Judeo-Christianity is patriarchal and repressive of women's rights. A superficial understanding of Judeo-Christianity and history encourages this view.

The real question that needs an answer is what are the effects of any belief system on the lives of people? It does not matter if it's a priest or a priestess, a prophet or a prophetess if the underlying message of a religion is immoral or insane. The underlying message in Judeo-Christianity is that "God is a Spirit: and they that worship him must worship him in spirit and in truth" (John 4:24). In primitive and pagan civilizations, women were mercilessly mistreated, and no amount of goddess worship changed that fact.

What history reveals about the characteristics of what was called the "Mother goddess" or "Earth goddess" are not flattering. Donald A. Mackenzie describes her in his book *Crete & Pre-Hellenic* as "the original mother goddess . . . worshipped and propitiated because she was feared . . . She gloried with callous heart in her power to destroy and was untouched by the tender emotions of mankind."[114]

In primitive societies, the treatment of young girls was especially horrendous. In his classic study of primitive cultures, James Frazer writes of how they were treated as they transitioned from girl to womanhood: "In New Ireland girls [Papua New Guinea] are confined four or five years in small cages, being kept in the dark and not allowed to set foot on the ground."[115] He states that in Borneo, "Girls at the age of eight . . . are shut up in a little room . . . none of her family may see her . . . her lonely confinement . . . often last seven years . . . the girl is in almost total darkness."[116]

Kate Millet, a feminist leader in the Women's Liberation Movement, was honest enough to confess that "primitive society practices its misogyny in terms of taboo . . . which evolve into explanatory myth . . . In ancient and preliterate societies women are generally not permitted to eat with men. Women eat apart today in a great number of cultures, chiefly those of the Near and Far East."[117]

Today, in those regions of the world where there is still dominant pagan influence, there remains a strong resistance to the acceptance of human rights and democracy. The acceptance of Judeo-Christian values and spiritual beliefs are necessary to the survival of human rights. If we examine the political record of those parts of the world where pagan culture is still dominant, we

114 Mackenzie, 60.
115 Frazer, 715.
116 Ibid, 716-17.
117 Kate Millet, "Theory of Sexual Politics," in *American Values in Transition: A Reader* (San Diego: Harcourt Brace Jovanovich, 1972), 116.

find a woeful spectacle of long-term, continuing political failure. The top ten countries with the worst human rights records are all countries where Judeo-Christian culture has had the least influence.

A survey of the world's longest-ruling, non-royal national leaders reveals eight countries that have not had democratic change and a leader who has ruled for at least twenty years. Four of these eight countries have maintained their undemocratic rule for over twenty-five years: Iran, Cambodia, Kazakhstan, and Tajikistan. Close behind these come Belarus, Malaysia, Nicaragua, and Samoa—all of which have leaders who have lasted at least twenty years.[118] In 2018, an article by Darin Graham stated, "There are only 19 full democracies on the planet . . . western Europe accounts for 14 of the 19 full democracies."[119]

A closer examination of these undemocratic regions reveals the full horror that affects their people's lives. If we start with the continent of Africa, the U.N. reported in 1998 that there were fourteen nations engaged in war. ReliefWeb, a leading humanitarian information source, says, "Conflict is still Africa's biggest challenge in 2020."[120] Patricia Danzi of the International Red Cross describes Africa's conflicts this way: "Conflicts last and they don't stop. And more are added."[121]

In the modern period of history since its de-colonization, Africa has been the scene of many wars, creating more refugees than any other part of the modern world. Africa has suffered from the most conflicts and the most prolonged conflicts in modern history. To give a few examples, war in western Sahara has lasted on and off for fifty years; a guerrilla war in Uganda

118   Zoe Ettinger, "After a Historic Vote, Vladimir Putin Could Remain in Power in Russia Until 2036. Here Are 15 of the World's Longest Serving Leaders," BusinessInsider online, July 2, 2020, https://africa.businessinsider.com/strategy/after-a-historic-vote-vladimir-putin-could-remain-in-power-in-russia-until-2036-here/122yjbz.amp.

119   Darin Graham, "Only 19 countries are still full democracies, report suggests," Indy100.com, February 2, 2018, https://www.indy100.com/news/democracy-index-economist-intelligence-unit-map-data-report-norway-democratic-united-states-8191501.

120   Simon Allison, "Conflict is still Africa's biggest challenge," Reliefweb.int, January 6, 2020, https://reliefweb.int/report/world/conflict-still-africa-s-biggest-challenge-2020.

121   Patricia Danzi, "ICRC Action in Africa - Interview of Patricia Danzi," International Committee of the Red Cross, July 11, 2018, YouTube video, 2:49, https://www.youtube.com/watch?v=JKWj0_LUFdE&t=1s.

has lasted thirty-three years; a war in Senegal lasted thirty-two years; and a war between Somalia and Ethiopia has lasted twenty-six years.[122]

In 1960, Yorick Blumenfeld wrote, "The major non-economic problem facing all these countries is how to achieve both political stability and freedom. The various political factions were united against colonial rule, but independence has freed them to follow separate ways and has produced large numbers of splinter factions."[123] Tribalism is rooted in Africa's long, pagan past. Pagan religious beliefs promote a belief in the particular, not the universal. Paganism works against the concepts of the universal brotherhood of humanity and equality under the universal moral law. On the harmful effects of tribalism, Blumenfeld goes on to write:

> African tribal customs and the political forms of democracy are in many ways poles apart . . . It is only the relatively few Africans who have received a higher education who think of themselves primarily as citizens of an African state . . . Whereas in most of Europe and America political education started long before the majority of the people were enfranchised, in Africa many tribesmen who have no political training have been given the vote.[124]

In his article "How tribalism stunts African democracy," Calestous Juma writes:

> The last 20 years of Somalia have shown the dangers of ethnic competition and underscore the importance of building nations around ideas rather than clan identities . . . Tribal interests have played a major role in armed conflict and civil unrest across the

---

122 Jeffrey Gettleman, "Africa's Forever Wars: Why the continent's conflicts never end," *Foreign Policy* online, February 11, 2010, https://foreignpolicy.com/2010/02/11/africas-forever-wars.

123 Yorick Blumenfeld, "Tribalism and Nationalism in Africa," *CQ Researcher* online, November 2, 1960, https://library.cqpress.com/cqresearcher/document.php?id=cqresrre1960110208.

124 Ibid.

continent . . . many African countries have reverted to tribal identities as foundations for political competition. Leaders often exploit tribal loyalty . . . tribes are not built on democratic ideas but thrive on zero-sum competition.[125]

Freedom House, which created an index called Freedom in the World, reported in 2018 that "the majority of sub-Saharan African states . . . were not free."[126] The vast majority of African nations are ruled by the military or by one-party dictatorships. Freedom House says only eleven percent of Africans are free. Even in those parts of Africa where there is a pretense of democracy and elections are held regularly, a survey of thirty-six African countries found that only forty percent of Africans believe their elections are "free and fair."[127] As a result of tribal hatred and the injustice it fosters, Africa lacks a long tradition of political stability and the rule of law. This is seen in the long and continuing record of coups, attempted coups, civil conflicts, and the number of single-party governments which rule the African continent.

Since the 1960s, Africa has experienced at least two hundred successful or failed coups. Since the year 2000, seventy percent of all the coup events in the world have taken place in Africa.[128] Of Africa's fifty-four countries, forty-eight are ruled by military or single-party governments.[129] To put a human face on all this political turmoil, we can look at three countries: Kenya, the Democratic Republic of Congo, and Uganda.

In an article published by the United States Holocaust Memorial Museum, Dr. Naupess K. Kibiswa wrote of the Congo, "The rate of killings of civilians . . . was multiplied more than 10 times . . . The bodies of Congolese women and

125 Calestous Juma, "Viewpoint: How tribalism stunts African democracy," BBC.com, November 27, 2012, https://www.bbc.com/news/world-africa-20465752.
126 Michael J. Abramowitz, "Democracy in Crisis," Freedom House.org, 2018, https://freedomhouse.org/report/freedom-world/2018/democracy-crisis.
127 Ibid.
128 Ibid.
129 Colleen Lowe Morna, "One Party Rule Dominates in Africa. FOR THE GOOD OF THE PEOPLE? Many Africans say traditions and development needs make pluralism a costly luxury," *The Christian Science Monitor online*, March 29, 1989, https://www.csmonitor.com/1989/0329/cone.html.

children are the battlefield for much of the violence . . . armed groups commit large scale mass rapes, often as a public event."[130] It has been estimated that thirty thousand children have taken part in this violence as armed gangs.

Brigitte Rohwerder describes the same kind of violence against women in Kenya: "Kenya is a large multi-ethnic country with over 40 different ethnic groups . . . It has high levels of sexual and gender-based violence and of intercommunal violence."[131] And finally, Peace Insight reported in 2017, "Uganda has suffered intermittent conflict since independence . . . Multiple military coups and violent regimes followed . . . and have since resulted in hundreds of thousands of deaths and the prolonged suffering of Ugandans. 55[sic] years since independence, the country is yet to witness a democratic handover of power."[132] The record of human rights abuse and civil conflict in Africa's modern history is exceptional only by degree.

A study of the modern political/social record in Asia, Latin America, and the Middle East shows if not the same level of turmoil, at least the same awful pattern. If we examine the Asian region of the world, we find an interesting political dichotomy. The smaller nations of Asia show a similar pattern to Africa of having multiple coups and ethnic conflicts. Their governments are less intrusive and operate based on more traditional pagan norms.

But if we examine the Far East's largest and most populous nations (i.e. People's Republic of China, North Korea, and Vietnam), we find an opposite historical pattern. There is relatively little political instability in these Communist countries, which practice totalitarian control of their societies. In these countries, any descent is quickly crushed under the weight of enormous security forces and a modern and pervasive system of surveillance.

---

130 Naupess K. Kibiswa, "Local Populations at Risk of Violence in the Democratic Republic of Congo," United States Holocaust Memorial Museum, July 19, 2021, https://www.ushmm.org/genocide-prevention/blog/local-populations-at-risk-of-violence-in-the-democratic-republic-of-congo.

131 Brigitte Rohwerder, "Conflict Analysis of Kenya," University of Birmingham online, May, 2015, https://gsdrc.org/publications/conflict-analysis-of-kenya.

132 Kibiswa, ibid.

One Earth Future, which provides an annual risk report on the probability of coups worldwide, stated in its 2019 report, "There have been 463 coup attempts worldwide since 1950 . . . 12% have taken place in Asia . . . since 1980 there have been 24 coup attempts [in Asia] and 12 successful coups."[133] The remaining ten percent of the worldwide coup attempts since 1950 have taken place in Latin America. The risk report of One Earth Future says Latin America is responsible for "142 total coup attempts between 1950-2018."[134]

The evidence shows that the smaller, poorer, and traditionally pagan societies are at greater risk of political instability and social turmoil. In Asia, the One Earth Future risk report warns that countries like East Timor, Nepal, Papua New Guinea, and Fiji are at greater risk. In Latin America, the risk report warns that those countries at greater risk of coup attempts are Bolivia, Haiti, Guatemala, Honduras, and Ecuador.

In Latin America, the political trend is heading in the wrong direction. *The Washington Post* reported in 2018, "Democracy is in crisis in Latin America." The author of the article, Luis Schenoni, wrote:

> Data . . . shows that democracy is weaker than it has been for decades. Public support for and satisfaction with democracy is also falling . . . Democracy has collapsed in Nicaragua and Venezuela and is in serious trouble in countries such as Bolivia and Honduras. In El Salvador, Guatemala, Honduras, and Mexico, just as in Brazil, criminal organizations ule the poorer parts of many cities, weakening democracy and the rule of law.[135]

The old scourge of slavery is making a major comeback worldwide but especially on the continents of Asia, Africa, and South America. According to

---

133 Jay Benson, Matthew Frank, et al., "Annual Risk of Coup Report-2019 (Vienna: One Earth Future 2019), https://oneearthfuture.org/publication/annual-risk-coup-report-2019.

134 Ibid.

135 Luis Schenoni, and Scott Mainwaring, "Democracy is in crisis in Latin America. Brazil may be the next trouble spot," The Washington Post online, October 22, 2018, https://www.washingtonpost.com/news/monkey-cage/wp/2018/10/22/democracy-is-in-crisis-in-latin-america-brazil-may-be-the-next-trouble-spot.

the Minderoo Foundation's Global Slavery Index in 2018, there are 24,990,000 living under conditions of slavery in Asia and the Pacific region, and "the prevalence of modern slavery was highest in Africa . . . This was followed by Asia and the Pacific . . . An estimated 40.3 million men, women, and children were living in modern slavery in 2016."[136]

Seven of the ten countries taking the most action to fight against modern slavery are in Europe. Still, among those who live in the ten countries doing the least to end slavery, nine are located in Asia or Africa, and the tenth is Russia. The Global Slavery Index also reported, "We know that 47 countries globally have not yet recognized human trafficking as a crime . . . Nearly 100 countries still fail to criminalize forced labor."[137] These terrible statistics should open the eyes of a complacent world to the great need for more humanitarian change in the world's largest and most populous regions.

---

136 Global Slavery Index, Minderoo Foundation, Accessed June 29, 2023, https://www.walkfree.org/global-slavery-index.
137 Ibid.

PART THREE
THE CREATIVE POWER OF CHRIST

CHAPTER EIGHT

THE SACRED INDIVIDUAL

WHEN PEOPLE STOP BELIEVING IN the sacredness of human life, there is less concern about preserving or protecting life. Without the belief in a personal soul, such concepts as a heroic sacrifice or the pursuit of moral excellence at any cost would be judged as vain attempts to validate a soul that does not exist. This view of life reduces everything to the animal level. Unlike other animals, human beings are creatures that feed on meaning and purpose and tend to self-destruct without it.

Most human beings aspire to something greater than mere survival. Without a sense of more significant meaning or purpose to their lives, they lapse into depression, viewing life as futile. The infamous serial killer Jeffrey Dahmer confessed that it was after he stopped believing in a soul and judgment in an afterlife that he no longer tried to restrain his homicidal impulses.

The word "soul" has been used in many cultures to express various meanings. In pagan cultures, it usually meant "that which imparts life." Beyond that fundamental belief, most often very little else was said. What we know of pagan views on the subject is a hodge-podge of ridiculous assertions: only men have souls; only their king has a soul; souls come in different shapes and sizes; or as previously discussed, human souls derive from plants and animals.

The most populous pagan faith system of today, Hinduism, is characterized by the belief in a one world soul they call "Paramatman." The idea of an individual, personal soul is criticized in Hinduism as an act of self-delusion. The primary purpose of Hinduism is to assist its followers in discovering and renouncing a personal soul as self-delusion. In Hinduism, spiritual individualism is an anathema. The Judeo-Christian meaning of the word "soul" is the morally conscious inner self—that which Jesus said we shouldn't trade away for the entire world. The Judeo-Christian tradition holds that the soul was made in the "image of God" (Gen. 1:26-27) and maintaining its wellbeing is the essential activity of human life.

In Judeo-Christianity, spiritual individualism is a Divine gift, and the highest purpose is for God to redeem and transform the individual soul, not to eradicate it. For the Christian believer, it provides powerful motivation for personal and social transformation. It can strengthen a person's resolve to resist evil and to do good. It can promote tolerance and concern for others. Instead of hating or desiring the destruction of a bad person, the person who believes they have a soul will seek to bring about their reformation and salvation. This is what Christian believers mean when they use the phrase, "reclaiming a lost soul."

The belief in a human soul that is of equal value to any other human soul has far-ranging social and moral consequences. There is little scope for compassion or social consciousness for those who view life as only the product of a random, material accident or view other people as competitive animals who share the same meaningless planet. Without belief in a soul, people are less likely to sacrifice their time, comforts, or money to promote the general welfare of others or seek to rescue a fallen individual from the errors of a bad life. In such a world, the prevailing attitude will be both selfish and cynical, which is the attitude and outlook that dominated the pagan world.

The great Jewish philosopher Moses Mendelssohn wrote of the pagan view of life, "Without God, Providence, and immortality, all the goods of life would lose their worth in my eyes, and our earthly life would be . . . like wandering in wind and weather without the consoling prospect of finding cover and protection at night."[138]

The ancient Jews provided the first view of God as the only supreme, moral Ruler of the universe, and they were the first people to spend a great deal of time thinking and writing about the moral character of one God. They wrote about what He hated and loved and how humankind can gain His favor or lose it based upon the quality of an individual's thoughts and actions. The genius of Judaism rests on its monotheistic belief in God. Without accepting this belief, no logical argument in favor of universal truth or moral law can be made. Where multiple gods rule, there can be no one standard nor one truth.

A great Jewish philosopher who wrote during the medieval period of history was Moses Maimonides. He established the following list of the principal beliefs of Judaism:

1. I believe with perfect faith that the Creator . . . is the Creator and Guide of everything that has been created.
2. I believe with perfect faith that the Creator . . . is One . . . and He alone is our God, who was, and is, and will be.
3. I believe with perfect faith that all the words of the prophets are true.
4. I believe with perfect faith that the prophecy of Moses our teacher . . . was true . . .
5. I believe with perfect faith that the Creator . . . knows all the deeds of human beings and all their thoughts.
6. I believe with perfect faith that the Creator . . . rewards those who keep His commandments and punishes those that transgress them.

138 Will and Ariel Durant, *Rousseau and Revolution*, Vol. 10, *The Story of Civilization* (New York: Simon & Schuster, 1972), 639.

7.   I believe with perfect faith in the coming of the Messiah . . .

8.   I believe with perfect faith that there will be a revival of the dead at the time when it shall please the Creator.[139]

Judeo-Christianity teaches that God is a Spirit of love, Who freely shares the gift of life and consciousness with His creation. In the Judeo-Christian view, the world's creation was a cosmic act of love. God's greatest joy is sharing His blessed, eternal life with others. In Acts 20:35, Paul says, "Remember the words of the Lord Jesus . . . it is more blessed to give than to receive."

Another aspect of Judaism that is fundamentally different from pagan belief is its linkage of the faith in one God with the pro-life principle of the sacred individual. This necessary linkage was established in the first book of the Holy Bible when God confronts Cain for killing his brother. "And he said, What hast thou done? the voice of thy brother's blood crieth unto me from the ground" (Gen. 4:10).

The pro-life principle is not limited to being against murder, abortion, euthanasia, or suicide. It is a Judeo-Christian belief with a far-reaching application. It supports and protects the dignity of humanity in multiple ways. The fourth of the Ten Commandments to "remember the sabbath day, to keep it holy" (Exod. 20:8) was a powerful, weekly reminder to God's people that God had created the world; and through Adam and Eve, all humanity were children from the same Divine source.

In Exodus 22-23, the Israelites are told by God through Moses how to treat the alien, widows, orphans, and the poor; to not spread lies; to not do wrong just because others do; to not be unjust; and to not show favoritism; These verses in both the Old and New Testaments are the basis of the famous Judeo-Christian concern for what people call "social justice."

---

139   Kenneth Seeskin, s.v. "Maimonides," in *Stanford Encyclopedia of Philosophy*, February 4, 2021, https://plato.stanford.edu/entries/maimonides.

The exclusiveness that both Judaism and Christianity teach is not intended to create artificial barriers between different cultures or peoples (those barriers already existed in the pagan world) but to draw a line between pro-life and anti-life belief systems. Deuteronomy 12:31 says, "Thou shalt not do so unto the LORD thy God: for every abomination to the LORD, which he hateth, have they done unto their gods; for even their sons and their daughters they have burnt in the fire to their gods."

Even in a world where war and slavery were universal, the ancient Jews demonstrated fidelity to the pro-life principle. Durant writes of their more humane treatment of enslaved people, "War captives and convicts were used as slaves . . . But the owner had no power of life and death over his slaves . . . typical institutions of the Near East were mitigated in Judea by generous charity, and a vigorous campaign, by priest and prophet, against exploitation."[140]

A new list of prohibitions comes in Leviticus. Most of these prohibitions are in reaction to the prevailing pagan customs of that day:

- "Moreover ye shall eat no manner of blood, whether it be of fowl or of beast, in any of your dwellings" (Lev. 7:26).
- "Ye shall not make any cuttings in your flesh for the dead, nor print any marks upon you: I am the LORD: (LEV. 19:28).
- "Regard not them that have familiar spirits, neither seek after wizards, to be defiled by them: I am the LORD your God" (Lev. 19:31).
- "And thou shalt not let any of thy seed pass through the fire to Molech, neither shalt thou profane the name of thy God: I am the LORD. Thou shalt not lie with mankind, as with womankind: it is abomination. Neither shalt thou lie with any beast to defile thyself therewith: neither shall any woman stand before a beast to lie down thereto: it is confusion" (Lev. 18:21-23).

---

140 Durant, Vol. 1, 337.

The core of the Mosaic Law was the Ten Commandments, a list of moral commands that are so self-evidently true that today they are automatically accepted as part of human nature. But when the Ten Commandments were first presented to the world, they were a revolutionary departure from the immoral thinking of the pagan world. The first four commandments in Exodus 20 were necessary to establish the authority of the following six from that same passage of Scripture:

1. Thou shalt have no other gods before me.
2. Thou shalt not make any graven image.
3. Thou shalt not take the name of the Lord thy God in vain.
4. Remember the sabbath day, to keep it holy.
5. Honour thy father and thy mother.
6. Thou shalt not kill.
7. Thou shalt not commit adultery.
8. Thou shalt not steal.
9. Thou shalt not bear false witness against thy neighbour.
10. Thou shalt not covet.

Early in the teachings of Judaism, we see the linkage between the pro-life principle and the principle of purity. It is impossible to honor one without honoring the other. All these commandments are meant to support and protect life. The Holy Bible states this clearly in Leviticus 18:5: "Ye shall therefore keep my statutes, and my judgments: which if a man do, he shall live."

This ancient Jewish commitment to the sacredness of human life was expanded in the teachings of Jesus Christ. Judaism called for the negation of certain negative behaviors, but Jesus' teachings were more about the general feelings and attitudes, which were the seedbed of all evil deeds. His famous sermon, the "Sermon on the Mount," illustrates this concept. Found in Matthew 5:3-12, Jesus' words provide a spiritual recipe for living a holy life:

Blessed are the poor in spirit: for theirs is the kingdom of heaven.

Blessed are they that mourn: for they shall be comforted.

Blessed are the meek: for they shall inherit the earth.

Blessed are they which do hunger and thirst after righteousness: for they shall be filled.

Blessed are the merciful: for they shall obtain mercy.

Blessed are the pure in heart: for they shall see God.

Blessed are the peacemakers: for they shall be called the children of God.

Blessed are they which are persecuted for righteousness' sake: for theirs is the kingdom of heaven.

Blessed are ye, when men shall revile you, and persecute you, and shall say all manner of evil against you falsely, for my sake.

Rejoice, and be exceeding glad: for great is your reward in heaven: for so persecuted they the prophets which were before you.

It is clear from a survey of these statements that the blessings Jesus promises are spiritual attitudes. They are blessings that the physical world cannot take away nor provide. These attitudes are blessings themselves, and the rewards they bring are spiritual. The last three of these beatitudes are incredibly spiritual, since they reference holding to them while being persecuted in the present world—meaning that any satisfaction in this world can only come from the mental pleasure of having been faithful to a God Who is transcendent. It is also clear that the spiritual attitudes which Jesus advocated are rooted in a far-reaching social consciousness: His concern was for the poor, the suffering, the humble, and those living without peace of mind or body.

In Will Durant's book *Caesar and Christ*, he goes to the essence of Jesus' message:

He was not hostile to the simple joys of life . . . he uttered no criticism of civil government . . . The revolution he sought was a far deeper one . . . If he could cleanse the human heart of selfish desire, cruelty, and lust, utopia would come of itself, and all those institutions that rise out of human greed and violence . . . would disappear . . . Christ was in this spiritual sense the greatest revolutionary in history."[141]

We will see later in this book that His spiritual message has been and still is the inspiration of countless human efforts to reform and improve this present world. The primary question is why did the life, words, and deeds of one working-class Jewish man living thousands of years ago in poverty and relative obscurity become the most-recognized moral standard of Western civilization? And how did He become the Lord and Savior of 2.2 billion people today? The answer is that both the message and the messenger were uniquely inspiring. His message was that because God loves humanity, every human life is sacred and worthy of respect.

The pro-life principle based upon the belief in the sacredness of the individual was clearly on the minds of early Christians. The apostle Paul wrote, "I beseech you therefore, brethren . . . present your bodies a living sacrifice, holy, acceptable unto God . . . And be not conformed to this world: but be ye transformed by the renewing of your mind, that ye may prove what is that good, and acceptable, and perfect, will of God" (Rom. 12:1-2).

In ancient times, where actual human sacrifice was universally practiced, Paul called for Christians to be "living sacrifices." This was the very opposite of the pagan view of sacrifice. The sacrifice he called for was denying one's selfish appetites and living transformed lives of goodness to the glory of God.

One pagan critic of early Christianity described them as "imbeciles . . . disdaining things terrestrial." This was a common pagan slander and a total

---

misunderstanding of the Judeo-Christian message. Nothing could have been more life-affirming or productive for human happiness on earth than Jesus' teachings to "love thy neighbour as thyself" (Mark 12:31). Still, Jesus even exceeded this lofty standard by adding in Matthew 5:44, "Love your enemies, bless them that curse you, do good to them that hate you." Multiple Christian apostles, disciples, writers, and pagan witnesses confirmed this was the essential Christian message.

While on earth, the Christian's duty was to endure. "Let us not be weary in well doing . . . As we have therefore opportunity, let us do good unto all men, especially unto them who are of the household of faith" (Gal. 6: 9-10). Like most modern Christians today, ancient Christians lived their lives in this well-doing. They and their Jewish brothers and sisters, who shared most of the same moral and spiritual beliefs, were famous for the wholesomeness of their family life and their many acts of charity.

Despite the Christians' moral goodness—or perhaps because of it—the pagans continued to promote unfounded slanders and persecutions against them. In this context, many Christian and Jewish writers attempted to set the historical record straight. The Roman Christian Tertullian, who died in A.D. 240, left thirty-one works of writing which still exist. His writings mainly aimed to defend Christian teaching against pagan slander. In the following passage, he argues against the charge that Christians were anti-social:

> We have filled all your . . . cities, islands . . . towns, marketplaces . . . unarmed and without rebellion but simply as dissenters . . . you prefer to call us enemies of the human race rather than enemies of human error . . . among us there is nothing to be said, nothing to be seen, nothing to be heard, of the madness of the circus, the immodesty of the theater, the brutality of the arena . . . We pray even for the emperors . . . for the condition of the world, that peace may prevail."[142]

---

142 Tertullian, *Apology, Faith of the Early Fathers,* Vol. 1, edited by William A. Jurgens (Collegeville, MN: The Liturgical Press, 1070), 115.

The pagan Roman writer Pliny, called "the Younger," confirmed this view in a report to the Roman emperor, Trajan.

In another of Tertullian's writings, he describes the nature and purpose of Christian worship: "we are a body joined together by religious conviction . . . We assemble in meeting and comprise a congregation, so that we might surround God with our prayers . . . Each one puts in a small amount on the monthly day . . . No one is compelled, and it is given freely . . . for the support . . . of the poor, boys and girls without parents . . . for the aged . . . for the shipwrecked . . . or in the prisons.[143]

As we see here, Christians were far from being anti-social and were not, as he says, "enemies of the human race." Early Christians lived peaceful lives, promoting charitable activities. Ancient Roman jails were full of anti-social people because of crimes motivated by lust, pride, hatred, or greed. On this very point, Tertullian writes, "It is with your own people (pagans) that the jail is always bulging . . . with your own people that the beast are always fattening . . . with your own people that the producers of gladiatorial shows always make flocks of criminals food for beasts. No one there is a Christian unless he is there for that very reason."[144] The very lack of respect for the sacredness of human life resulted in these Roman pastimes and pleasures.

Another Roman Christian writer of this same period of history, Marcus Minucius Felix, contrasted the pagan lifestyle with that of the Christian:

> We maintain modesty not on the surface but in the mind. We cling freely to the bond of one marriage . . . The banquets we attend are not only modest but sober . . . we temper our joyousness with gravity . . . You forbid adultery, yet you do it . . . You punish crimes when they are committed. With us, it is a sin even to consider a crime. You fear witnesses. We fear even our

---

143 Ibid, 116-17.
144 Ibid.

own conscience . . . the jails are full of your people; but there is
no Christian there, unless his crime be his religion.[145]

Christianity was not a pie-in-the-sky religion; it offered a change in
how people both thought about life and how they lived it. Its benefits were
practical and spiritual and could be measured in the everyday life experience
of ordinary people. Unlike pagan religions and philosophies, it was offered
freely, and its benefits were immediately and personally felt. Jesus called
individuals to have a personal relationship with Him, and anyone who heard
His message and believed could have that relationship. It was a matter of free
choice made by one individual to another; and no government, elder, tribe,
culture, or nation could stop that choice from being made.

The goal of Judaism and Christianity was to end the human enslavement
to sin, which causes all social and political evils. Changing the human heart
from selfishness to selfless love would undermine the concept and practice
of a masterclass, a master-race, a master-male-female relationship. The only
Master would be the God of agape love.

The word "holy" is used in the Bible 611 times, and the word "righteous"
is used over five hundred times in the Old Testament and over two hundred
times in the New Testament. They are used to describe both God and those
human beings who follow His teaching. Before Judaism and Christianity,
there was no philosophy or religion which had, as its primary purpose, the
universal salvation of all humankind. Other religions and philosophies
produced moral codes, but none, before Judeo-Christianity, sought as its
primary purpose the moral transformation of the entire world based upon
following one perfect example of one perfect God.

145 Marcus Minucius Felix, *A Source Book of Theological and Historical Passages, The Faith
of the Early Fathers*, Vol. 1, edited by William A. Jurgens (Collegeville: Liturgical Press,
1970), 110-111.

The Buddha was a wise man, as far as wise men go, but he never claimed to be God or even claimed that there was one true God. He told his followers that they had to be "a lamp unto themselves."[146] In other words, his followers were on their own when discovering the truth. At the beginning of Buddhism, there was little provision for women to follow his example or seek enlightenment. This is also true for the earliest stage of Islam. Mohammed taught that very few women would go to Heaven because of their inferior nature.

Contrast these views with what is the beginning statement found in the Gospel of John—"For God so loved the world, that he gave his only begotten Son, that whosoever believeth in him should not perish, but have everlasting life" (John 3:16)—and his Great Commission statement found in the book of Matthew—"Go ye therefore, and teach all nations, baptizing them in the name of the Father, and of the Son, and of the Holy Spirit: Teaching them to observe all things whatsoever I have commanded you: and, lo, I am with you always, even unto the end of the world. Amen" (Matt. 28:19-20).

By the fifth century B.C., some of the world's greatest philosophers, such as Socrates and Plato, began to promote the belief that each individual had an eternal soul. Socrates, Plato's teacher, shifted the whole direction of philosophical inquiry. He insisted that "the unexamined life is not worth living" and that "no harm can come to a good man in this life or the next."[147] Jews and Christians would engage in this same moral inquiry but would not leave the answers to fallible men.

When reflecting on this kind of moral inquiry, we see the difference between philosophy and theology. Philosophy is the search for truth or wisdom, but theology is a study of revealed truth or wisdom. Philosophy's search is limited to the confines of human thought, while theology unites

---

146 J. Krishnamurti, "Be a Light unto Yourself," Awakin.org, Accessed October 18, 2022, https://www.awakin.org/v2/read/view.php?tid=183.

147 J.O. Famakinwa, "Is the Unexamined Life Worth Living or Not?" *Think* 11, No. 31 (2012): 97-103, https://doi.org/10.1017/S1477175612000073.

human reason with Divine revelation. Rene Descartes' philosophy started with a blank slate and doubted everything except thought—*cogito, ergo sum*.[148]

In practical terms, the philosopher's way is too slow, time-consuming, and uncertain to provide a large-scale, immediate benefit to a suffering world. A sick world needs simple, easily accessible truth that speaks to a universal human heart and mind. It requires a belief system that has been tested over thousands of years and proven correct. This is what Judeo-Christianity provides and has always provided. We see that Jesus' mission was not some partial application of earthly wisdom to enhance the lives of only some people. His mission was the total transformation of the entire human race.

The only thing that could justify such a Great Commission was the acceptance of Him as God. He had to be God to command such authority; and to be God, He had to be perfect. John 3:16 is profound because it encompasses the entire world in God's love, and the Great Commission is profound because it includes the whole world in God's action plan.

This comprehensive plan to transform and redeem the entire world depended on there being something worth saving. It depended on the belief that there was something about human beings that was sacred and, by definition, something that connected them to God and made them worthy of awe and respect. The belief in a soul is the belief that human life has a value and existence that transcends the temporary and the immediate. Unlike the pagan gods, God did not create a world that was an accident—without meaning or purpose. Life is a Divine gift, and no human being can alter God's intention or purpose for it.

If one can believe in an eternal, loving God, then one should also be able to believe that He wants to share eternal life with them. This is such a positive, hopeful message that anyone who comes to believe it will have a life infused with a strong sense of joy and peace. The practical results of

---

148 Bertrand Russell, *The Story of Western Philosophy* (New York: Simon & Schuster, 1972), 563-64.

that infusion of lasting joy will be the positive transformation of both the individual and society.

———————————◆———————————

The history of Judaism reveals that Moses Maimonides' definition of Jewish beliefs remained the Orthodox view well into the twentieth century. Since then, Reform Judaism—a much more liberal belief system—represents the views of most modern Jews who still practice Judaism.[149] Pew Research reported in 2021 that "there are more than twice as many self-identified Jewish liberals as conservative . . . Roughly half of Orthodox Jews describe themselves as political conservatives . . . Orthodox Jews more closely resemble evangelical Protestants."[150] Reform Jews are less likely to believe in an afterlife, a Messiah, or the unchanging moral code of Orthodox Jewish morality.

American historian George Bancroft gave a speech in 1835, which included the following:

> Nature is the same. For her no new forces are generated . . . The earth turns on its axis, and perfects its revolutions, and renews its seasons, without increase or advancement . . . The world can advance only through the culture of the moral and intellectual powers of the people . . . The measure of the progress of civilization is the progress of the people. It is alone by infusing great principles into the common mind that revolutions in human society are brought about.[151]

Judeo-Christianity has shown itself to be the ideal vehicle in the history of the world for "infusing great principles into the common mind."[152] Viewed

149 Becka A. Alper and Alan Cooperman, "10 Key Findings about Jewish Americans," Pew Research Center, May 11, 2021, https://www.pewresearch.org/fact-tank/2021/05/11/10-key-findings-about-jewish-americans.
150 Ibid.
151 George Bancroft, "The Office of the People in Art, Government, and Religion," in *American Values in Transition; A Reader* (Harcourt Brace Jovanovich, 1972), 291-93.
152 Ibid.

through the long lens of history, one can see the partial justification for the many Jewish ritual requirements and strict kosher practices. They defended the existence of Judaism against the constant onslaught of paganism. They were a highly effective defensive strategy meant to keep pagan culture and theology at arm's length. But on the negative side, they hindered the Jews and non-Jews from having an easier access to the great moral/spiritual truths of Judaism.

This is what Jesus was referring to when He said, "For they bind heavy burdens and grievous to be borne, and lay them on men's shoulders; but they themselves will not move them with one of their fingers" (Matt. 23:4). The old beliefs of Judaism were clarified and magnified by Jesus Christ, Who came to explain and super-charge Judaism.

Jesus said as much when He stated, "Think not that I am come to destroy the law, or the prophets: I am not come to destroy, but to fulfill" (Matt. 5:17). When He was asked which was the greatest commandment in the Law, His response left no doubt that He was speaking as a devout Jew. His answer summed up the essence of Judaism by quoting the Torah's Shema: "And thou shalt love the Lord thy God with all thy heart, and with all thy soul, and with all thy mind, and with all thy strength: this is the first commandment. And the second is like, namely this, Thou shalt love thy neighbour as thyself. There is none other commandment greater than these" (Mark 12:30-31).

As reported in the book of Matthew 22:35-40, Jesus added, "On these two commandments hang all the law and the prophets." What Jesus taught by both word and deed was the message of Judaism, simplified and empowered. He did not come to preach the end of Judaism but to unlock its great, holy potential and release its truest meaning into the world.

Christianity was not a refutation of Judaism but the most powerful affirmation of its essential truths. Those fundamental truths were embodied in the life of one perfect Man. All the glorious, abstract truths of Judaism were now visible in the life of Jesus Christ. Moral perfection and the most inspiring example of Divine and human love were joined in one Person.

Because His message met universally critical human needs, it spread like wildfire, especially among women, poor, sick, afflicted, and oppressed. Christianity provided the most positive, hopeful message that the world has ever heard.

CHAPTER NINE

THE FREE INDIVIDUAL

A "CALLING" REQUIRES A RECEPTIVE heart and mind. No one can be a faithful Christian without freely choosing to be one. The idea of faith as a free choice can be traced back to Genesis 3:3-24. The story of Adam and Eve in the garden is about human freedom and the consequences of choosing wrongly. More confirmation of this comes in the story of Noah and the flood (see Gen. 6-9). Noah believed in God and freely chose to build the ark. Those who decided not to join him perished in the flood. The story of the prophet Jonah is an even more straightforward example. Jonah initially refused God's calling to preach repentance to the wicked city of Nineveh but later repents.

Judaism and Christianity are both religious callings. God called Abraham, but Abraham had a choice. God called Moses, but Moses had a choice. God called the Jewish prophets, and they all had a choice. Throughout the history of Christianity, we see precisely the same thing, people were asked to step into a calling. Jesus invited numerous individuals and large groups of people, but they all had a choice as free individuals to answer the call or not. His apostles and disciples traveled about the ancient Roman world repeating His invitation to follow Him.

God explicitly endorsed the concept of free will in Genesis 4:7 after Cain murdered his brother Abel. The Lord said, "If thou doest well, shalt thou not be accepted? and if thou doest not well, sin lieth at the door. And unto thee shall be his desire, and thou shalt rule over him'" Saying, "sin lieth at your door" is another way of saying you are responsible for your actions, and "thou shalt rule over him" is another way of saying you have free will.

Jesus accepting His crucifixion was a choice. When speaking in the Garden of Gethsemane, He said: "Father, all things are possible unto thee: take away this cup from me: nevertheless not what I will, but what thou wilt" (Mark 14:32-36). There are so many examples in the Bible of free will that one could write a book on it alone.

On the other hand, there are no biblical examples of anyone being ordered or compelled to accept the call to become a Christian. There are consequences for rejecting this call, but the Bible clarifies that any punishment for refusing God's calling belongs to God alone. Disobedience to God is disobedience to God, not to man. Acts of disobedience have spiritual consequences, but no human being has a right to impose penalties on any other human for non-belief.

The Bible teaches that even an infallible God with every right to judge His world is long-suffering. The Bible provides thirteen verses in both Old and New Testament that state this: Exodus 34:6, Numbers 14:18, Psalm 86:15, 2 Peter 3:15, Luke 13:9, Romans 2:4, 2 Peter 3:9, Joel 2:13, Romans 3:25, Isaiah 30:18, Ezekiel 20:17, Romans 9:22, and 1 Peter 3:20. If the holy God is long-suffering, who is sinful man to take it on himself to administer punishment to non-believers for spiritual offenses? Not only are the use of force or coercion explicitly condemned in the New Testament, but Christians also understand them to be completely counterproductive. They are counter to the very essence of the Gospel, which is a free invitation to love God and love others.

The Bible teaches that man can only punish sins if those sins produce criminal consequences. Acts of incest, murder, theft, and child abuse are examples of punishable sins; but even then, Christians are called to pray for sinners, to forgive their past behavior, and to lead them to a better way of life. Like Jesus, the Christian's primary role is healing and reconciliation, not condemnation and punishment. Jesus said of Himself, "God sent not his Son into the world to condemn the world; but that the world through him might be saved" (John 3:17).

In the Old Testament, there is a great deal about God commanding the ancient Jews to carry out ruthless warfare against their pagan enemies. Ancient Israel was a theocracy, a type of government where God Himself is in charge. Like the modern state of Israel, the ancient Jews were constantly threatened with complete destruction or enslavement by outside groups. In fact, they were conquered and enslaved several times in their ancient history.

Israel was a national state under the indirect rule of God through their prophets, judges, priests, and anointed kings and only believed in free will within the context of a one religion. The Christians began as outsiders, a small group of believing Jews who were not accepted by either the state of Israel or the pagan Roman Empire. Christians had to acknowledge and promote tolerance because their numbers were too small to believe or promote anything else.

The Judeo-Christian tradition, unlike paganism, did not call for blind faith in an irrational, cruel spirit world. It called for each person to search their conscience and expand their spiritual understanding by diligently studying God's Word. The Judeo-Christian tradition did not dethrone human reason. It conjoined it with a higher level of truth, or as St. Augustine wrote, "I believe that I might understand." It called for the free individual to begin a long journey of enlightenment based upon an ever-increasing knowledge of a perfect God. In social and practical terms, it called for increasing efforts at the moral transformation of the self and of society.

If we look at the primary sources in the New Testament, which give a record of both Jesus' words and deeds, we find a large amount of evidence that Jesus supported the belief in a free individual. If we start with some of His most important parables that focus on presenting the Gospel message and how human beings choose to respond to it, we get a clear statement confirming belief in the free individual and rejecting anything but voluntary conversion. In the parable of the Sower, Jesus says:

> Behold, a sower went forth to sow; And when he sowed, some seeds fell by the way side, and the fowls came and devoured them up: Some fell upon stony places, where they had not much earth: and forthwith they sprung up, because they had no deepness of earth: And when the sun was up, they were scorched; and because they had no root, they withered away. And some fell among thorns; and the thorns sprung up, and choked them: But other fell into good ground, and brought forth fruit, some an hundredfold, some sixtyfold, some thirtyfold (Matt. 13:3-8).

In Luke 8:11-15, Jesus explained the meaning of the Parable:

> The seed is the word of God. Those by the wayside are they that hear; then cometh the devil, and taketh away the word out of their hearts, lest they should believe and be saved. They on the rock are they, which, when they hear, receive the word with joy; and these have no root, which for a while believe, and in time of temptation fall away. And that which fell among thorns are they, which, when they have heard, go forth, and are choked with cares and riches and pleasures of this life, and bring no fruit to perfection. But that on the good ground are they, which in an honest and good heart, having heard the word, keep it, and bring forth fruit with patience.

In this parable, Jesus' explanation makes clear that conversion is based upon an individual's intellectual and emotional response to the Gospel message. In each case where there is a failure to respond or maintain one's faith, the loss is based upon subjective reasons under the individual's control. Repeatedly in the parable, Jesus refers to the condition of the individual's heart, desires, concerns, and problems. He ends His explanation by saying that only those with an "honest and good heart . . .

bring forth fruit." Clearly, the Christian message is all about free choices made by individual people.

In Matthew 13:24-30, Jesus provides another parable about sowing—a parable that explicitly makes an iron-clad case against the use of force on non-believers:

> The kingdom of heaven is likened unto a man which sowed good seed in his field: But while men slept, his enemy came and sowed tares among the wheat . . . But when the blade was sprung up, and brought forth fruit, then appeared the tares also. So the servants of the householder came and said unto him . . . Wilt thou then that we go and gather them up? But he said, Nay; lest while ye gather up the tares ye root up also the wheat with them. Let both grow together until the harvest.

The harvest Jesus is speaking of is the Final Judgment by God, an action solely under the direction and control of God. This statement by Jesus rejects the use of human efforts to compel religious conformity or to use force to rid the world of false teachings. It is a message consistent with the statement by the Lord in the Torah: "To me belongeth vengeance" (Deut. 32:35). In the New Testament, it is confirmed in Romans 12:17-19: "Recompense to no man evil for evil. Provide things honest in the sight of all men. If it be possible, as much as lieth in you, live peaceably with all men. Dearly beloved, avenge not yourselves, but rather give place unto wrath: for it is written, Vengeance is mine; I will repay, saith the Lord."

The famous parable of the Prodigal Son in Luke 15 also confirms the same message of a long-suffering God Whose goodness and patience are rewarded when a rebellious son finally comes to his senses. The son represents universal human rebellion to God's will. The father in the parable does not compel the son to honor or respect his will but leaves it to the son to make a free choice of repentance based on his own life experience and reasoning. The Prodigal Son leaves his father's house based on free will and returns to his father's house based upon another act of free will. We find in one of Paul's letters to the Romans the same essential truth expressed this way: "Despisest thou the riches of his goodness and forbearance and longsuffering; not knowing that the goodness of God leadeth thee to repentance?" (Rom. 2:4).

Supporting this evidence in the Old and New Testaments are also words and examples from Jesus' life experiences. In Matthew 26:52-53, we have the record of the arrest of Jesus when an angry Peter used a sword to assault someone. Jesus told him, "Put up again thy sword into his place: for all they that take the sword shall perish with the sword. Thinkest thou that I cannot now pray to my Father, and he shall presently give me more than twelve legions of angels?" Here, Jesus clarifies to His followers that it would not be by force that His Kingdom will rule, spread, or be maintained.

In Luke 9:52-55, we find Jesus' response to those of His followers who desired Him to use His supernatural powers to punish unbelievers who had just rejected hearing the Gospel message: "[Jesus] sent messengers before his face: and they went, and entered into a village of the Samaritans, to make ready for him. And they did not receive him . . . And when his disciples . . . saw this, they said, Lord, wilt thou that we command fire to come down from heaven, and consume them, even as Elias did? But he turned and rebuked them."

Later, after Jesus' teachings had alarmed both the Jewish religious authorities and the Roman political authorities, Jesus gave a definitive answer to the Roman governor, Pilate: "My kingdom is not of this world: if my kingdom were of this world, then would my servants fight" (John 18:36). Jesus had already engaged with the Pharisees on this same question about the coming of His kingdom in Luke 17:21: "the kingdom of God is within you." This was another definitive statement that on earth, God's will is to rule over the hearts and minds of people and not through governments or force.

Jesus had come into the world to abolish humanity's enslavement to a sinful heart and a selfish ego. He made this clear in the Gospel of John when He said, "If ye continue in my word, then are ye my disciples indeed; And ye shall know the truth, and the truth shall make you free" (John 8:31-32).

H.J. Pos, in a UNESCO report investigating freedom in the world, explained the importance of this belief:

> Christianity brought an entirely different meaning, namely free will . . . the liberty to choose between good and evil . . . Christianity has singularly strengthened the role of the (conscience) by teaching that one must "obey God before men." To the present day, Christianity has inspired acts of resistance against tyrannical and criminal governments and upheld the rights of the religious conscience . . . Christianity handed down to Western civilization the struggle for moral liberty.[153]

The ancient pagan Roman philosopher, Pliny, recognized the uniquely democratic character of the early Christian church. In a letter to the emperor Trajan in A.D. 112, he wrote, "In the provinces of Asia Minor . . . the temples of the gods were almost forsaken, and the Christians were everywhere a multitude. The members were of every class, from the noblest rank down to the slaves . . . But in the church, its services and its officers, the slave was treated as the equal of the noble. A slave might be a bishop, while his master was only and ordinary member.[154]

Early Christian worship also reflected this democratic character. Ordinary members of the church could freely and spontaneously offer prayer. The apostle Paul agreed with having several Christian members freely taking part in the worship services, but he cautioned that "all things be done decently and in order" (1 Cor. 14:40). Some of the earliest Christian writings after the New Testament held the same position—namely, that God had created man a free moral agent. It was for each person to, as Paul wrote, "work out [their] own salvation with fear and trembling" (Phil. 2:12).

---

153   Robert E. Dewey, James A. Gould, and H.J. Pos, "Unesco Report on the Investigation Concerning Freedom," in *Freedom: Its History, Nature and Varieties*, (London: Macmillan, 1970), 60, 63-64.
154   Paul Pavao, "Pliny the Younger: Letter to Trajan," *Christian History for Everyman*, Accessed January 4, 2023, https://www.christian-history.org/pliny-the-younger.html.

Bishop Theophilus of Antioch, who lived from A.D. 169-183, wrote in a letter, "To Autolycus [his pagan friend] . . . God made man free and self-determining . . . Thus if he should incline to the ways of immortality, keeping the command of God, she should receive from God the reward of immortality . . . If, however, he turns aside to the ways of death, disobeying God, he should become for himself the cause of death."[155]

In an earlier letter called "Letter to Diognetus," written about A.D. 130 by a disciple named Mathetes, we find the same insistence that faith is a voluntary matter between God and man. "Who did God send to bring truth to the world? He sent the very Designer and Creator of the universe . . . But did he send him, as one might suppose, in despotism and fear and terror? Not so. Rather, in gentleness and meekness . . . He sent him for saving and persuading, but not for compelling. Compulsion, you see, is not an attribute of God."[156]

The Greek bishop, known later as St. Irenaeus (A.D. 130-A.D. 202), made the same case. He quoted Jesus' plea to Israel: "How often would I have gathered your children together, but you would not" and then added, "[make] clear the ancient law of human liberty; for God made man free from the beginning, so that he possessed his own power just as his own soul, to follow God's will freely, not being compelled by God, for with God there is no coercion."[157]

St. Augustine, a greater name in Christian literature, was still defending this view in the fourth century A.D., writing, "No one should be coerced into the unity of Christ . . . we must fight only by arguments, and prevail only by force of reason."[158] Unfortunately, for the Catholic church and the cause of Christ in general, its leadership began to stir her policy in a different direction.

155 W.A. Jurgens, "Bishop Theophilus of Antioch, 'Letter to Autolycus,'" In *The Faith of the Early Fathers*, Vol. 1, (Collegeville: Liturgical Press, 1970), 1-76.
156 Ibid.
157 Ibid, 98.
158 "Augustine—Letter 93 to Vincentius (*Cogite Intrare*)," Early Church Texts, Accessed October 20, 2022, https://www.earlychurchtexts.com/main/augustine/letter_93_to_vincentius_cogite_intrare.shtml.

By the fourth century A.D., its leadership had become too closely attached to Rome's imperial government, and soon, flushed with new political power, it began to adopt rationales justifying the use of force in matters of faith. This was not a position that all Catholics took. Many of her holiest and most saintly followers objected to using force in matters of faith. Many others blindly followed the authority of her leadership. Finally, under the courageous direction of John Paul II, an official apology was offered to the world. The *New York Times* published his apology on March 13, 2000, under the title, "Pope Asks Forgiveness for Errors of the Church Over 2,000 Years."[159]

The New Testament uses the word "teacher" seventy-one times and the word "preach" 141 times. The meaning of the word *preach* means to "advocate earnestly." For the first three hundred years after the death of Jesus Christ, the rapid growth of the Christian church was solely advanced by teaching and preaching. Christianity proved its ability to convert large numbers of people without pressure or force. Paul wrote in his second letter to the Corinthian church, "All things are of God, who hath reconciled us to himself . . . and hath given to us the ministry of reconciliation . . . Now then we are ambassadors for Christ" (2 Cor. 5:18-20).

Mark wrote, "And he ordained twelve that they should be with him, and that he might send them forth to preach" (Mark 3:14). Paul's letter to the Roman Church declares, "I am debtor both to the Greeks, and to the Barbarians; both to the wise, and to the unwise. So, as much as in me is, I am ready to preach the gospel to you that are at Rome also" (Rom. 1:14-15).

These apostolic letters were intended to recruit all willing Christians to join the Great Commission of preaching the Gospel. Paul's letter to the church at Colossae makes this very plain: "Let the word of Christ dwell in you richly in all wisdom; teaching and admonishing one another in psalms and hymns and spiritual songs from the Spirit, singing with grace in your

---

159 "List of Apologies Made by Pope John Paul II," Wikipedia Foundation, last modified June 26, 2022, https://en.wikipedia.org/wiki/List_of_apologies_made_by_Pope_John_Paul_II.

hearts to the Lord" (Col. 3:16). His second letter to Timothy calls for the same evangelism: "Preach the word; be instant in season, out of season; reprove, rebuke, and exhort" (2 Tim. 4:2).

Most of what one reads in the New Testament is about teaching and preaching, and people either accept or reject the Gospel message of their free will. This is the method that Jesus used and commanded His followers to use; anything else is anti-Christian. By combining the beliefs that humans are both sacred and free, a new stage in the development of human rights was reached. What remained was its logical extension to the governance of men.

Historian Herbert J. Muller said, "The most vital force in the last centuries of Rome . . . was Christianity. It had the potentialities for freedom inherited from Judaism, emphasized by the more insistent gospel of love and brotherhood preached by Jesus." Muller continued in his praise of the influence of the Judeo-Christian tradition, "Its most obvious contribution was the ideal of social justice preached by the great prophets . . . rejecting the fatalistic resignation common to other Eastern peoples . . . they introduced the novel, portentous idea of the Messiah . . . the germs of the dynamic idea of progress."[160]

Muller also explained that the ancient Jewish kings were not like medieval or modern kings and explained the difference as "kingship in Israel was essentially different from the sacred monarchy . . . the king was in no sense divine or eligible for deification . . . his power was not absolute; he was always subject to a higher law . . . he could be openly denounced . . . as he often was by the prophets and even the high priests."[161]

As the ancient Roman civilization began to collapse under the weight of Germanic invasions, Europe entered a Dark Age. Any widespread acceptance of human rights or democratic forms of governance would have to wait another one thousand years. But even during this period, dissenting Catholic

---

160 Herbert J. Muller, "Freedom and Justice in History," in *Freedom: Its History, Nature and Varieties*, edited by James Gould and Robert E, Dewey (London: Macmillian 1970), 20-21.
161 Ibid.

voices spoke up for freedom against the tide of suppression promoted by their church leadership. People who in later Catholic church history were named saints—like Francis of Assisi, Teresa of Avila, and Thomas Aquinas—spoke in favor of increasing freedom of thought. So did many famous Catholic philosophers—Peter Abelard, William of Ockham, Marsilius of Padua, and Desiderius Erasmus. Finally, we can add these Catholic theologians, John Wycliffe, John Huss, and Martin Luther; they all "spoke truth to power."

Between the twelfth and sixteenth centuries, there were numerous movements within the Catholic Church to reform itself. Many of these movements had in common the belief that individuals should be free to read and study the Bible in their language. Freedom of conscience or thought is the beginning of individual freedoms. Actions are the product of thoughts, and thoughts must be free before actions can be free. The Protestant Reformation movement was not the beginning of these beliefs but the culmination of an ongoing tension within the Catholic Church that had been building for multiple centuries. The Catholic historian Lord Acton (1834-1902) did give extra credit to the seventeenth century Protestants for revitalizing this ancient Judeo-Christian principal of human freedom. Lord Acton wrote:

> The idea that religious liberty is the generating principle of civil, and that civil liberty is the necessary condition of religious, was a discovery reserved for the seventeenth century . . . there were men among the independent congregations (Protestants) who grasped . . . the principle that it is only by abridging the authority of States that the liberty of Churches can be assured. That great political idea, sanctifying freedom and consecrating it to God . . . has been the soul of what is great and good in the progress of the last two hundred years.[162]

162 Robert E. Dewey, James A. Gould, and Lord Acton, "The History of Freedom in Ancient and Modern Europe," in *Freedom: Its History, Nature and Varieties* (London: Macmillan, 1970), 45.

The Protestant Reformation was a movement to rediscover and practice the original teachings of Christianity. Protestant theologian, Paul Tillich, confirmed this when writing, "In principle, Christianity has always maintained the unconditional moral responsibility of the individual person in the Pauline doctrine of conscience."[163] Many of the greatest voices of Catholicism (mentioned above in this chapter) were in total agreement with this doctrine. Tillich gives credit to the Catholic philosopher Thomas Aquinas (1225-1274), writing, "Aquinas states that he must disobey the command of a superior to whom he has made a vow of obedience, if the superior asks something against his conscience."[164]

Some of Thomas Aquinas' political views were ahead of his time. He wrote in *On the Rule of Princes*, "The prince holds the power of legislating only so far as he represents the will of the people."[165] This view of politics is essentially the Social Contract theory, which the English philosopher John Locke explained and defended in the late 1600s, and it is the same view of politics that became the basis of the U.S. Constitution and was expressed in Thomas Jefferson's document, the Declaration of Independence.

Before Thomas Aquinas, another famous medieval philosopher, Peter Abelard (1079-1142), had argued that false religious teaching should only be refuted by reason and not by force.[166] Other prominent Catholics, such as St. Bernard, disagreed on this issue, and during this period, Pope Innocent II ruled in favor of suppressing free thought, ordering Abelard to practice complete silence.

Long before Luther, a Dutch Catholic deacon named Gerard Groote (1340-1384) preached the Gospel in his language and created a widespread following among the working class in the Netherlands. His most famous follower was Thomas á Kempis, the author of the classic in Christian literature, *The*

---

163 Tillich, 139.
164 Ibid.
165 R.W. Dyson, *St. Thomas Aquinas: Political Writings* (Cambridge: Cambridge University Press, 2002).
166 Will Durant, *The Reformation*, Vol. 6, *The Story of Civilization* (New York: Simon and Schuster, 2011), 328.

Imitation of Christ. Groote is credited for the Christian movement known as the Brethren of the Common Life, which Thomas á Kempis joined. Groote, Thomas á Kempis, and other followers preached the need to return to a simple life devoted to Jesus Christ. What made this movement stand out was its devotion to studying the Bible and preaching in the vernacular language, as well as the fact that most of its followers were laymen, not clergy.[167]

During this pre-Reformation period, we see the same hunger among certain German Christian mystics to be free to seek and discover religious truth on their own. Historian Will Durant wrote of these mystics, "The Church looked with some concern upon the mystics who ignored most of her dogmas, neglected her ritual, and claimed to reach God without the help of priests . . . Here lay in germ the Reformation doctrines of private judgment, and every man a priest, and justification not by good works but by transcendent faith."[168]

The Catholic Church was correct that some of these mystics, or "Free Spirits," held heretical doctrines. But the issue was not whether some of these people were heretics, but rather, do heretics have a right as free individuals to be heretical. The word "heretic" comes from the Greek and means "individual choice." Throughout its long history, the Catholic Church battled against many forms of heresy. Unfortunately, in defending Christian truth, it stumbled into its own heresy of justifying the use of force against non-believers.

Before the Reformation became a popular social/political movement, it had been preceded by an intellectual movement. During the thirteenth, fourteenth, and early fifteenth centuries, some of the Catholic Church's greatest philosophers had written in support of freedom of thought and against the use of force to combat heresy. Marsilius of Padua (1275-1342) wrote "The Defender of Peace," a tract that proposed the separation of religious and secular authority. Marsilius advocated that crime should be punished by secular governments on earth, and sins should be punished by God in the next life.[169]

---

167 Ibid, 253-54.
168 Ibid, 256.
169 Ibid, 253-54.

The English philosopher and Franciscan William of Ockham proposed the same separation of secular and religious authority. By the fifteenth century, Nicholas of Cusa (1401-1464), a philosopher and cardinal in the Catholic Church, had written, "Since by nature all men are free, then every government . . . exists solely by the agreement and consent of the subjects."[170]

The most famous Catholic writer during the fifteenth century was the Dutch Humanist Erasmus. He was famous for both his satirical prose and his biblical scholarship. He was an ardent supporter of Catholic Church reform and freedom of conscience, and he drew the line regarding using force to promote religious conformity. In one of his most influential writings, the *Philosophy of Christ*, he stated:

> The yoke of Christ would be sweet, and his burden light, if petty human institutions added nothing to what he himself imposed. He commanded us nothing save love for one another . . . nothing accords better with the nature of man than the philosophy of Christ . . . I would that men were content to let Christ rule by the laws of the Gospel . . . We shall better overcome the Turks (Muslims) by the piety of our lives than by arms; the empire of Christianity will thus be defended by the same means by which it was originally established.[171]

Erasmus and other Catholic writers, philosophers, and churchmen were beginning to connect the dots between the need for freedom of thought and the democratic exercise of government. The earlier attempts at reformation by John Wycliffe in England and John Huss in Bohemia failed. Still, the beliefs upon which they were based—the right of free conscience, the right to read the Bible in one's own language, and the right of professing one's understanding of it without censure or punishment—survived and thrived under Martin Luther's efforts, beginning in 1521. His answer to the charge

---

170 Ibid, 256.
171 Ibid, 284-85.

of heresy was, "Unless I am convicted by the testimony of Sacred Scripture or by reason . . . my conscience is captive to the Word of God. I cannot and will not recant anything, for to go against my conscience is neither right nor safe. God help me. Amen."[172] This one quote expressed the essence of the Protestant Reformation.

In his essay, "The Changing Content of Freedom in History," Harold J. Laski wrote that the Reformation was "the most important factor in revitalizing the . . . doctrine of the primacy of the individual and in giving a new emphasis to individual rights . . . By the time of Locke the idea of the individual as the embodiment of certain natural and imprescriptible rights which authority is not entitled to invade had become commonplace."[173]

From the Protestant Reformation on, there is a clear line of historical development that proves the freedoms and democracy we now celebrate in Western civilization were the culmination of ideas that were contained in original Judeo-Christian teaching. Those areas of Europe where Protestantism flourished and became dominant are the same areas of the world where freedom and democracy first took root (i.e., England, Netherlands, Switzerland).

The same observation can also be made when comparing the colonial settlements in the New World of the Americas. The English colonies were populated by many immigrants seeking religious freedom. The colonies of France, Spain, and Portugal were known for their authoritarian governments and religious intolerance. Historian Paul Johnson described the cultural difference between the English colonies and the French: "by Continental standards Britain was a liberal state with a minimalist government and a tradition of freedom of speech, assembly, the press . . . France still had a divine right absolute monarchy . . . it was a Catholic state which did not

---

172 Williston Walker, *A History of The Christian Church* (New York: Charles Scribner's Son, 1970), 310.

173 Harold J. Laski, "The Changing Content of Freedom in History," in *Freedom: Its History, Nature and Varieties*, Eds. James A. Gould and Robert E. Dewey (London: Macmillan Company, 1970), 49-50.

practice toleration . . . The English settling in America brought with them this (English) political tradition."[174]

As the Reformation movement progressed between 1630 and 1660, Johnson wrote, "In England a veritable explosion of political argument and experiment, in which, perhaps for the first time in history, the fundamentals of participatory and democratic politics were discussed . . . and the English settlers in America were, in a sense, participants in this process."[175]

In the English colonies during this period, we began to see increasing support for representative democracy and religious tolerance. Roger Williams wrote, "It is impossible for any man or men to maintain their Christ by the sword, and to worship a true Christ."[176] The charter for his Rhode Island colony stated, "No person, within the said colony, at any time hereafter, shall be in any way molested, punished, disquieted or called in question, for any difference in opinion in matters of religion."[177]

In the colony of Connecticut, Thomas Hooker preached, "That all authority, in state or religion, must rest in the people's consent."[178] In Pennsylvania, Johnson wrote that William Penn "was determined to create a 'tolerance settlement' for Quakers and other persecuted sects from all over Europe."[179] In like manner, Catholics fleeing persecution from intolerant Protestants in Europe were also part of this changing attitude and thought. In their colony of Maryland, they passed the Toleration Act in 1649.

Before the American Revolution, the type of religious belief in the colonies was described by Paul Johnson as "under the control of laity . . . concerned itself with behavior . . . was voluntary and multi-denominational, and thus expressed freedom rather than restricted it."[180]

---

174 Johnson, 70.
175 Ibid, 71.
176 Ibid, 49.
177 Ibid, 50.
178 Ibid, 54.
179 Ibid, 64.
180 Ibid, 109.

Before the American Revolution, England, Scotland, and the Netherlands had already concluded their struggles to resist absolute monarchy and secure a measure of religious toleration. The most influential voice in England was John Locke. Will Durant described Locke's theory this way:

> He imagined that individuals in the "state of nature" were free and equal . . . no man had by nature more rights than any other . . . By reason . . . men came to agreement-made a "social contract" . . . Hence the community is the real sovereign. By majority vote it selects a chief administrator to implement its will . . . When the American colonists rebelled against the . . . monarchy of George III they adopted the ideas . . . almost the words, of Locke to express their Declaration of Independence.[181]

Before the American War for Independence, Paul Johnson identified the Protestant, colonial-wide revival known as the Great Awakening as a significant reason for the success of the American Revolution. Johnson also held that the American War for Independence had both a religious and political cause.[182] The widespread religious revival strengthened the patriots' belief that freedom and faith were inseparable beliefs ordained by God. Its influence was most felt among the Presbyterians and least among the Anglicans, who generally supported the Loyalists' cause. It is not an exaggeration to say that the most extraordinary political gift given to the world by Judeo-Christianity was the free United States of America.

Indeed, the great leaders who went on to devise and create America's republic would agree that faith and freedom were inseparable. John Adams wrote, "The Revolution was effected before the War commenced. The Revolution was in the minds and hearts of the people: and change in their religious sentiments of their duties and obligations."[183] The famous skeptic

---

181   Will and Ariel Durant, *The Age of Louis XIV*, Vol. 8. *The Story of Civilization* (New York: Simon and Schuster, 2011), 583.
182   Johnson, 116-17.
183   Ibid.

Thomas Jefferson agreed that there was an inseparable link between the sacred individual and the free individual writing, "The God who gave us life, gave us liberty at the same time: the hand of force may destroy, but cannot disjoin them."[184] On the other side of the issue, even King George III agreed. He called the American Revolution "a Presbyterian Rebellion."[185] Finally, let us end with the authoritative quote of John Adams that the settlement of America was part of God's plan, "for the illumination . . . and emancipation of the slavish part of mankind."[186]

---

184 Ibid.
185 Ibid, 173.
186 Ibid, 179.

CHAPTER TEN

THE LOVING AND FORGIVING INDIVIDUAL

IT IS CLEAR FROM THE historical record that there was no pagan concept of, or belief in, the universal brotherhood of man. A few wise individuals in that world (e.g., Socrates, Buddha, and Confucius) promoted something close to that view, but their understanding was alien to the prevailing cultures to which they belonged. The Jews became the first culture to promote a universal standard of morality. Their sense of social justice extended to the foreigner as much as to themselves (see Lev. 19:34). In the same way, their concept of love was more varied and advanced. The pagan Greek words for "love" included *philia*, which means "friendship," *philautia*, which means "self-love," and *eros*, which means "sexual love." Like other pagan cultures, their uses of the word "love" were more physical, narrowly focused, and ethnocentric. The ancient Jews added new meaning to the lexicon of love.

In the Jewish Mishnah, which is the rabbinic interpretation of the Torah, the rabbis wrote that the universe rests on three things: the Torah (God's Law), *avodah* (service to God), and *g'milut chasadim* (acts of lovingkindness). If we join these three beliefs together, we get something like, "Follow the law, in service to God, by showing acts of loving kindness." Another Hebrew word for "love" is *ahabah*, meaning, "God's love for His people." There is nothing in pagan myths about the gods having a general concern or love for all people.

The Old Testament is comprised of 622,700 words; of these, the word "love" is used 131 times. The New Testament is composed of 184,600 words; of these, the word "love" is used 310 times in the King James Version. God's message is always the same: "Love the Lord thy God with all thy heart, and with all thy soul, and with all thy mind" (Matt. 22:37) and "Love thy neighbour as thyself" (Mark 12:31). As we can see from the "love" word count, the New Testament placed a greater focus on the message of love than the Old Testament. This difference can be explained by the different missions or roles played by pre- and post-Messianic Judaism.

Moses and the pre-Christian prophets had as their primary role the establishment of the Torah. Most of their prophecy was about condemning evil and warning about the disastrous results of continued apostasy. It is only reasonable to believe that the Messiah's message to the world would be more hopeful, more explicit, and more consistent with the theme of love since the concept of the Messiah was based upon the expectation of God's future spiritual dominance in the world. This is what Jesus the Messiah was referring to when He prayed to His Father, "Thy kingdom come, Thy will be done in earth, as it is in heaven" (Matt. 6:10).

The Jews had been waiting for their Messiah for a reason. If He hadn't provided a more straightforward, more powerful message of God's intent beyond what they already knew, what were they waiting for? Their prophets knew that and said as much. In Jeremiah 31:31, we read, "'Behold the days are coming, declares the LORD, when I will make a new covenant with the house of Israel." And in Isaiah 61:1, the prophet declared, "The LORD has anointed me to bring good news to the poor; he has sent me to bind up the brokenhearted, to proclaim liberty to the captives, and the opening of the prison to those who are bound."

Isaiah 49:6 says, "It is too small a thing for you to be my servant to restore the tribes of Jacob and bring back those of Israel . . . I will also make you a light for the Gentiles, that my salvation may reach to the ends of the earth." It is only reasonable that God Himself (in the flesh) would provide a purer understanding of His nature and purposes beyond what an inspired, human intermediary could reveal. God knows His mind beyond what human beings can understand. Jesus was the final, perfect Message of Judaism. Orthodox Judaism teaches that the ancient temple in Jerusalem had to be rebuilt so all 613 commandments could be observed. Jesus said in John 2:19, "'Destroy this temple, and in three days I will raise it up.'" Jesus' reference was to His death and resurrection, not the Jewish temple. The temple was a symbol of God's authority and truth on earth, but now Jesus was saying He was the final Authority and Truth. In John 14:6, He explicitly stated, "'I am the way, and the truth, and the life. No one comes to the Father except through me.'"

Christianity is the only religion in the world that has introduced itself to the world by saying, "'For God so loved the world, that he gave his only Son . . . that the world might be saved" (John 3:16-17). God's plan was world redemption by the process of spreading His special, agape love throughout the world. Jesus was the Vehicle of that special love and set the pattern for the Church to follow through His life and words. No organization in history has as consistently over as long a period of history provided the world with more acts of charity than the Christian Church. Imitating its Founder, every Christian church is a charitable institution. The core message of Christianity is love—love of God and love of man—in that order.

Like no other religious book in history, the New Testament is saturated with statements promoting and explaining the true meaning of God's agape love. This unique love is both the nature of God and His mission on earth through His Son, Jesus Christ. *Agape* comes from the Greek, meaning "unconditional love" or "God love." It was a word developed and used by the early Christians to describe God and their relationship to God through their Intermediary, Jesus Christ. In the New Testament, we find the most extended list of statements about it:

- Do everything in love (1 Cor. 6:14).
- Put on love above all else (Col. 3:14).

- Never let go of love and faithfulness (Prov. 3:3).
- God is love (1 John 4:8).
- "We love . . . because he loved us" (1 John 4:19).
- Most importantly, "love each other deeply" (1 Peter 4:8).
- Love each other as He has loved us (John 15:12).
- Devote yourselves to one another in love (Rom. 12:10).
- God lives in us and makes His love perfect in us (1 John 4:12).
- "There is no fear in love" (1 John 4:18).
- Allow the Lord to increase your love increase (1 Thess. 3:12).
- Love your neighbor (Mark 12:31).
- Love your enemies and pray for them (Matt. 5:44).
- "Love *is* the fulfilling of the law" (Rom. 13:10).
- "The fruit of the Spirit is love" (Gal. 5:22).
- "Walk in love" (Eph. 5:2).
- Because you love God, keep His commands (John 14:15).
- God's love is spread in our hearts through the Holy Spirit (Rom. 5:5).
- If you obey God, you will always be loved by Him (John 15:10).
- The only thing that matters is faith through love (Gal. 5:6).

Another holy word found in the New Testament more often than any other ancient religious text is the word *forgiveness*. It is used in the New Testament fourteen times and once in the Old Testament. The Old Testament uses the word *forgive* forty-two times, and the New Testament uses it thirty-three times. From the Christian point of view, the themes of love and forgiveness are inseparable. It is impossible to experience agape love without being able to forgive. Remember, agape love is Who God is and how He loves. He loves the unlovable and forgives the sinner.

Jesus Himself made forgiving others a condition of our receiving forgiveness. He said in Matthew 6:14-15, "For if ye forgive men their trespasses, your heavenly Father will also forgive you. But if ye forgive not their trespasses, neither will your Father forgive your trespasses."

The apostles, who established the first Christian churches, continued the same message: "Forbearing one another, and forgiving one another . . . As Christ forgave you, so also do ye" (Col. 3:13). Agape is not just being saved from our sins and remaining the same people we were before being rescued. Agape is taking on the character and spiritual qualities of Jesus, then providing that example to the world. Since His two most remarkable qualities are love and forgiveness, they are required of every true Christian.

Forgiveness is not just a gracious thing to do. Forgiveness is itself an act of love. It was Jesus Christ's supreme act of love that He demonstrated by mounting the cross. He said, "Father, forgive them; for they know not what they do" (Luke 23:34). He was completing His mission of love on earth. While on earth, He had already set the pattern of love and forgiveness for every other Christian believer to follow. Crystal McDowell listed them in the *7 Different Ways Jesus Showed Love*:

1. Jesus healed the sick.
2. Jesus raised the dead.
3. Jesus fed the hungry.
4. Jesus preached the kingdom in love.
5. Jesus cast out demons.
6. Jesus interceded for his disciples . . .
7. Jesus gave his life for the world.[187]

Throughout Jesus' three-year ministry on earth, He did what He calls all His followers to do—"[speak] the truth in love" (Eph. 4:15). We find no examples when He was confronted verbally or with violence that He

---

187 Crystal McDowell, "7 Different Ways Jesus Showed Love," Telling Ministries, LLC, Accessed October 21, 2022, https://www.whatchristianswanttoknow.com/7-attributes-of-god-you-may-not-know/.

responded in like manner. He certainly had many opportunities to show a darker side of His humanity, but He didn't just teach forgiveness; He lived it. Non-forgiveness poisons the well of love, and it is impossible to practice the type of supernatural, agape love where non-forgiveness holds sway.

The apostle Peter took note of Jesus' perfect response to His enemies when he wrote in 1 Peter 2:21-24, "For even hereunto were ye: because Christ also suffered for us, leaving us an example, that ye should follow his steps . . . when he was reviled, reviled not again; when he suffered, he threatened not."

No other religion in history has as consistently and repeatedly told its followers to love and forgive others. The Bible teaches that the Christian life is "joy, peace, and righteousness" (Rom. 14:17). Out of this life flows all the activities of the Church: benevolence, worship, teaching, preaching—all the ways one can confess Jesus Christ before men. These "fruits of the Spirit" are effects of the Christian life but not the cause of it. Its cause is the indwelling Holy Spirit—the agape spirit of love.

The Christian life is, in a sense, both its fruit and its seed. Out of joy, we seek to bring joy; out of the peace of mind, we aim to be peacemakers. In pursuit of these ends—such as joy, peace, and righteousness—Christians renew their motivational forces of actions and thoughts to encourage each other. Joy, peace, and righteousness are, however, not external activities but spiritual attitudes or conditions of the soul. Christian love and living the Christian life are far more subtle than just doling out food stamps or public housing. The Christian life includes all conceivable acts of charity and the less tangible virtues that Jesus demonstrated.

The apostle Peter promoted these in his second epistle. "Add to your faith virtue; and to virtue knowledge; and to knowledge temperance; and to temperance patience; and to patience godliness; and to godliness brotherly kindness; and to brotherly kindness charity" (2 Peter 1:5-7). As we can see here, Peter's last virtue is charity—the visible external charity of good works. Peter would not have listed these other virtues as a necessary part of the Christian

THE LOVING AND FORGIVING INDIVIDUAL   133

life if good works were the total of the Christian life. Turning the other cheek, blessing people who abuse us, and praying for those who curse us are also acts of charity.

In Mark 12:41-44, it is recorded, "Jesus sat over against the treasury, and beheld how the people cast money into the treasury: and many that were rich cast in much. And there came a certain poor widow, and she threw in two mites . . . And he called unto him his disciples, and saith unto them . . . this poor widow hath cast more in . . . For all they did cast in of their abundance; but she of her want."

Here we see that quantity becomes irrelevant, and quality becomes paramount. The widow's story continues to challenge us and inspire us, even in the absence of any perceptibly physical change caused by the widow's gift. The starving masses remained, but the widow's example of unselfishness is a powerful stimulant to the hearts of those who have the wealth to satisfy those human needs.

The social/political philosophies of the nineteenth century (socialism, communism) ignored the causal relationship between individual sin and group misery. Jesus' statement that "the love of money is the root of all evil" (1 Tim. 6:10) was suddenly altered to mean, "The lack of money is the root of all evil." These philosophies were largely group-orientated. They taught men that the individual's condition couldn't change until the whole of society was radically altered. The results of this theory have been bloody revolutions, genocide, and individual immorality; for if an individual's life did not count, neither could it be blamed for its crimes, and without blame, neither could there be individual responsibility. One of the great wisdoms of Judeo-Christianity is that we can only make society better by making individuals better or, as Jesus said, "Except a man be born again, he cannot see the kingdom of God" (John 3:2).

As we have established, the Christian is a free individual. Still, because of his relationship to Christ as a redeemed citizen of the Kingdom of God, he is also an obligated servant. This is one of the many paradoxes which

Christianity teaches. The apostle Paul wrote, "When ye were the servants of sin, ye were free from righteousness" (Rom. 6:20). The opposite is also true: to be freed from the control of selfishness and sin places us under the obligation and responsibility to serve God. In life, there is no middle ground or place of moral neutrality. It is like the Bob Dylan song says, "You're going to have to serve somebody / Well, it may be the devil or it may be the Lord / But you're going to have to serve somebody."[188]

The Protestant reformer Martin Luther had already written a great deal on this subject before his ex-communication in 1521. In his essay, "On Secular Authority," he wrote, "Over the soul God can and will let no one rule but himself . . . Since belief or unbelief is a matter of everyone's conscience."[189] But in "On the Liberty of a Christian Man" he explained, "A Christian is a perfect free lord of all, subject to none. A Christian is a perfectly dutiful servant of all, subject to all."[190] Luther went on to explain this paradox by quoting St. Paul's explanation: "For though I am free from all men, yet have I made myself servant unto all" (1 Cor. 9:19). He also quoted Romans 13:8, which says, "Owe no man anything, but to love one another." Luther agreed, adding, "Love by its very nature is ready to serve and be subject to him who is loved. So Christ, although he was Lord of all . . . was at the same time a free man and a servant."[191]

All actual Christian charity comes from an attitude of love and thankfulness. St. Paul's extraordinary letter on the nature of love found in 1 Corinthians 13:1-13 provides the definitive proof that this is the valid Christian message. "Though I have the gift of prophecy, and understand all mysteries, and all knowledge; and though I have all faith, so that I could remove mountains, and have not charity,

188 Bob Dylan, "Gotta Serve Somebody," 1 1072 on *Gotta Serve Somebody*, Columbia Records, 1979.
189 Joseph Loconte, "Martin Luther and the Long March to Freedom of Conscience," National Geographic online, October 27, 2017, https://www.nationalgeographic.com/history/article/martin-luther-freedom-protestant-reformation-500.
190 Martin Luther, "On the Liberty of a Christian Man," in *Freedom: Its History, Nature and Varieties*, edited by James A. Gould and Robert E. Dewey (London: Macmillan, 1970), 174.
191 Ibid, 179.

I am nothing. And though I bestow all my goods to feed the poor, and though I give my body to be burned and have not charity, it profitieth me nothing."

Because Martin Luther spent so much time teaching that human beings were saved by "faith alone," he was careful to also promote a doctrine of doing good works. He knew his enemies would say he only cared about having faith and neglected good deeds. To preempt or counter this slander, he wrote, "A man does not live for himself alone in this mortal body . . . he lives for all men on earth . . . and to this end he brings his body into subjection, that he may the more sincerely and freely serve others."[192] Furthermore, "this rule for the life of Christians that we should devote all our work to the welfare of others, since each has abundant riches in his faith, that all his other works and his whole life are a surplus with which he can by voluntary benevolence do good to his neighbor."[193]

And Luther also said, "I will therefore give myself as a Christ to my neighbor, just as Christ offered himself to me; I will do nothing in this life except what I see necessary, profitable and salutary to my neighbor, since through faith I have an abundance of all good things in Christ."[194]

For thousands of years, the Judeo-Christian message has been the most positive, transformative message the world has ever known. Starting with its application in the ancient Roman world and continuing to the present, no other belief system has benefited the world more. Sociological statistics, worldwide historical facts, and modern psychological studies all confirm the truth of this statement. The Judeo-Christian message is responsible for billions of individual acts of charity and has also been the catalyst for numerous social, political, and economic reforms.

192 Ibid.
193 Ibid, 181.
194 Ibid.

The historian Will Durant writes of the changing ethical message brought about by the spread of Christianity in the ancient, pagan Roman world:

> For the first time in European history the teachers of mankind preached an ethic of kindliness . . . humility, patience, mercy, purity, chastity . . . the Church . . . demanded a single standard of fidelity for both sexes in marriage . . . she raised the morals of the home . . . she raised the security and dignity of the wife . . . the Church blessed abundant motherhood, and sternly forbade abortion and infanticide . . . the Romans had maintained hospitals for their soldiers: but it was Christian charity that gave the institution a wide development."[195]

After the fall of Rome in A.D. 476, it was the Church that, over time, established fifty percent of the hospitals that now exist in modern Europe. It was the Church that "suppressed the gladiatorial shows, denounced the enslavement of prisoners . . . taught men a new respect for human life . . . softened the penalties exacted by Roman and barbarian law . . . with Christianity . . . the treatment of slaves . . . became more humane; legal rights were given to them . . . and emancipation was sanctioned and encouraged."[196]

The great universities of Europe and the most prestigious ones founded in colonial America (e.g. Harvard, Princeton, Yale, and Dartmouth) had their beginnings as servants of the Judeo-Christian message. Most of Western civilization's art, architecture, classical music, drama, literature, philosophy, law, and science are the products of the fusion of Greco-Roman culture and Judeo-Christian culture. Wherever this hybrid culture has been spread and taken root, it has produced the same civilizing effects.

It was not only western Europe and its colonial settlements which have benefited from Judeo-Christian culture's spiritual/moral values. Eastern European countries such as Russia, Poland, and Hungary were improved by

---

195 Will Durant *The Age of Faith*, Vol. 4, *The Story of Civilization* (New York: Simon and Schuster, 1950), 76.
196 Ibid, 77.

it as well. Durant writes, "The Slavs would have continued to be an almost totally illiterate people had it not been for the efforts of the missionary Cyril. Cyril invented the Slavonic alphabet and . . . This made possible a huge advance in education and civilization."[197] Without Cyril's alphabet, the world would never have had the great masters of Russian literature: Leo Tolstoy, Fyodor Dostoevsky, Aleksander Solzhenitsyn. In the big picture, without the civilizing and unifying influence of Judeo-Christian culture on Europe, both west and east, there would have been perpetual domination by pagan invaders like German tribes, Vikings, Huns, and Mongols. The development of a strong, culturally unified, Western civilization would have been lacking to prevent a permanent pagan Dark Age.

Not only did Judeo-Christianity provide a moral/spiritual foundation upon which European civilization could be resurrected after the Dark Ages, but it also has, for multiple centuries, shown its spiritual resiliency by being a catalyst for numerous reform movements. The Protestant Reformation triggered the most remarkable moral/spiritual revival ever known. The Reformation increased literacy and educational reforms. New educational curriculums were created that promoted the advanced study of science, history, mathematics, music, and art.[198] The Protestant reformers believed that everyone should be able to read, including girls. The Reformation doctrine said that every Christian is his own priest and must know and practice what the Bible teaches. This belief placed the primary responsibility for religion and education on the individual.[199]

Before the Reformation, the old, medieval view held that "ignorance is the mother of piety." The medieval Church had greatly restricted the publication of written materials, especially the Bible. Based upon the fear of spreading heresy, the Church operated on a need-to-know basis. In their view, the clergy

---

197 Ibid, 535-36.
198 Hugh Whelchel, "How the Reformation Changed Education Forever," Institute For Faith, Work & Economics, June 26, 2017, https://tifwe.org/how-the-reformation-changed-education-forever.
199 Ibid.

needed to know, and the laity was required to receive and accept what they were taught without questioning.

When the Reformation spread to Scotland, it established a national school system with the primary focus on children being able to read the Bible.[200] In *How The Scots Invented the Modern World*, Arthur Herman wrote that by 1696, "nearly every parish in Scotland had some sort of school . . . Scotland's literacy rate would be higher than that of any other country by the end of the eighteenth century."[201] Herman explains that out of this widespread improvement in learning, Scotland became an influential source of Enlightenment and progress for itself and the rest of the world. Great names in literature, science, engineering, and political and economic theory were the result: James Watt, Adam Smith, David Hume, Francis Hutcheson, Robert Burns, and Sir Walter Scott—to name only a few.

The Protestant emphasis on free individuals, freely studying and spreading what they called "the Word of God," produced the same remarkable results in the English colonies during the First Great Awakening. Beyond the political influence of encouraging the American Revolution, it caused a widespread increase in schooling and literacy.[202] It was created by preachers carrying the Word of God to simple frontier people. Historian Paul Johnson explains, "These preachers were anxious not just to deliver a message but to get their hearers to learn it themselves by studying the Bible; and to do that they needed to read . . . an important element of the Great Awakening was the provision of some kind of basic education."[203]

As a result of this sincere desire to evangelize the people of the Frontier, William Tennent established what he called "Log Colleges," teaching the basics of education along with religious instruction. One of these Log Colleges

200 Arthur Herman, *How the Scots Invented the Modern World* (New York: Three Rivers Press, 2001), 22-23.
201 Ibid
202 Johnson, 114.
203 Ibid, 110.

became, in time, Princeton University.[204] The Second Great Awakening, which took place in the early to mid-nineteenth century, produced a similar effort to spread literacy and education.

Paul Johnson describes these efforts: "By 1850 (Methodists and Baptists) . . . had penetrated every existing state and had a major theological college in almost all of them . . . This kind of intense religion seemed to give to the lives of ordinary people a focus and motivation which turned them into pioneers, entrepreneurs, and innovators on a heroic scale."[205]

As in all periods of history, one sees causes producing effects that also become causes; these are the back-and-forth influences of different areas of the world. It was during the First Great Awakening that John Wesley visited America and was stirred by the teachings of Jonathan Edwards, who was one of the great preachers of that movement. He eventually returned to England and, with his brother Charles, initiated the greatest evangelical movement in modern British history.[206] John and Charles traveled thousands of miles preaching to both small and large audience of poor working-class people— people who the established Church of England had largely neglected. Because the official church of England condemned their evangelical efforts, most of their evangelism was conducted outside in public.

Although Wesley was a pastor in the Church of England, his experience in America led him to embrace a more emotional, less-intellectual style of evangelism. Like the others of the Great Awakening movement, he believed that true religious conversion had to elicit a response from both the heart and the mind. It was out of the efforts of the Wesley brothers that the Methodist Church was established.[207] Not only did Methodism raise the moral standards in England, but it also promoted a greater concern for the welfare of the ordinary person. The Methodist Church (e.g., the Quakers,

---

204 Ibid, 113.
205 Ibid.
206 Ibid, 297.
207 Walker, ibid.

Unitarians, and Congregationalists) became a home for many in the British anti-slavery movement.[208] This was a natural fit, since Methodism spoke to the poor and oppressed and many Methodists had been jailed and persecuted for their beliefs.

In Great Britain, the leader of the opposition to the slave trade was William Wilberforce. Will Durant describes Wilberforce's motivation and efforts to end the slave trade when he wrote, "Feeling the influence of the Evangelical Movement . . . he protested that a nation officially Christian still tolerated the trade in African slaves . . . Wilberforce . . . formed the Society for the Abolition of the slave trade."[209] Wilberforce introduced an anti-slave trade bill to Parliament four different times. He died in 1833, and a month later, a bill was passed that abolished slavery in all British territories.[210]

From this period forward, a growing number of people inspired by the Judeo-Christian message of love in Great Britain and America would be instrumental in protesting and calling for social, political, and humanitarian reforms. In 1774, John Howard presented a report to Parliament calling for prison reform. Durant writes of John Howard, "Howard took Christianity not as a system of law but as an appeal to the heart . . . he was appalled by the conditions in the local prison . . . most prisoners wore chains . . . No heat was provided in winter . . . some died of slow starvation."[211] It has been calculated that John Howard traveled over forty-two thousand miles, recording the conditions under which prisoners were kept.

In America, Dorothea Dix, another remarkable individual, replicated the method used by John Howard to study the conditions under which the mentally ill were kept.[212] In the end, like Howard, her ongoing research and lobbying of the government eventually led to significant reforms.

---

208 Ibid, 469-70.
209 Durant, Vol. 10, 733.
210 Ibid, Vol 11, 367-68.
211 Ibid, Vol 10, 737-38.
212 Dorothea Dix, Wikimedia Foundation, last modified December 5, 2022, https://en.wikipedia.org/wiki/Dorothea_Dix.

The lives of people like Wesley, Wilberforce, Howard, and Dix are potent examples of the importance of individual lives inspired by the Judeo-Christian message of love. What has been presented here is only the tiniest tip of the humanitarian iceberg inspired by Judeo-Christianity. In more modern times, the American Civil Rights movement of the 1960s, the anti-apartheid movement in South Africa in the 1970s-80s, and the Catholic Church's support of the Solidarity Movement in communist-ruled Poland in the 1980s are all examples of the continuing influence of the Judeo-Christian message to bring about reform.

What do the facts today show about the average person of faith in the United States of America regarding charitable giving and voluntary efforts to help others in need? There is strong evidence that people of religious belief are much more giving and concerned about the welfare of others than secular people. The evidence also shows that the level of personal involvement in one's religious belief system is correlated strongly to the amount of time and money they are willing to give to help others.

In the United States of America, close to seventy-five percent of all charitable giving is faith-based, and the vast majority is Christian.[213] America today, with all of its problems, is still the most religious country among the developed countries of the world.[214] As a nation, America donates seven times as much to charity as the nations of Europe.[215]

Not only is there a strong correlation between religious faith and giving, but there is also a correlation between the decline in spiritual practice and giving. Based on a study by *Chronicle of Philanthropy*, "from 2000-2014 the share of American households donating to charity dropped by nearly 11 points, from 66.2 percent to 55.5 percent." The bottom line is that as America becomes more

213 Karl Zinsmeister, "Less God, Less Giving?," *Philanthropy Roundtable*, Winter 2019, https://www.philanthropyroundtable.org/magazine/less-god-less-giving.
214 Ibid.
215 David Harsanyi, "Americans are more generous than Europeans—by a large margin," New York Post online, October 23, 2021, https://nypost.com/2021/10/23/americans-are-more-generous-than-europeans-by-a-large-margin/.

secular, it also becomes less charitable. Americans provided $449.54 billion in charity in 2019, and of that amount, sixty-nine percent came from individuals.[216]

The World Giving Index ranked America as one of the most generous countries in the world.[217] American private charity exceeds the foreign aid provided by the U.S. government.[218] It is not by accident that Communist China ranks among the lowest on a survey of charitable giving by nations based on their GNP.[219] Chairman Mao, the founder of Red China, stated in his Communist bible, the *Little Red Book*, "Communism has nothing to do with love,[sic] it is just an excellent hammer for smashing one's enemies."[220] Contrast that statement with what Jesus told His followers: "By this shall all men know that ye are my disciples, if ye have love one to another" (John 13:35).

Even in a highly religious society like India, Christians stand out for their charitable giving. A national survey of per-household religious contributions found that Christian Indians give the largest amount per household of all religious communities.[221]

If love and forgiveness are the starting point of the Christian life, joy and peace are its supernatural results.

---

216 "Share of Households Donating to Charity Drops to Lowest Level in Nearly 20 Years," *The Chronicle of Philanthropy*, July 27, 2021, https://www.philanthropy.com/newsletter/philanthrophy-today/2021-07-27.

217 Charities Aid Foundation, "CAF World Giving Index, 2021" (London: CAF Publications, 2021), https://www.cafonline.org/docs/default-source/about-us-research/cafworldgivingindex2021_report_web2_100621.pdf.

218 "Giving USA: Total U.S, charitable giving remained strong in 2021, reaching $484.85 billion" Lilly Family School of Philanthropy, June 21, 2022, https://philanthropy.iupui.edu/news-events/news-item/giving-usa:--total-u.s.-charitable-giving-remained-strong-in-2021,-reaching-$484.85-billion.html?id=392#:~:text=Giving%20USA%3A%20Total%20U.S.%20charitable,in%202021%2C%20reaching%20%24484.85%20billion&text=Giving%20USA%202022%3A%20The%20Annual,to%20U.S.%20charities%20in%202021.

219 "Bill Gates, in Communist newspaper, urges more in China to help poor," Reuters.com, April 28, 2014, https://www.reuters.com/article/us-china-philanthropy-gates/bill-gates-in-communist-newspaper-urges-more-in-china-to-help-poor-idUKKBN0DE0QY20140428.

220 "Foreword to the Second Edition of the Quotations of Chairman Mao, 1966," USC US China Institute, December 16, 1966, https://china.usc.edu/foreword-second-edition-quotations-chairman-mao-1966.

221 Suvojit Bagchi, "Christian, Muslim Households Top in Donation for Charity," THG publishing PVT, Ltd., July 15, 2017, https://www.thehindu.com/news/national/christian-muslim-households-top-in-donations-for-charity/article19285920.ece.

CHAPTER ELEVEN

THE JOYFUL AND PEACEFUL INDIVIDUAL

MY FAVORITE QUOTE FROM THE classic Christian literature of St. Augustine's *Confessions* is, "Thou hast made us for thyself, O Lord, and our heart is restless until it finds its rest in thee."[222] His confessions detail his life as a pagan—the sins, the crimes, and vain attempts to find happiness outside God's love. He describes in beautiful poetry and profound philosophical insight the fruitless journey to find happiness in physical pleasure, fame, honor, and wealth. He concludes, "For whither so ever the soul of man turns itself, unless towards Thee, it is riveted upon sorrows."[223]

He admits that there are many good things to experience in life, but none provide lasting pleasure or joy. They are only fleeting moments. When they are lost or taken away, we are left in desolation, depression, or worse, despair. This was the life he knew until he found lasting joy and peace in the Lord. Augustine prayed to God, "Out of all these things [pleasures] let my soul praise Thee, O God, Creator of all; yet let not my soul be riveted unto these things . . . For they go whither they were to go, that they might not be . . . in these things is no place of repose; they abide not, they flee . . . abide forever before God, who abideth and standeth fast forever."[224]

After losing both my parents, I remember thinking that the only thing that does not decay, lessen in time, or become less meaningful was the love

---

222 St. Augustine, *Confessions* (London: Everyman's Library, 1975), 1.
223 Ibid, 60.
224 Ibid, 60-61.

I felt for them. This is what St. Augustine was expressing—that our love for God and God's love for us endures. It is always fresh, active, and alive.

Unhappiness is the absence of joy, and restlessness is the absence of peace. The greatest thieves of joy and peace are fear and guilt. Only by removing these impediments can the human soul know joy and peace. That is what Christianity makes possible—experiencing God's love and forgiveness results in joy and peace. This is what Christians experience when their minds are on God in worship. When they pray to him, sing praise, or meditate on his extraordinary greatness and goodness, they are overwhelmed with joy and a sense of inner peace.

The joy of the Lord and the peace of the Lord are beneficial in times of physical pain and emotional suffering. Knowing these does not do away with pain but mitigates its intensity. Joy and peace are candles of hope in the darkness. Thomas Jefferson, a skeptic of the supernatural, admitted after the death of his young daughter that if he had had more religious faith, his grief would not have been as great. He recognized how faith had helped others to cope with their grief, but he did not have the necessary faith to help himself.

Pain, suffering, and grief are all part of the universal human condition. Buddha made a whole philosophy out of it.[225] Suffering without hope soon turns to cynicism. As we discussed when we studied paganism, pagans had no answer for this problem. In the face of suffering, they thought the gods were uncaring, evil, or attempted to bribe them into doing their will. Like the words love and forgiveness, the Old and New Testaments have much to say about joy and peace.

In another of St. Augustine's classics, The City of God, he explained that all people face suffering, but people with Christian faith, because of their different attitude about life, do not lose hope or become cynical.[226] Unlike the pagans, the Christian believes in a good God Who controls his future. In Jesus, the Christian has both a Friend and a Savior. Whether you call it

---

225 Barbara O'Brien, "What Are the Four Noble Truths of Buddhism?," Learn Religions, April 23, 2019, https://www.learnreligions.com/the-four-noble-truths-450095.
226 St. Augustine, The City of God (Garden City, NY: Doubleday, 1958), 448.

THE JOYFUL AND PEACEFUL INDIVIDUAL 145

"karma" or the "wages of sin," most good people are blessed in this life, and most evil people suffer for doing wrong. God's grace is free for everyone, but each person must access it by traveling the road of love and forgiveness.

No love and forgiveness mean no joy and peace. In Philippians 4:6-7, we see that the experience of joy and peace are joined together. "Be careful for nothing; but in every thing by prayer . . . with thanksgiving let your requests be made known unto God. And the peace of God, which passes all understanding, shall keep your hearts and minds through Christ Jesus." The kind of peace that Jesus promises His followers is a unique peace that only they can know. He describes this special peace in John 14:27: "My peace I give unto you; not as the world giveth, give I unto you. Let not your heart be troubled, neither let it be afraid." Without knowing Him and loving Him, the joy and peace He speaks of are unattainable.

One of the all-time great misconceptions about Christianity is that its primary focus is on keeping rules, that it is a kill-joy religion of do's and don'ts. If this had been true, early Christianity would not have had the explosive growth in the first century A.D. A religion of do's and don'ts could not have motivated early Christians to risk persecution and martyrdom.

In the writings of the Early Church, we find a constant reference to human emotions such as love, joy, and peace. Like the long list of New Testaments statements on love and forgiveness, we find the same copious exhortations to experience joy and peace:

- "These things have I spoken unto you, that my joy might remain in you, and that your joy might be full" (John 15:11).
- "Your heart shall rejoice, and your joy no man taketh from you" (John 16:22).
- "Ask, and ye shall receive, that your joy may be full" (John 16:24).
- "Rejoice in the Lord always" (Rom. 4:4).
- "Rejoicing in hope" (Rom. 12:12).

- "The kingdom of God is . . . peace, and joy" (Rom. 14:17).
- "Now the God of hope fill you with all joy and peace" (Rom. 15:13).
- "I am exceedingly joyful" (2 Cor. 7:4).
- "But the fruit of the Spirit is love, joy, peace" (Gal. 5:22).
- "Count it all joy" (James 1:2).
- "Yet believing, ye rejoice with joy unspeakable" (1 Peter 1:8).

The early Christians were known for their moral rectitude and for living peaceful, humble, and joyful lives. Because their lifestyle produced less conflict with other people, they had a greater opportunity to experience joy and peace. Where pride, lust, and selfishness ruled, there were increased levels of stress and conflict. The outer harmony of the world is contingent upon the inner peace of individuals. The Early Church was constantly reminded of its primary mission of spreading the Gospel of love, which included joy and peace.

We see this in the many appeals of the apostles. The writer of Hebrews said, "Follow peace with all men" (Heb. 12:14). Timothy told them, "The servant of the Lord must not strive; but be gentle unto all men . . . that they may recover themselves out of the snare of the devil" (2 Tim. 2:24-26). James wrote, "Where envying and strife is, there is confusion and every evil work . . . And the fruit of Righteousness is sown in peace of them that make peace" (James 3:16-18).

The early Christians promoted a "Peace Agenda." They were "not of the world" (John 15:19). Their behavior was based upon a higher standard of "righteousness, and peace, and joy" (Rom. 14:17).

Stress and conflict increase the incidents of mental illness. A review of 129 psychological and sociological studies showed a marked increase in depression, anxiety, bipolar disorder, and even schizophrenia related to different conflict zones in the world.[227] Having faith and hope in a blessed afterlife gave early Christians a significant advantage over pagans who either did not believe in an afterlife or feared it was a place of eternal punishment. This fear was openly written about in Hebrews 2:14-15: "that through death he [Jesus] might destroy him that had the power of death, that is the devil . . . And deliver them who through fear of death were all their lifetime subject to bondage."

In 2 Timothy 1:7, we see the specific promise made by God to every Christian when Paul writes, "For God hath not given us the spirit of fear; but of power, and of love, and of a sound mind." In John 4:18, the connection between Christian love and perfect peace is established: "There is no fear in love, but perfect love casteth out fear."

When I write about the creative power of Christ, these are the innovative thoughts and behavioral changes about which I am writing. Just as we learned in the previous chapter that loving and forgiving individuals promoted positive social reform and acts of charity, the joyful and peaceful individual experiences greater mental health. Unlike paganism, which exalts fear and increases conflict, the new Christian paradigm promotes love, forgiveness, joy, and peace.

A great deal of modern research done by the social sciences supports this thesis. People of religious faith are generally happier and suffer less mental illness when compared to secular-minded individuals. Most of these social-science studies have been conducted on the American public where most religious belief is still Christian. In an article published in the *Psychiatric Times*, entitled "Religion, Spirituality, and Mental Health," Simon Dein explains:

> Lower rates of depressive symptoms in persons who were more religious . . . greater religiousness predicted mild symptoms and faster remission at follow-up . . . Religion has been found

227 Steven Reinberg, "1 In 5 People Living in Conflict Areas Has a Mental Health Problem," HealthDay.com, June, 12, 2019, https://consumer.healthday.com/public-health-information-30/war-health-news-788/1-in-5-people-living-in-conflict-areas-has-a-mental-health-problem-747297.html.

to enhance remission in patients with medical and psychiatric disease . . . 57 studies reported fewer suicides . . . among the more religious . . . social support, comfort, and meaning derived from religious belief also are important . . . loss of faith correlates with higher depression . . . religion has been found to positively affect the ability to cope with trauma . . . in a review of 134 studies that examined . . . religious involvement and substance abuse, 90% found less substance abuse among the religious.[228]

Sociological studies have shown over a long period of time that faith-based counseling/treatment programs have a much higher success rate than secular treatments alone. This is because faith-based therapies deal with the existential cause of human unhappiness—the lack of meaning and purpose in a human being's life. The faith-based approach to helping people is not just about stopping problematic behaviors, such as alcohol and drug abuse, but also changing the values and beliefs that motivate human behavior.

The proof of the success of a faith-based life is found in sociological statistics of adolescents and young adults who commit a crime. In a sociological report entitled "Effects of Religious Practice on Crime Rates," the following facts were reported: "States with more religious populations tend to have fewer homicides and fewer suicides. Religious attendance is associated with direct decreases in both minor and major forms of crime . . . There is a 57 percent decrease in the likelihood to deal drugs and a 39 percent decrease in likelihood to commit a crime among the young, black inner- city population if they attend religious services regularly."[229]

The secular world is very familiar with the concept of "positive mental attitude" (PMA) and the good that can come from it. But the secular world is missing an accurate understanding of what it takes to create it. Secularists

---

228 Simon Dein, "Religion, Spirituality, and Mental Health," Psychiatric Times online, January 10, 2010, https://www.psychiatrictimes.com/view/religion-spirituality-and-mental-health.

229 "Effects of Religious Practice on Crime Rates," Marripedia.org, Accessed July 1, 2023, https://www.marripedia.org/effects_of_religious_practice_on_crime_rates.

attempt to raise low self-esteem without examining the sin-based condition that perpetuates it. People must start with an accurate understanding of human nature, both good and bad, before they can work to increase the good and decrease the bad. They must also have a perfect moral yardstick on which to base that performance. Judeo-Christianity provides that ideal standard. Most importantly, it provides the primary motivation that a loving and forgiving God brings to a broken world, and without that, all true and lasting joy and peace are impossible.

CHAPTER TWELVE

THE PURE INDIVIDUAL

IN OUR MODERN AMERICAN SOCIETY, if one were to ask if you believe in sexual purity before marriage, we would expect to hear a crowd laughing in the background. There is no question that Hollywood, the music/entertainment industry, America's academic elites, and most of today's youth would be part of that crowd. America's iconic debauchee Hugh Hefner was a famous libertine but, until recently, resided outside America's mainstream culture. If he had lived only a few more years, he would have become the patriarch of our present culture. His anti-Judeo-Christian vision for America has now been realized.

The most recent Gallup survey of American attitudes related to sexual morality proves that the majority now share Hefner's views. Over sixty percent of Americans accept homosexual rights, producing children out of wedlock, and easy divorce. Other questions asked on the survey showed a significant increase in the acceptance of polygamy, pornography, and sex between un-married teens.[230]

Even in today's communities of practicing Christians, there is evidence of the increasing acceptance of the pagan standard for sexual morality. The most recent Pew Research survey of adult Christians found that "half of Christians say casual sex between consenting adults . . . is sometimes

---

230 Frank Newport, "Continuing Change in U.S. Views on Sex and Marriage," Gallup online, June 18, 2021, https://news.gallup.com/opinion/polling-matters/351326/continuing-change-views-sex-marriage.aspx.

or always acceptable. The number in the same survey for people who were religiously unaffiliated was 84% and for atheists 94%."[231]

Liberals and secular humanists see the words "sexual purity" as an anachronism—a verbal relic of an old-fashion belief called "sexual morality." Containing sex within marriage has always been a tricky proposition. Most primitive, pagan cultures did not seem to try. Historian Will Durant provided a peek into the bedroom of primitive people when he wrote:

> Marriage by purchase and parental arrangement was the rule in early societies . . . In all these forms and varieties of marriage there is hardly a trace of romantic love . . . Chastity is a correspondingly late development . . . Union seldom lasted more than a few years among the American Indians . . . African women hardly differed from slaves . . . Half of the primitive peoples known to us attach no great importance to the sin of adultery.[232]

Durant describes the primitive practice of group marriage as a group of brothers marrying a group of sisters. The wife could pick another mate if he left home and was gone for over a year and a day. They lived a communal lifestyle, sharing tools, weapons, and food. Sex was often viewed the same way. The pagan civilizations that developed out of the primitive societies were also highly promiscuous.[233]

The social pattern in the pagan world included polygamy, religious and secular prostitution, easy divorce, and, as we have discussed, festivals of sexual license. Ancient Judaism provided the first cultural pattern that departed from this easy sexual paradigm, and Christianity inherited and advanced this higher standard of behavior. The ancient Jewish/Christian belief about

231 Jeff Diamant, "Half of U.S. Christians Say Casual Sex between Consenting Adults Is Sometimes or Always Acceptable," Pew Research Center, August 31, 2020, https://www.pewresearch.org/fact-tank/2020/08/31/half-of-u-s-christians-say-casual-sex-between-consenting-adults-is-sometimes-or-always-acceptable.
232 Durant, Vol. 1, 43-44.
233 Ibid, 36-39.

sexual morality was non-existent in any purely pagan culture. Buddhism and Confucianism also promoted very conservative codes of sexual conduct, but their views contradicted their prevailing cultures.

The Jews were the first civilization to establish sexual purity as national law. During the period of the Roman Empire, the great philosophers and historians Josephus and Philo of Alexandria stated their commitment to this higher standard of sexual morality.

Philo lived in Egypt under Roman rule and was part of a body of Jews who traveled to Rome to speak in favor of their national customs. He explained to the Roman government, "We Hebrews follow our own laws . . . The sons of other people, after they turn fourteen, are freely allowed to go to prostitutes . . . In our society . . . We never sleep with a woman before legally valid marriage, and both men and women approach each other as virgins."[234]

The Jewish historian Flavius Josephus, who lived from 37 to 100 A.D. and is known for providing two of the earliest non-Christian statements about Jesus, supported the view of Philo, stating, "What are our laws concerning sexual ethics? The law [Jewish] only accepts natural intercourse with woman . . . Intercourse between men is strictly prohibited . . . A husband has an intimate relationship only with his wife and everything else is ungodly."[235]

Thousands of years later, these are still the views of both Orthodox Judaism and Orthodox Christianity. In an article entitled "Kosher Sex," the Orthodox Jewish view of sexuality is explained this way:

> In Jewish law, sex is not considered shameful, sinful or obscene
> . . . sexual desire . . . like hunger, thirst or other basic instincts . . .
> must be controlled and channeled, satisfied at the proper time,

---

234 William Loader, "'Not as the Gentiles': Sexual Issues at the Interface between Judaism and Its Greco-Roman World," Multidisciplinary Digital Publishing Institute, August 28, 2018, https://www.mdpi.com/2077-1444/9/9/258.

235 Eberhard Bons, "Marriage and Family in Flavius Josephus's Contra Apionem (II, § 199–206) Against Its Hellenistic Background," in *Family and Kinship in the Deuterocanonical and Cognate Literature* by De Gruyter, Accessed December 12, 2013, https://www.degruyter.com/document/doi/10.1515/9783110310436.455/html.

place and manner. But when sexual desire is satisfied between a husband and a wife . . . out of mutual love . . . sex is a mitzvah . . . The primary purpose of sex is to reinforce the loving marital bond . . . Procreation is also a reason for sex, but it is not the only reason . . . Jewish sexuality involves both the heart, and the mind, not merely the body.[236]

In "How did Judaism and early Church face contemporary sexual morality?," Erkki Koskenniemi explains that during ancient Roman times, young pagans "spent a period of time called ludus that, was meant for . . . searching for sexual experiences . . . Both girl and boy slaves as well as brothels were part of young men's sexual education . . . later in life . . . sexual relations outside marriage, whether straight or gay, were not considered improper."[237] Koskenniemi quotes the famous Greek orator Demosthenes: "We have lovers for pleasure, housemates for daily sexual needs, and wives for receiving legal offspring." Since thirty to forty percent of the population were enslaved, this would have been a paradise for the rich, powerful few—a world tailor-fit for Hugh Hefner, Jeffrey Epstein, or human trafficking and pedophilia.

Modern feminists who lack an accurate understanding of the Bible and the long history of the pagan world are highly critical of the Judeo-Christian tradition. Theirs is a simplistic critique focusing on the narrow question of patriarchy. But as we have seen, all patriarchies are not the same. Judaism was patriarchal, as almost every culture in pre-history and history were, but its values and treatment of women differed vastly from every other ancient culture. The ancient Jews did not see women as soulless sex machines. Marriage for the Jews was called a "holy act," and the Torah taught that the husband was responsible for fulfilling his wife's needs as a person. Judaism

236 "Issues in Jewish Ethics: 'Kosher' Sex," Jewish Virtual Library, Accessed October 22, 2022, https://www.jewishvirtuallibrary.org/quot-kosher-quot-sex.
237 Erkki Koskenniemi, "How did Judaism and early Church face contemporary sexual morality?," Translated by Elina Salminen, Lutheran Evangelical Association of Finland, Accessed October 22, 2022, https://www.bibletoolbox.net/en/bible/sexual-morality.

taught that the husband should never force his wife to engage in sex.[238] Jesus and the early Christian Church accepted this superior sexual morality and advanced it even higher.

Based upon Jesus' teaching, which linked the concepts of the sacred and the pure Christian, morality transitioned from polygamy to monogamy. By making that change, the rights and treatment of women were greatly advanced and was one of the reasons Christianity spread so fast among women. Because of four little verses that Jesus uttered, the old beliefs in polygamy and easy divorce crumbled. "From the beginning of the creation God made them male and female. For this cause shall a man leave his father and mother, and cleave to his wife; And they twain shall be one flesh; so then they are no more twain, but one flesh. What therefore God hath joined together, let not man put asunder" (Mark 10:6-9).

Throughout these verses, Jesus refers only to a husband and a wife, or male and female. He says the "twain shall become one . . . no more twain." Jesus always called people to live by the highest standard of love. He never advocated half-measures in morality. He called people to seek moral/spiritual perfection. His wise understanding was that to achieve the greatest level of intimacy and devotion between husband and wife, their relationship needed to be monogamous. Two could equally join and become one flesh, but three or four could not. Ask any married couple today, and they will tell you that even two becoming one is not easy. It takes years of selfless acts and learning to compromise.

Unlike the Old Testament, the New Testament never references polygamy. Monogamy is always assumed when the apostles speak of marriage or the relationship between a husband and wife. In 1 Timothy 3:12, we find, "Let the deacons be the husbands of one wife." Ephesians 5:25 says, "Husbands, love your wives, even as Christ also loved the church, and gave himself for it." Notice, it doesn't say for a husband to love all his wives.

---

238 "Judaism and Sexuality," My Jewish Learning, Accessed October 22, 2021, https://www.myjewishlearning.com/article/judaism-and-sexuality/.

In other Scripture, the Church is called the "bride" of Christ, not "brides" of Christ. St. Paul continues in Ephesians to promote the new model for relationships within monogamy: "So ought men to love their wives as their own bodies. He that loveth his wife loveth himself. For no man ever yet hated their own flesh; but nourish and cherisheth it, even as the Lord the church . . . For this cause shall a man leave his father and mother, and shall be joined unto his wife, and they two shall be one flesh . . . every one of you in particular so love his wife even as himself; and the wife see that she reverence her husband" (Eph. 5:28-33).

During the high point of moral decay in ancient Rome, one finds the same social trends taking place in America today with high rates of abortion, infanticide, an increasing percentage of adults not getting married, and many unwanted children abandoned. Everywhere throughout history where sexual promiscuity has been the rule, people have suffered and societies have become unraveled, such as ancient Greece, ancient Rome, Renaissance Italy, Revolutionary France, Weimar Germany, and now modern America.

As Christianity spread throughout the Roman empire, so did the practice of monogamy, as another example of the creative power of Christ. Historian Will Durant describes its effects on Western civilization: "Christian monogamy . . . kept the sexual impulse within bounds, and slowly raised the status of woman . . . the Church enforced monogamy, insisted upon a single standard of morals for both sexes . . . defended woman's right to the inheritance of property."[239]

Women's rights, like all human rights, took time to develop and become widespread, but it was in Western civilization, influenced by Judeo-Christian culture, that they developed first. Before the spread of Judeo-Christian culture, eighty-three percent of indigenous non-Western cultures were polygamous.[240] What the history of the world shows is that, outside of Western civilization, women's rights and human rights, in general, have been slow to advance.

---

239 Durant, Vol. IV, 77.
240 Robert VerBruggen, "Is Monagamy Unnatural?," Institute of Family Studies, March 29, 2016, https://ifstudies.org/blog/is-monogamy-unnatural.

Everywhere and every time there has been an experiment in "free love," women and children have suffered the most. "Free love" was a euphemism used by the hippies in the radical 1960s to '70s to justify selfish acts of lust. It was based upon the naïve belief that since freedom is a positive good, absolute freedom must be perfection.

A second erroneous belief connected to "free love" was that since the natural world is good, human beings should be free to express their natural desires whenever they feel the urges. These young apostles of absolute freedom and nature had not lived long enough to discover the core difference between nature's laws and human nature, which is that nature is all it can be without free choice. Nature acts according to the laws and instincts which God has decreed them. But human beings are not predetermined to act a certain way, and they must learn how and when to use their freedom over time. Five thousand years of human conflict and crime have shown that humans often misused that freedom.

In short, human beings need wisdom in knowing how to use one's freedom. A study of history and modern sociological and psychological research reveals that the standard Jesus called the world to adopt is not only optional for the good of humanity but imperative. Most of the problems the modern world faces today are a by-product of human selfishness. Most people would concede that greed is evil, but lust is a kind of sexual greed, putting one's short-term desires before the moral and spiritual good of another. Examining global problems like crime, human trafficking, prostitution, illegitimacy, single-parent families, and poverty provides us with indisputable, factual evidence that each of these are linked to the problem of uncontrolled lust or what I call the "lust-greed nexus."

The United States now has the world's highest rate of children born into single-parent households.[241] In 1970, only thirteen percent of American children were born into single-parent households; by 1996, the number had

241 Ibid.

increased to twenty-five percent. The 2010 Census reported that twenty-seven percent of children were part of a single-parent family.[242] In 2018, Pew Research announced this number had reached thirty-five percent. Since 1960, the number of adult Americans who have never married has increased to fifty percent. The Pew survey found that fifty percent of Americans consider a person just as well-off if people have other priorities than marriage.

Both national and international statistics prove that young people born out of wedlock and raised in single-parent families are on a fast track to crime, violence, poverty, and low educational achievement.[243] Back in the 1970s, when the Democratic Party still had honest, courageous, intelligent leadership, Daniel Patrick Moynihan sounded the national alarm over the destruction of the black family. He warned the nation that the Afro-American family was disintegrating because of its rising out-of-wedlock childbirths.

Since Moynihan's early warning, the problem has grown from twenty-five percent to seventy-two percent. Most telling is the statistic provided by the liberal think-tank Progressive Policy Institute that shows if you removed the factor of single-parent families from the crime reports, the rates of crime committed by whites and blacks are almost the same.[244] An even newer study by "Child Trends," which calls itself "the nation's leading research organization focused . . . on improving the lives of children," reported in 2018 that "40% of births in the United States now occur outside marriage, up from 28% in 1990."[245]

242 Stephanie Kramer, "U.S. Has World's Highest Rate of Children Living in Single-Parent Households," Pew Research Center, May 28, 2021, https://www.pewresearch.org/fact-tank/2019/12/12/u-s-children-more-likely-than-children-in-other-countries-to-live-with-just-one-parent.

243 U.S. Census Bureau, "2010 Overview," United States Census Bureau, 2010, https://www.census.gov/history/www/through_the_decades/overview/2010_overview_1.html.

244 Ron Palmer, "Fatherless Single Mother Home Statistics," Fix Family Courts, 2017, https://www.fixfamilycourts.com/single-mother-home-statistics.

245 Elizabeth Wildsmith, Jennifer Manlove, and Elizabeth Cook, "Dramatic Increase in the Proportion of Births Outside of Marriage in the United States from 1990 to 2016," Child Trends, August 8, 2018, https://www.childtrends.org/publications/dramatic-increase-in-percentage-of-births-outside-marriage-among-whites-hispanics-and-women-with-higher-education-levels.

It is clear from these statistics that the problem of illegitimacy is not only a problem for the African American community, but it is a problem for the all-American community. If we consult the statistics outside the United States, we find that it is an world problem. If we combine America's over sixty percent approval of having sex outside marriage with her over forty percent divorce rate, it is inevitable that in the future, most young Americans will be born or raised in single-parent homes. America's current divorce rate is bad enough, but if we factor in the reality that second marriages fail sixty-three percent of the time and third marriages fail seventy-three percent of the time, the situation gets worse. The only thing that has kept the divorce rate down in America and Europe is the increasing percentage of people not getting married.

The facts about divorce and remarriage disprove the old liberal canard that the wise person should have multiple sexual experiences before marrying. Research shows that people who live together before marriage "increase the chance of getting divorced by as much as 40% . . . a woman who has lived with more than one partner before her first marriage is 40% more likely to get divorced . . . women with six or more premarital sexual partners are almost three times less likely to be in a stable marriage."[246]

Eighty-five percent of single-parent households have women at the head. The 2020 U.S. Census has reported that 18.3 million children are living without a father and are at a greater risk for "poverty . . . behavioral problems . . . more likely to go to prison . . . to commit crime . . . to be abused . . . to abuse drugs and alcohol and to . . . drop out of school."[247] Liberal social critics whose morals are mostly un-tethered from religious faith are eager to preach about America's problems like class, race, sex, education,

---

246 Gretchen Livingston, "The Changing Profile of Unmarried Parents," Pew Research Center, April 25, 2018. https://www.pewresearch.org/social-trends/2018/04/25/the-changing-profile-of-unmarried-parents.

247 Melissa Byers, "The Father Absence Crisis in America [Infographic]," National Fatherhood Initiative, Accessed October 22, 2022, https://www.fatherhood.org/championing-fatherhood/the-father-absence-crisis-in-america.

unemployment, and mental illness but ignore the elephant in the room, which is the absence of sexual morality. The mass of illegal immigrants crossing the U.S southern border are young people uprooted by poverty and crime, but the Liberal news outlets never focus on the large numbers of single mothers with young children.

One exception to this rule was a report by NPR in 2015 stating, "All Across Latin America Unwed Mothers are the Norm . . . In Columbia 84% of all children are born to unmarried mothers . . . Argentina, Mexico, Chile, and others have similar numbers."[248] If we change continents, we find the same thing in Africa and Asia. All these places have large numbers of single female-led homes with multiple children living in poverty. Out of this witch's brew, we find examples like the extremely violent Northern Triangle of Central America, an area of the earth that makes up only eight percent of the world's population but is responsible for thirty percent of the world's murders.[249] In Africa, the same out-of-control scenario of children without fathers has fueled the modern horror of children's armies used in bloody tribal wars.

The modern horror of human trafficking is seventy-nine percent related to sexual exploitation. It is a world crisis that feeds on the mass-availability of unwanted, uncared-for-children born to single mothers. In India alone, 1.2 million children are working as prostitutes.[250] In Thailand, forty percent of prostitutes are children.[251] Every major city in Sub-Saharan Africa is a significant source of child prostitution.

---

248 Lulu Garcia-Navarro, "All Across Latin America, Unwed Mothers Are Now the Norm," NPR online, December 14, 2015, https://www.npr.org/sections/parallels/2015/12/14/459098779/all-across-latin-america-unwed-mothers-are-now-the-norm.

249 Amelia Cheatham and Diana Roy, "Central America's Turbulent Northern Triangle," Council on Foreign Relations, June 22, 2022, https://www.cfr.org/backgrounder/central-americas-turbulent-northern-triangle.

250 "Official: More than 1M Child Prostitutes in India," CNN online, Accessed October 22, 2022, https://www.cnn.com/2009/WORLD/asiapcf/05/11/india.prostitution.children/index.html.

251 "Child Prostitution and Pedophiles in Thailand," Facts and Details, Accessed October 22, 2022, https://factsanddetails.com/southeast-asia/Thailand/sub5_8d/entry-3247.html.

U.S. Homeland Security has defined human trafficking as "the use of force, fraud, or coercion to obtain some type of labor or commercial sex act. Every year, millions of men, women, and children are trafficked worldwide."[252] The National Human Trafficking Hotline reported in 2018:

> Internationally there are between 20-40 million people in modern slavery . . . Human trafficking earns global profits of . . . $150 billion a year . . . $99 billion of which comes from commercial sexual exploitation . . . Globally, an estimated 71% of enslaved people are women and girls, while men and boys account for 29% . . . In 2018, over half of the cases active in the U.S. were sex trafficking cases involving only children.[253]

The motivation for human trafficking, especially its sexual component of sex tourism, clearly illustrates what I call the "lust-greed nexus." The providers of those who are trafficked care only about the money, and the consumers of this illicit trade in human flesh are only motivated by lust. The consumers are heterosexual and homosexual individuals who are sexually obsessed, travel long distances, and pay top dollar to realize their fantasies. Many consumers are from wealthy nations, and their victims are the poorest of the poor in Third World countries. Ten of the largest sites for sex tourism are The Netherlands, Germany, Spain, Malaysia, Kenya, the Philippines, Colombia, Thailand, Dominican Republic, and Brazil. If we remove the three European nations, we are left with seven poor, less developed nations, all of which have high out-of-wedlock birth rates. The poor nations of the world are supplying the human flesh that is being peddled to the richer nations of the world.[254]

---

252 "What Is Human Trafficking?," DHS.gov, Accessed October 22, 2022, https://www.dhs.gov/blue-campaign/what-human-trafficking.

253 "National Statistics," National Human Trafficking Hotline, Accessed October 22, 2022, https://humantraffickinghotline.org/en/statistics.

254 PTI, "Handling of Human Trafficking Cases in India 'Disproportionately Low': US Report," Deccan Chronicle, June 29, 2018, https://www.deccanchronicle.com/world/america/290618/handling-of-human-trafficking-cases-in-india-disproportionately-low.html.

The lust-greed nexus is the basis of human trafficking, prostitution, and pornography, along with the wealth, glamor, and fame upon which Hollywood rests.

During the 1950s when America reached a high point in modern religious attendance, movies like *The Ten Commandments* in 1956 and *Ben-Hur* in 1959 were being made. The actors, writers, producers, and directors of that period were not significantly more religious than those who run Hollywood today but were mindful of the fact that the average American consumer was. Today, secular-humanist, neo-pagan Hollywood no longer needs to wear a mask of decency. Our national standard for sexual morality is now so low that they no longer fear a broad-based, adverse public reaction. The most recent statistics in 2021 show that only 24 percent of American viewers are bothered by seeing sex on TV.[255]

Hollywood has played a significant role in the sixty-year-long slide that has produced this pagan America. They are the number one institutional cheerleader for the LGBTQ community. Their efforts, along with others in America's music/entertainment industry, national media, and academic elites, have successfully brought our nation to eat out of one mass-cultural slop trough. Americans can't pretend to be surprised by this change. A poll published by *The Hollywood Reporter* in 2008 stated, "Sixty-one percent of those surveyed said that religious values in America are 'under attack' and 59% agreed that 'the people who run the TV networks and the major movies studios do not share the religious and moral values of most Americans.'"[256]

Not content with rubbing Judeo-Christianity's nose into the mud of depravity, they are now spending billions of dollars to make movies and TV programming that openly attack and disparage the Judeo-Christian faith. As early as 1976, Hollywood was experimenting with anti-Judeo-Christian themes. Movies like *Carrie, Priest, Footloose, Dogma, Jesus Camp, The Name of*

255 Julia Stoll, "Opinion on sex in TV shows in the U.S. 2019," January 13, 2021, Statista. com, https://www.statista.com/statistics/990852/sex-tv-shows-us.

256 Gregg Kilday, "Hollywood Out of Step with American Morals: Poll," Reuters. com, November 17, 2008, https://www.reuters.com/article/us-poll-idUSTRE4AG0VK20081117.

the Rose, The Magdalene Sisters, The Boys of St. Vincent, and Monty Python's *The Meaning of Life* are only a few examples.[257]

As successful as the motion picture industry has been in undermining America's traditional culture, the movie business now takes second place to television. This change began in the 1960s when average daily TV viewing significantly increased, but theater attendance dropped sharply, reaching a twenty-five-year low in 2017. The moral degradation which Hollywood initiated has been consummated by TV. From a logistical point of view, it makes perfect sense. Why hold America's youth captive for two to three hours a week at a walk-in theater when the entertainment industry can invade every American home 24-7? Now with the new streaming services like Netflix, Amazon, and HBO, uncensored programming is available to any household that can afford it. And with a handheld mobile device in almost every kid's hand, hardcore pornography is only a touch away.

Over a sixty-year period of these changes, we have received multiple warnings from Pew Research, Kaiser Family Foundation, Rand Corporation, and many other psychological/sociological studies that have documented the disaster we now call the "modern American family." The research shows that, in the 1990s, fifty-six percent of television programming included sexual content, and by 2001, that number increased to sixty-six percent.[258] Only four years later, that number reached seventy percent. The Rand Corporation reported in 2004 that the "average American teenager watches 3 hours of television a day . . . Sex is often presented as a casual activity without risks or consequences . . . Watching TV shows with sexual content . . . hastens the initiation of teen sexual activity."[259]

---

257 "10 Most Anti-Christian Movies of All Time," Vulture online, December 7, 2007, https://www.vulture.com/2007/12/list_antireligious_movies.html.

258 Brian Lowry, "Sexual Content Becomes More Prevalent on TV, Study Finds," Los Angeles Times online, February 7, 2001, https://www.latimes.com/archives/la-xpm-2001-feb-07-ca-21942-story.html.

259 Rebecca L. Collins, et al., "Does Watching Sex on Television Influence Teens' Sexual Activity?," RAND Corporation, January 1, 2004, https://www.rand.org/pubs/research_briefs/RB9068.html.

More recent studies found, "The content of media to which adolescents are exposed is concerning given representations of men as violent and women as sexual.[260] Ybarra's 2014 study confirmed this and expressed its logical effect: "youth . . . exposure to sexual media content was linked to higher odds of sexual violence."[261] Movies and TV have played the greatest role in indoctrinating the young with pagan values. Still, other media have helped to shape this culture. "Sexually objectifying of women appears in 52% of magazines . . . 59% of music videos . . . 27% of teen-rated video games."[262] The young are receiving unofficial sex education "online via the use of pornography." A study by Wright and Donnerstein in 2014 found that forty-two percent of children from ten to seventeen years of age had viewed pornography.[263]

The Conversation.com reported, "Children and young people are encountering porn in greater numbers at younger ages . . . 88% of scenes show aggression . . . people who watched violent porn were six times as likely to engage in sexually aggressive behavior."[264]

Young children are not only viewing pornography, but they are also the subject of much of it. The National Center for Missing and Exploited Children reported, "There has been a 774% increase in the number of child pornography

260 Amy Bleakley, "Trends of Sexual and Violent Content by Gender in Top-Grossing U.S. Films, 1950-2006," *The Journal of Adolescent Health* 51, No. 1 (July 2021): 73-9, https://pubmed.ncbi.nlm.nih.gov/22727080.

261 Michele L. Ybarra, "Sexual Media Exposure, Sexual Behavior, and Sexual Violence Victimization in Adolescence," *Clinical Pediatrics* 53, No. 15 (November 2014): 1239-47, https://pubmed.ncbi.nlm.nih.gov/24928575.

262 Peter Koval, Elise Holland, and Michelle Stratemeyer, "Sexually Objectifying Women Leads Women to Objectify Themselves, and Harms Emotional Well-Being," The Conversation online, July 23, 2019, https://theconversation.com/sexually-objectifying-women-leads-women-to-objectify-themselves-and-harms-emotional-well-being-120762.

263 Paul J. Wright and Edward I. Donnerstein, "Sex Online: Pornography, Sexual Solicitation, and Sexting," *Adolescent Medicine State of the Art Reviews* 25, No. 3 (December 2014): 574-89, https://experts.arizona.edu/en/publications/sex-online-pornography-sexual-solicitation-and-sexting.

264 Michael Flood, "Pornography Has Deeply Troubling Effects on Young People, but There Are Ways We Can Minimise the Harm," The Conversation.com, January 5, 2020, https://theconversation.com/pornography-has-deeply-troubling-effects-on-young-people-but-there-are-ways-we-can-minimise-the-harm-127319.

images and videos . . . the U.S. remains one of the largest producers and consumers of child porn."[265] Having increasingly exposed American's young to a steady diet of permissive morality, Hollywood and the entertainment industry have them exactly where they want them—totally enslaved to the product they create and sell.

America's young are showing the signs of sexual addiction. In every survey of attitudes related to sexual behavior, young people score as more liberal and permissive in their attitudes compared to older Americans. In 1988, only eleven percent of Americans surveyed approved of homosexual marriage. By 2010, that number was forty-six percent, and currently, it is sixty percent. Most alarming is that seventy percent of young adults now approve of homosexual marriage.[266] We find the same generation gap when it comes to surveying the American public on the issue of the legalization of prostitution. In 1995, only nineteen percent of Americans favored the legalization of prostitution; but today, fifty-two percent of Americans give their approval, and most alarming is the fact that sixty-six percent of young adults approve.[267]

One of the great Liberal myths is that morality is subjective—right and wrong are only a matter of opinion. Liberals favor concepts like victimless crime, consenting adults, and safe sex. Their mantra is, "Since people can't agree on one standard of morality, then all standards must be equal," with the best social policy being to judge everything by a standard of practical utility—or the greatest good for the greatest number. The major flaw in their reasoning is that life is more than its short-term effects. Either morality is universal or, as the nihilist thinks, it doesn't exist. If it exists, it is rooted in the overall cause

265 Patricia Davis, "100,000,000 The race to save children behind the staggering number," Missing Kids.org, December 1, 2021, https://www.missingkids.org/blog/2021/100,000,000-the-race-to-save-children-behind-the-staggering-number.

266 Tom W. Smith, "Public Attitudes toward Homosexuality," NORC/University of Chicago, September 2011, https://www.norc.org/PDFs/2011%20GSS%20Reports/GSS_Public%20Attitudes%20Toward%20Homosexuality_Sept2011.pdf.

267 Elizabeth Nolan Brown, "What Americans Think About Prostitution Laws," Reason.com, February 6, 2020, https://reason.com/2020/02/06/what-americans-think-about-prostitution-laws.

and purpose of life and is not based upon what a person feels or thinks at any given moment. Being concerned with only short-term effects leaves societies vulnerable to what people call "unintentional consequences." The greatest risk to society is giving up on the concept of a universal standard of morality and only attempting to mitigate the adverse effects of an immoral society.

The declining sexual morality in Europe and America has increased prostitution, and the rich Western countries serve as colossal magnates, drawing in the impoverished women and children of Asia, Africa, Latin America, and Eastern Europe to satisfy their demands for lust. In Europe, the Netherlands was the first country to legalize prostitution in 1999, followed by Denmark. As the saying goes, "The road to Hell is paved with good intentions." Their intentions were to improve public health, improve the lives of prostitutes, and reduce the level of human trafficking. The facts show that by legalizing prostitution, the demand for it increased forty percent and resulted in an increase in human trafficking. In Sweden, where prostitution remained illegal and punishment was directed toward customers, they did not experience an increase in prostitution or human trafficking. In the Netherlands, "60% of women prostitutes suffered physical assaults . . . 57% have been victims of sexual abuse as children."[268]

An article published in *Forbes* in 2016 by Simon Hedlin stated, "A study of . . . trafficking data in Europe . . . concluded that sex trafficking is most prevalent in countries where prostitution is legal."[269] Prostitutes are not just deviants or criminals; they are highly damaged human beings who began their lives as innocent victims. In those countries where prostitution has been legalized and their earnings taxed, governments are substituting themselves for the traditional pimps.

---

268 Jacqueline Saffy, "Child Sexual Abuse as a Precursor to Prostitution," *Social Work* 39, No. 2 (August 2014), https://www.researchgate.net/publication/276320820_Child_sexual_abuse_as_a_precursor_to_prostitution.

269 Simon Hedlin, "Why Legalizing Prostitution May Not Work," Forbes online, October 17, 2016, https://www.forbes.com/sites/realspin/2016/10/17/why-legalizing-prostitution-may-not-work.

Business Insider.com reported in 2019 that "most sex workers . . . come from (poor) Eastern European countries and many are coerced or trafficked."[270] In Southeast Asia, notorious for human trafficking, eighty percent of the men in Cambodia and seventy-five percent of the men in Thailand have paid for sex. Even in an Asian society as advanced as Japan, almost forty percent have purchased sex. These permissive attitudes and the poor treatment of women and children that it produces have long been an accepted part of pagan culture.

What is now new is that Western civilization is increasing its acceptance of the same pagan standard. A recent poll in the United States found that sixty percent of men surveyed believed that it was morally acceptable to exchange money for sex. Most prostitutes come from dysfunctional families, are runaways attempting to escape physical and sexual abuse, or come from home environments where drugs and alcohol addiction are prevalent. These facts do not seem to be part of today's moral calculation. Many studies in the U.S. and Europe support these facts. "In several studies, child sexual abuse had been identified as a characteristic of adolescent prostitution."[271] "A study of 200 street prostitutes documented a high prevalence of alcohol and drug abuse in their family of origin, during the drift into prostitution."[272] "70% of female and 56% of male drug users had been sexually abused as children."[273] "A study conducted by the National Treatment Agency . . . UK revealed that 95% of the women that are involved with street prostitution are heroin or crack cocaine users."[274] A Colorado Springs study found that the "death rate

---

270 "Prostitution Is Legal in Countries across Europe, but It's Nothing like What You Think," *Business Insider* online, March 13, 2019, https://www.businessinsider.in/ miscellaneous/prostitution-is-legal-in-countries-across-europe-but-its-nothing-like-what-you-think/slidelist/68397375.cms.

271 MJ Seng, "Child Sexual Abuse and Adolescent Prostitution: A Comparative Analysis," *Adolescence* 24, No. 95 (1989): 665-75, https://pubmed.ncbi.nlm.nih.gov/2801287.

272 MH Silbert, "Substance Abuse and Prostitution," *Psychoactive Drugs* 14, No. 3 (July 1982): 193-7, https://pubmed.ncbi.nlm.nih.gov/7143150.

273 Sunny Hyucksun Shin, "Childhood Sexual Abuse and Adolescent Substance Use: A Latent Class Analysis," *Drug Alcohol Depend* 109, Nos. 1-3 (June 2010): 226-35, https:// pubmed.ncbi.nlm.nih.gov/20197217.

274 Dr. Joanna Kesten, "Drug Use in Street Sex Workers: The DUSSK Study," ARC West, Accessed January 11, 2021, https://arc-w.nihr.ac.uk/research/projects/reducing-drug-use-female-street-sex-workers-feasibility-study.

among active prostitutes is 5.9 times that of the general population." How can honest, caring people inside and outside the government not see the harm of prostitution? It does not matter if it is legal or illegal—it still destroys lives.

For a Christian or any person with a moral conscience, it is not enough to simply ignore the suffering of sex workers. It is not enough to only focus on reducing some negative after-effects of such a lifestyle. Like all other problematic social issues, this issue brings us back to the question of is human life sacred? If the answer is no, societies can only focus on practical effects. The history of Judeo-Christian culture proves that the higher the moral standards are, the higher the positive social results will be. If societies aim low in terms of moral expectations, they will achieve even lower results.

CHAPTER THIRTEEN

THE GAY CRUSADE

IN AMERICA AND EUROPE OVER the last sixty years, the average citizen has been brainwashed into believing that the issue of homosexuality is only about someone's sexual orientation and fooled into thinking that the problem is about inequality. What has intentionally been left out of this presentation are the hardcore facts that characterize this radically different lifestyle. It is also about sexual obsession and addiction that in most cases respects no moral order and depersonalizes the people it touches.

This issue has been presented by those who control the mass-cultural media as a broad-minded, tolerant, social justice, and human rights issue versus the narrow-minded and intolerant. Any discussion on the definition of sexual morality must include some analysis of homosexuality and the rights of homosexuals. Critical questions to ask are a) is the homosexual lifestyle healthy and b) is homosexuality capable of producing human happiness? If the answer to these fundamental questions is no, what should the proper response of society be?

Homosexual rights in recent years have become a literal cause célèbre and obsession of Hollywood and the liberal mass media. This crusade has resulted in changing the meaning of the Constitution and even celebrating homosexual marriage by projecting a rainbow of color on the White House.

First, everyone should admit that homosexuals are human beings who deserve the same protection and rights of "life, liberty, and the pursuit of happiness" that all American citizens claim. The question that must be answered is at what point does abnormal sexual behavior require social/legal restrictions?

Since the beginning of the world, societies have placed restrictions on specific sexual behaviors. At first, this was done through customs and later with the development of civilization through laws. The primary aim of these restrictions was to limit behaviors that the majority considered adverse to the good of the group. Sexual behaviors such as incest, prostitution, rape, and homosexuality were all eventually subject to some restrictions or control. In many cases, the issue was decided based upon a "consenting adult" standard. Rape and incest are examples of this standard being applied. In cases like prostitution, adultery, and homosexuality, a consenting adult standard should not be the only one that has to be met, but societies must also decide if the behavior is antithetical to the good of the community.

There are many types of sinful behavior that people commit in private but depending on the circumstances are either wicked but not criminal or sinful and criminal. For a free society, deciding this is a delicate balancing act between human freedom and human responsibility. If behaviors which begin in private can be shown through fact to harm those outside the private world, then in those cases, law enforcement has a legitimate right to investigate and stop those destructive behaviors. In an intimate setting, sexual conduct between consenting adults may be allowed by law but remain morally abhorrent, and if children are present in that environment, it should be an illegal activity.

During the early spread of the AIDS pandemic in 1984, the city of San Francisco hotly debated whether to close the city's bathhouses, which were the places where homosexuals would meet and engage in sexual activities that accelerated the spread of HIV. In an article entitled "The Bathhouse War," *The Washington Post* quoted letters to the editor of the gay-supporting San Francisco newspaper, the *Bay Area Reporter.* These letters showed how passionate the homosexuals were to keep the bathhouses open, despite the danger of spreading AIDS. The following quotes were directed against a sergeant within the local sheriff's department, who was gay and had come out in support of closing the bathhouses: "homophobic pig," "morality cowboy," "homophobic slime," "Alice-in-Wonderland do-gooder."[275]

In San Francisco, the spread of HIV/AIDS started in the early 1970s, and by the 2000s, a total of 27,422 had contracted HIV, and 18,549 people had died. Homosexual activities were responsible for seventy-seven percent of HIV infections, and injecting illegal drugs was responsible for thirteen percent.[276] On September 13, 2020, the *San Francisco Chronicle* reported, "Bathhouse ban revoked: Amid one pandemic [Covid], SF confronts legacy of another."[277] Under pressure from the homosexual lobby, the bathhouses reopened.

As recent as 2018, people in San Francisco were still being infected with HIV, but as terrible as the San Francisco AIDS pandemic was, it was only a tiny piece of the global AIDS disaster. At the end of 2019, over thirty-two million people had died from AIDS, and thirty-eight million people were living with AIDS. The World Health Organization has identified these populations as most at-risk: sex workers, transgender people, people who inject drugs, and men who have sex with men. Sexual behaviors account for sixty-two percent of new HIV infections.[278] Two-thirds of people with HIV infection live in Africa. The three main drivers of HIV infection in Africa are prostitution, sexual violence directed against women, and those who inject drugs. Homosexuality and prostitution did not cause the AIDS pandemic, but both are the major drivers of its rapid spread. Also worth noting is the

275 "The Bathhouse War," The Washington Post online, April 19, 1984, https://www. washingtonpost.com/archive/lifestyle/1984/04/19/the-bathhouse-war/5c864455-2310-4f9e-ac70-e0f57083a511.

276 Willi McFarland, ed., "HIV/AIDS Programs & Research," Department of Public Health | HIV Epidemiology Section, Accessed October 24, 2022, https://www.sfdph.org/dph/files/reports/RptsHIVAIDS/HIVAIDSAtlas1981-2000.pdf.

277 Ryan Kost, "Bathhouse Ban Revoked: Amid One Pandemic, SF Confronts Legacy of Another," San Francisco Chronicle online, September 14, 2020, https://www. sfchronicle.com/bayarea/article/Bathhouse-ban-revoked-Amid-one-pandemic-San-15558609.php.

278 Nikolay Doychinov, "The Global Health Observatory, HIV/AIDS," World Health Organization, 2022, https://www.who.int/data/gho/data/themes/hiv-aids.

extreme promiscuity of their lifestyle accounts for eighty-three percent of the primary and secondary cases of syphilis.[279]

The argument favoring homosexual marriage is based upon the Hollywood myth of the happy, well-adjusted gay person. This myth says that the homosexual lifestyle is not very different from the normal heterosexual lifestyle. Once this myth was accepted, it logically followed that homosexuals should be allowed to adopt children, and the decision by the Supreme Court in favor of homosexual marriage has now opened the flood gates to that reality.

The myth of the well-adjusted homosexual breaks down under the pressure of cold, hard facts. The sociological statistics prove that most homosexuals do not live in stable, long-term relationships that are monogamous. The statistics also shows that the average homosexual is deviant in both physical and mental health. Even if one accepts the central Liberal premise that homosexuality is a natural, predetermined trait, there is still the issue of their extreme sexual promiscuity. Joe Kort, Ph.D., wrote the following description in *Psychology Today* in 2018:

> Research shows that around 50 percent of gay male couples manage open relationships . . . cheating has less of a negative impact than for heterosexuals . . . gay men . . . think that cheating is a "natural part of any relationship" . . . Gay male couples often report that what works best from them is to engage in sexual encounters based on sexual attraction only and not emotions or affection . . . Many straight couples—especially millennials— are now doing the same thing.[280]

Even when predispositions or controlling addictions exist, a moral society expects individuals to attempt to resist or restrain their negative

279 "Syphilis Statistics," Centers for Disease Control and Prevention, April 11, 2023, https://www.cdc.gov/std/syphilis/stats.htm.
280 Joe Kort, "Monogamy: It's Not What You Think," Psychology Today online, 2018, https://www.psychologytoday.com/us/blog/understanding-the-erotic-code/201809/monogamy-it-s-not-what-you-think.

behaviors. It is not considered acceptable for alcoholics, drug addicts, rapists, adulterers, and pedophiles to act on their urges. An ethical society does not tell its deviants to organize parades and celebrate their perversion.

As imperfect as heterosexual-marriage relationships are, a U.S. Census study in 2002 found that "70.7 percent of women . . . reached their tenth anniversary and 57.7 percent [stay] married for twenty years or longer."[281] On the issue of fidelity, the *Journal of Sex* published a finding that eighty-eight percent of heterosexual women and seventy-seven percent of heterosexual men remained faithful to their spouses.[282]

Bell and Weinberg's classic study of female and male homosexuals found that "43 percent of male homosexuals had sex with 500 or more partners, with 28 percent having a thousand or more sex partners."[283] In a study by McWhirter and Mattison, they found that "most homosexual men understood sexual relations outside the relationship to be the norm."[284]

More research shows that only a few homosexual relationships last more than two years. A Dutch study published in the journal *AIDS* found that homosexual relationships last only 1.5 years on average, and even when they have a steady partner, they continue to have up to eight other sexual partners a year.[285] The average homosexual, by this definition, would have to be described as having a sexual addiction.

Timothy J. Daily, wrote in his journal, *Comparing the Lifestyles of Homosexual couples to Married Heterosexual Couples*, "Even committed homosexual

281 Timothy J. Dailey, "Part 2: Harmful Aspects of The Homosexual Lifestyle," in "Homesexual Parenting: Placing Children at Risk,"Family Research Council, 2007, https://ac21doj.org/contents/homosexuality/homosexualParentingPlacingChildrenAtRisk-Part2.html.
282 Stephen Cranney and Aleksander Stulhofer, "'Whosoever Looketh on a Person to Lust After Them': Religiosity, the Use of Mainstream and Nonmainstream Sexually Explicit Material, and Sexual Satisfaction in Heterosexual Men and Women," *Journal of Sex* 54, No. 6, 694–705, https://doi.org/10.1080/00224499.2016.1216068.
283 Kort, ibid.
284 Dailey, ibid.
285 Joseph Nicolosi, "An Open Secret: The Truth about Gay Male Couples," Reparative Therapy, April 26, 2017, https://www.josephnicolosi.com/collection/2015/5/28/an-open-secret-the-truth-about-gay-male-couples.

relationships display a fundamental incapacity for faithfulness."[286] What explains the atypical pattern in homosexual relationships compared with heterosexual ones? The problems of the homosexual community are often blamed on heterosexuals for not accepting their lifestyle. The facts show there is an actual problem with homosexuality—a problem based upon underlying mental health issues, the dysfunctional nature of a homosexual relationship, and a low level of sexual morality.

In 2017, the American Psychiatric Association reported its findings under the title of their article, "Mental Health Disparities," saying, "LGBTQ individuals are more than twice as likely as heterosexual men and women to have mental health disorder . . . they are more than 2.5 times more likely to experience depression, anxiety and substance misuse compared to heterosexuals . . . their rate of suicide attempts are four times greater . . . than that of heterosexuals."[287] The new statistics put out by the CDC reported on April 20, 2021, says that "gay and bisexual youth are almost five times as likely to have attempted suicide as their straight peers . . . 40 percent of LGBTQ youths ages 13-24 had seriously considered attempting suicide in the previous 12 months."[288]

Each decade in America since the 1970s has shown an increasing acceptance of gay rights and even the acceptance of gay marriage by most young adults, but gay youth are still attempting suicide at a rate five times greater than normal. LGBTQ youth are overrepresented in the criminal justice system, and over a third of the women in America's prisons/jails are lesbian but make-up less than three percent of the overall population.[289]

286 Timothy J. Daily, "Comparing the Lifestyles of Homosexual Couples to Married Couples," United Productions, Accessed January 1, 2023, https://unite-production. s3.amazonaws.com/tenants/mtcalvaryhuron/attachments/75957/Comparing_the_ Lifestyles_of_Homosexual_Couples_to_Married_Couples.pdf.

287 "Mental Health Disparities: Diverse Populations," Psychiatry.org, Accessed October 14, 2017, https://www.psychiatry.org/psychiatrists/cultural-competency/education/ mental-health-facts.

288 "Disparities in Suicide," Centers for Disease Control and Prevention, Accessed October 22, 2022, https://www.cdc.gov/suicide/facts/disparities-in-suicide.html.

289 Julie Moreau, "'Overwhelming Number of Lesbians, Bisexual Women Incarcerated,'" NBCNews online, March 3, 2017, https://www.nbcnews.com/feature/nbc-out/ overwhelming-number-lesbians-bisexual-women-incarcerated-n728666.

The facts show that the combination of increased levels of depression, anxiety, and substance abuse contributes to a higher level of LGBTQ domestic violence. The numbers show that "43.8% of lesbian women and 61.1% of bisexual women have experienced rape, physical violence . . . by an intimate partner . . . as opposed to 35% of heterosexual women."[290] Maya Shwayder, in an article published in *The Atlantic* (2013), called the problem "A Same Sex Domestic Violence Epidemic."[291] On the male side of the issue, the CDC reported that "40 percent of gay and 47 percent of bisexual men have experienced sexual violence . . . compared to 21 percent of heterosexual men."[292]

The words "gay" and "straight" are words favored by homosexuals. These words became commonly used in the 1960s as part of the organized campaign to change American attitudes about homosexuality and increase its acceptance. The word "homophobia" was invented by George Weinberg, an American psychologist who used the term in his pro-homosexual writings like "Society and the Healthy Homosexual."[293] His psychological theory held that if heterosexuals had a strong dislike of homosexuality, it was because they were themselves latent homosexuals. Until Weinberg and other psychologists began to advocate this view, homosexuality had been defined and treated as a form of mental illness.

Then in 1973, the American Psychiatric Association voted to remove homosexuality from the medical list of disorders of the mind. The vital thing to note here is that removing homosexuality from the list of defined mental illnesses was not a unanimous decision based upon indisputable scientific

---

290 "Domestic Violence and the LGBTQ Community," National Coalition Against Domestic Violence, June 6, 2018, https://ncadv.org/blog/posts/domestic-violence-and-the-lgbtq-community.

291 Maya Shwayder, "A Same-Sex Domestic Violence Epidemic Is Silent," Atlantic Media Company, November 5, 2013, https://www.theatlantic.com/health/archive/2013/11/a-same-sex-domestic-violence-epidemic-is-silent/281131.

292 "The National Intimate Partner and Sexual Violence Survey (NISVS)," CDC.gov, Accessed June 30, 2023, https://www.cdc.gov/violenceprevention/datasources/nisvs/index.html.

293 William Grimes, "George Weinberg Dies at 87; Coined 'Homophobia' after Seeing Fear of Gays," The New York Times online, March 22, 2017, https://www.nytimes.com/2017/03/22/us/george-weinberg-dead-coined-homophobia.html.

evidence. It was a statement of fashionable belief and part of the counter-cultural movement of the radical 1960s and '70s. After the vote, some studies in genetics did follow, but the results were a mixed bag. Some said heredity accounted for up to seventy percent of sexual orientation, but others found much less at forty percent.

The most recent study published in *Scientific America* in 2019 stated, "Analysis of half a million people suggests genetics may have limited contribution to sexual orientation . . . a new study claims to dispel the notion that a single gene or handful of genes make a person prone to same-sex behavior."[294] As interesting as this new study may be, focusing on sexual orientation is less important than focusing on human behavior. Protecting children and adolescents is more critical than deciding if homosexuals are "born that way" or sociologically shaped to become that way. Even if we accept their predispositions or inherited traits, they still have an ethical responsibility to exercise self-control and not abuse other people.

Even discounting orientation as the cause of immoral behavior, homosexuals must still answer for the extreme promiscuity of their lifestyle. Their extreme level of promiscuity contributes to their being involved in a higher number of cases of sexual abuse. The most egregious example of homosexual dysfunction is their disproportionate involvement in pedophilia/hebephilia. When the issue of pedophilia/hebephilia behavior is raised, the typical response is that homosexuals don't perpetrate more than heterosexuals do or that homosexuality has nothing to do with pedophilia.

The first thing a person notices when reading homosexual literature on this topic is to attempt to take the focus off homosexual behavior by engaging in wordplay. Homosexual advocates like to restrict the definition of pedophilia to mean, "A consenting adult being sexually attracted to young children." By engaging in wordplay, they distract the honest person from the much-broader

294 Sara Reardon, "Massive Study Finds No Single Genetic Cause of Same-Sex Sexual Behavior," Scientific American online, August 29, 2019, https://www.scientificamerican.com/article/massive-study-finds-no-single-genetic-cause-of-same-sex-sexual-behavior.

category of sexual abuse, including hebephilia or sexual attraction by an adult to adolescent children. Common sense tells us that based upon their small 2.5 to four percent of the overall national population, homosexuals would feel sexual pressure to seek out new sexual conquests early and often and would be far less scrupulous about respecting the "age of consent" laws.

The heterosexual population faces a different dating and mating situation. There are 7.43 million more women than men in our population. If you combine the following factors: a low level of sexual morality, a smaller pool of individuals with whom to engage in sex, and homosexual obsession, this leads homosexuals away from the ethical or legal standards of society.

Those crusading for the advancement of homosexual acceptance will scream to the high heavens that the homosexual lifestyle has nothing to do with pedophilia or hebephiliac. Like Hollywood and the entertainment industry, they try to paint a sentimental picture of homosexuals as innocent victims of bigotry and hate, but the facts are the facts.

In the year 2000, a critical case was decided in the Supreme Court, called "Boy Scouts of America v. Dale." In it, Liberals and the homosexual lobby had pressured the Boy Scouts to allow openly homosexual people to become scoutmasters in the leadership program. Still, the Supreme Court ruled in the Boy Scouts' favor. Under continuing social pressure, the organization relented in 2008, allowing homosexuals to become scoutmasters. On February 18, 2020, CNN reported, "Boy Scouts of America files for bankruptcy. Hundreds of sexual abuse lawsuits are now on hold."[295] In this situation, it is not hard to see the connection between homosexuality and hebephilia at work.

The Gay Report, a book by Karla Jay and Allen Young, found "that 73 percent of (homosexuals) surveyed had had sexual relations with males 16-19 or younger."[296] In gay travel information, it is common to find advertisements

295 Laura Ly, "Boy Scouts of America files for bankruptcy. Hundreds of sexual abuse lawsuits are now on hold," Cable News Network online, February 18, 2020, https://www.cnn.com/2020/02/18/us/boy-scouts-bankruptcy/index.html.
296 Karla Jay, The Gay Report: Lesbians and Gay Men Speak Out About Sexual Experiences and Lifestyles (Mandaluyong: Summit Books, 1979).

of palaces around the world where boys are willing to engage in sex. A significant part of sex tourism is related to homosexual activity. Analysis of the sexual abuse of children in the Catholic Church found that eighty percent of those abused were male, and ninety percent of the abusers were male.[297] This abuse, which reached as far back as the 1980s, has cost the Catholic Church four billion dollars, as of 2020.[298]

We have the record of NAMBLA: the "North American Man/Boy Love Association." This was the first homosexual group to lobby for the right to engage in pedophilia openly. In 2005, the *San Diego Union Tribune* published the following statement about NAMBLA: "While NAMBLA's membership numbers are small, the group has a dangerous ripple effect through the Internet by sanctioning the behavior of those who would abuse children."[299] Though the average homosexual is quick to say they are against the philosophy that sexual relations between men and adolescent boys are appropriate, the International Lesbian and Gay Association allowed NAMBLA to be part of their organization in 1993. The United Nations suspended ILGA membership at the U.N. for allowing NAMBLA to be part of ILGA's membership.[300] The ILGA was well-aware of the NAMBLA philosophy that: "man/boy love is by definition homosexual . . . man/boy lovers are part of the gay movement and central to gay history and culture . . . homosexuals denying that it is 'not gay' to be attracted to adolescent boys are just as ludicrous as heterosexuals saying it's 'not heterosexual' to be attracted to adolescent girls."[301]

297 Karen J. Terry and Joshua D. Freilich, "Understanding Child Sexual Abuse by Catholic Priests From a Situational Perspective," *Journal of Child Sexual Abuse* 21, No. 4 (July 2012): 437-55, DOI: 10.1080/10538712.2012.693579.

298 "How Much Has the Catholic Church Paid to Abuse Victims," Massey Law Firm, December 13, 2021, https://dmasseylaw.com/how-much-catholic-church-paid-abuse-victims.

299 Onell R. Soto, "'FBI Targets Pedophila Advocates,'" The San Diego Union-Tribune online, 2005, https://www.sandiegouniontribune.com.

300 "U.N. Suspends Group in Dispute Over Pedophilia," The New York Times online, September 18, 1994. https://www.nytimes.com/1994/09/18/world/un-suspends-group-in-dispute-over-pedophilia.html.

301 Mary deYoung, "The World According to NAMBLA: Accounting for Deviance," *Journal of Sociology & Social Welfare* 16, No. 1 (1989), https://scholarworks.wmich.edu/jssw/vol16/iss1/9.

Because of social pressure from the public and increased law enforcement scrutiny, NAMBLA stopped holding public meetings in the late 1990s. It would take until 1994 for the New York LGBTQ group to ban NAMBLA's right to march in their international parade.[302] Even then, NAMBLA was still active. It joined the Gay Liberation Front group and conducted its own parade. For most homosexuals, the repudiation of NAMBLA was not based upon a higher standard of sexual morality.

It was a strategic decision based upon NAMBLA becoming a lightning rod drawing unwanted publicity that was damaging the gay rights campaign in general. This all happened when the main homosexual lobby was trying to convince everyday Americans that homosexuals were normal Americans and, as such, deserved the rights to both marry and raise children. This victory was achieved on June 26, 2015, when five U.S. Supreme Court justices ruled in favor of legalizing homosexual marriage.

With the help of sixty years of Hollywood and mass-media indoctrination, the American public has collectively buried its moral head in the sand. Instead of protecting the most innocent and vulnerable among us—our children— most Americans have become convinced that the rights of a tiny and morally confused group of people are more important. Most Americans believe that a radical change in America's standard of sexual morality poses no danger to our future. The "silent majority" has now become the "immoral majority" and has forgotten what the Savior said about the abuse of children: "Whoso shall offend one of these little ones which believe in me, it were better for him that a millstone were hanged about his neck, and that he were drowned in the depth of the sea" (Matt. 18:6).

---

302 Kim I. Mills, "Gay Groups Try to Put Distance Between Themselves and Pedophile Group," AP NEWS online, February 13, 1994, https://apnews.com/ c64e816cac5b0fa1194dd40f576813b2.

PART FOUR

REHEARSALS FOR THE FALL OF JUDEO-CHRISTIAN CULTURE

CHAPTER FOURTEEN

THE DANCE OF HISTORY

IN SOME WAYS, THE HISTORY of the world can be described as a continual dance with steps in many directions. Then, a new dance pattern emerges with an alternating partner leading the way. This is especially true in Western civilization since the Scientific Revolution and the Enlightenment. Even in the non-Western world, one finds evidence of the continuing struggle between rationalism and mysticism, such as with the Mu'tazilites and Sufism in Islam, Confucianism, Taoism in China, and Buddhism/Hinduism in India.

The difference between Western civilization and the non-Western world is its dominant trend toward secularism and the fact that the beliefs of Judeo-Christianity do not inhibit scientific advancement. Judeo-Christianity, with its unique concept of a Creator God Who is responsible for all of nature but is not part of nature, conditions the human mind to respect the difference between the world as objective and God and humanity as subjective. For this reason, we find some of the greatest minds of Western science like Galileo, Newton, and Kepler, pushing the boundaries of scientific discovery but remaining highly religious in their overall thought. By conceiving the world in this way, the laws of nature are respected, as are the laws of God.

Those in Western civilization who previously rejected the Judeo-Christian view of the world were left with competing and opposite directions of beliefs of secular humanism or neo-paganism. Judeo-Christianity and these other two influences are responsible for most of the cultural changes which have taken place in our history. Other than the status quo of Judeo-Christianity, the alternating dance partners of secular humanism and neo-paganism have led the way.

GNOSTICISM

Those who hate Judeo-Christianity begin their analysis based upon a false narrative of its history and beliefs. Their muddled misunderstanding associates Judeo-Christianity with the multiple competing doctrines that filled the ancient pagan world, such as Gnosticism, Donatism, Montanism, Manicheism, cynicism, stoicism, and Neoplatonism. These -isms were based on a pessimistic view and a strong aversion to the natural world. These competing philosophies and religions, especially Gnosticism and Manicheism, presented the first significant hurdle Christianity had to overcome on the road to surviving as a belief system. Gnosticism and Manicheism were Christianity's first rehearsal for the fall of Judeo-Christian culture.

The Christian church experienced tremendous growth from the first through second centuries A.D. It was inevitable that with such a large part of its membership coming from ordinary, un-educated people from various cultures, the Church would eventually be infected with some false notions. In this context, the false tar of Gnosticism was smeared on the Christian Church. The teachings of Gnosticism were never part of original Judaism or Christianity, and the teachings of Gnosticism were a frontal attack on the central beliefs of both.

The eminent Christian Church historian Williston Walker identified Gnosticism as "pre-Christian in origin . . . which may be traced back to Babylonian religious conceptions."[303] He also identified its Egyptian influences. Other scholars on the subject have identified other possible sources for Gnostic belief like Hellenistic Judaism, the cult of the Essenes, Persian Zoroastrianism, and even possibly Buddhism and Hinduism.

---

303 Walker, ibid.

Gnosticism taught that the physical world was evil, and because of that fact, Jesus Christ could not have been born in the flesh, nor could He have died on the cross and been resurrected. According to Gnostic teaching, Jesus was an angel or a phantom spirit, and He was not really the Son of God but only part of a spiritual source they called "the Monad" or "the pleroma" (a.k.a., "the fullness"). Like the concept of an avatar in Hinduism, the Gnostics believed that Jesus came to reveal esoteric, mystical truths that would assist human beings to escape an evil material world and rejoin the pleroma (e.g. in Hinduism, this is the world soul).

Gnosticism is a mixture of mythology and philosophy. Like all pagan conceptions of ultimate truth, it is overly complicated and packed with strange notions and esoteric terminology intended to impress the ignorant and gullible. Instead of the straightforward presentation of the Gospels, which Jesus explained in simple language and parables, the Gnostics created a great hierarchy of mystical knowledge one had to master:

> According to Gnostic mythology we, humanity, are existing in this realm because a member of the transcendent godhead, Sophia desired to actualize her innate potential for creativity without the approval of her partner the divine consort . . . Her hubris, in this regard, stood forth as raw materiality, and her desire which was for the mysterious ineffable . . . manifested itself as . . . the Demiurge, that renegade principle of generation and corruption which, by its unalterable necessity, brings all beings to life.[304]

To achieve salvation, the Gnostics taught one had to ascend a great ladder of spiritual steps based on one's knowledge (i.e., gnosis). A partial listing of the levels of knowledge one had to pass through included "Realms of Chaos, Outer Worlds of Darkness, 12 Universes, Fallen Worlds of Mixture, Cause

---

304 *Internet Encyclopedia of Philosophy*, s.v. "Gnosticism," Accessed October 24, 2022, https://iep.utm.edu/gnostic.

of Events, Virgin of Light, 13th Aeon, The Height-Upper Universe, Midway Councils, Spiritual Hierarchies Councils, Region of the Right-Unfallen Worlds, The plan-Emanations, programs of Pure Energy Being, Universal Mind, The Ineffable."[305]

One of the main differences between Gnosticism and Christianity is the fact Gnosticism makes its appeal to an elite few. Judaism and Christianity have compassion and concern for the salvation of all people. In Judeo-Christianity, no one is thought to be above or below the message. The Judeo-Christian message is simple, practical, and reasonable. No one must become a rocket scientist to share in its blessings or truth.

On the other hand, the Gnostic message is all about being more intelligent and knowing more than someone else. Gnosticism is about special people with special knowledge finding a way to salvation. Their method was not "love your neighbor as yourself" but rather knowing more than what your neighbor knows. St. Paul gave the perfect response to Gnosticism when he stated, "We all have knowledge. Knowledge puffeth up, but charity edifieth. And if any man think that he knoweth anything, he knoweth nothing yet as he ought to know. But if man love God, the same is known by him" (1 Cor. 8:1).

The Judeo-Christian message starts with humility and seeks to maintain it. Judeo-Christianity focuses on the greatness of God, but Gnosticism focuses on the greatness of self. Gnosticism strokes the human ego by teaching that if we have special knowledge, we can become gods. Their view of the material world differed equally from Judeo-Christianity and was similarly insidious. Their mythology was a direct attack against the fundamental basis of Judaism.

The Gnostics taught that the natural world was evil—the product of a fake god who they called the "Demiurge." They identified this Demiurge with the Hebrew Creator God, Who they claimed was not the real God but only a foolish "craftsman" who tried and failed to imitate the real god (Pleroma). Like the "great" religions of the Far East—such as Hinduism, Jainism, and

---

305 G.R.S. Mead, *Pistis Sophia* (London: The Theosophical Publishing Society, 1896), 206-21.

Buddhism—Gnosticism taught that we are trapped in an evil world of suffering, and only by acquiring special knowledge from special people could we escape this suffering. Some scholars have supported the thesis that Hinduism and Buddhism may have been a source for Gnosticism's disdain for the physical world. The highest level of Hindu philosophy is found in writings known as the "Upanishads." One of its foundational statements is "what is the good of enjoyment of desires? . . . we see that this whole world is decaying like gnats . . . what is the good of enjoyment of desires, when, after a man has fed upon them, there is seen repeatedly his return here to earth?"[306]

Buddha rejected many of the central teachings of Hinduism, including its belief in over three hundred million gods, the Vedic myths, and the control of religion by Hindu priests. But he accepted its quintessential beliefs in reincarnation and the need to escape a hostile world of continual suffering. Historian Will Durant described Buddha's view of life in this way: "Buddha was convinced that pain so overbalanced pleasure in human life that it would be better never to have been born . . . Every pleasure seemed poisoned for him by its brevity . . . above all, sexual desire, for that leads to reproduction, which stretches out the chain of life into new suffering aimlessly."[307]

Among the first rules Buddhist monks were to practice was, "To shun all amusements of sense or flesh . . . have nothing to do with business . . . live apart from women, in perfect chastity."[308]

Williston Walker says the Gnostic Marcion (85-160 A.D.) taught that "since the material world is evil, the ascetic life is to be embraced. Meat-eating and sexual intercourse only play into the hands of the (evil) creator god."[309]

Manicheism held the same view that the natural world was dark and evil. Women were a creation of the devil. The good God was pure Light,

---

306 Max Müller, "Maitrâyana-Brâhmana-Upanishad: FIRST PRAPÂTHAKA," in *The Upanishads,* Part 2, 1879, https://www.sacred-texts.com/hin/sbe15/sbe15112.htm.
307 Durant, 430.
308 Barbara O'Brien, "The First Buddhist Monks," Learn Religions, April 30, 2019, https://www.learnreligions.com/the-first-buddhist-monks-450082.
309 Walker, 54.

and men had to abstain from sexual activity and practice vegetarianism to be saved. A large part of St. Augustine's famous book *Confessions* describes his eventual rejection of this life-hating philosophy and his reasons for accepting Christianity as the truth. He describes his change of thinking this way:

> I perceived . . . that Thou madest all things good, nor is there any substance at all, which Thou madest not . . . And I enquired what iniquity was, and found it to be no substance, but perversion of will, turned aside from Thee, O God, the Supreme, towards these lower things . . . Persons are in Scripture called enemies of God, who not by nature but by sins, oppose his government . . . Nor by their wickedness do they effect that under the rule, power, and wisdom of the All-ruling God, the beauty and order of the universe should in any way be deformed.[310]

Augustine's view was the orthodox Christian view of nature. St. Irenaeus, who lived from A.D. 180-199, condemned Gnosticism for its anti-material, anti-sexual view of the world. Irenaeus wrote about Marcion's activities: "Marcion . . . mutilated the Gospel . . . removing all that is written about the generation of the Lord; and he removed much teaching . . . in which the Lord is recorded as confessing most clearly that his Father is the Maker of the universe . . . Creation itself reveals Him that created it; and the work is itself suggestive of him that made it; and the world manifests Him that arranged it.[311] Hundreds of years before Augustine and Irenaeus had expressed this orthodox Christian view of nature, St. Paul had said the same thing: "For the invisible things of him from the creation of the world are clearly seen, being understood by the things that are made, even his eternal power and Godhead; so that they are without excuse" (Rom. 1:20). Paul and the other New Testament apostles had already realized the growing danger of Gnosticism's big lie.

---

310   St. Augustine, *Confessions: Book XII* (New York: J.M. Dent & Sons, 1975).
311   St. Irenaeus, *Detection and Overthrow of the Gnosis Falsely So Called* (Collegeville: The Liturgical Press, 1970), 87.

The apostle Timothy warned of those "forbidding to marry, and commanding to abstain from meats, which God hath created . . . For every creature of God is good" (1 Tim. 4:3-4). The apostle James states, "Every good gift and every perfect gift is from above and cometh down from the Father" (James 1:2). In 2 John 1:7, the apostle directly contradicted the Gnostic belief that Jesus was a spirit without a physical body: "For many deceivers are entered into the world, who confess not that Jesus Christ is come in the flesh. This is a deceiver and an antichrist."

The Judeo-Christian view of life on earth is radically different. Judaism, the parent of Christianity, begins its introduction to the world by describing the miracle of Creation; and after a detailed description of various parts of Creation, it concludes by repeating over and over "that it was good . . . God saw that it was good . . . and God saw . . . it was very good" (Gen. 1:4-31). After the Fall, when Adam and Eve were no longer allowed to live in the Garden paradise, they continued to live on earth, which science agrees is the most beautiful, wonderful, and life-sustaining place in the universe. Humanity's relationship with God had changed, but the natural world that He created was still His and was still governed by the natural laws which He decreed.

In the first five books of the Old Testament, the same message is consistently presented that God still loves humanity and will bless us if we follow His laws and refrain from sin. A short list of these nature-affirming statements include:

- "And God blessed them, and God said unto them, Be fruitful, and multiply, and replenish the earth" (Gen. 1:28).
- "Honour thy father and thy mother: that thy days may be long upon the land" (Exod. 20:12).
- "When thou hast eaten and art full, then shalt thou bless the LORD thy God for the good land which he has given thee" (Deut. 8:10).

- "Behold, the heaven and the heaven of heavens is the Lord's thy God, the earth also, with all that therein is." (Deut. 10:14).
- "The heavens declare the glory of God; and the firmament sheweth his handywork" (Psalm 19:1).
- "But the meek shall inherit the earth; and shall delight themselves in the abundance of peace" (Psalm 37:34).[312]
- "Let heaven and earth praise him, the seas, and everything that moveth therein" (Psalm 69:34).
- "Let the heavens rejoice, and let the earth be glad; let the sea roar . . . Let the field be joyful, and all that is therein" (Psalm 96:11-12).
- "Praise ye him, sun and moon; praise him, all ye stars of light" (Psalm 148:3-4).

Many of the same nature-affirming verses are repeated in the New Testament. The last book of the New Testament, Revelation, includes, "Thou art worthy, O Lord, to receive glory and honour and power: for thou hast created all things, and for thy pleasure, they are and were created . . . every creature which is in heaven, and on the earth, and under the earth, and such as are in the sea, and all that are in them, heard I saying, Blessing, and honour, and glory, and power, be unto him that sitteth upon the throne" (Rev. 4:11, 5:13).

Not only does the New Testament confirm the Old Testament's respect for the natural world, but it also introduces the concept that Jesus, as part of the Godhead, was the primary Agent of the act of creation. This is stated at the beginning of the Gospel of John in chapter 1:1-4: "In the beginning was the Word [Jesus] . . . All things were made by him; and without him was not anything made . . . In him was life; and the life was the light of men." In Colossians 1:16-17, we get the same message: "For by him were all things created, that are in heaven, and that are in earth . . . all things were created by him . . . And he is before all things, and by him all things consist."

---

312 Jesus repeated this statement in the Gospels—Matthew, Mark, Luke, and John.

Probably the most significant refutation of Gnosticism was the simple facts about the life of Jesus Christ. He was born in the flesh and lived an everyday life of family, work, and study. He suffered physical and emotional pain and was tempted like all people. He ate food and drank wine, had friends, and showed His admiration for nature. He said, "Consider the lilies how they grow: they toil not, they spin not; and yet I say unto you, that Solomon in all his glory was not arrayed like one of these" (Luke 12:27).

Almost all of Jesus' teachings and miracles center around relieving ordinary people's physical or mental suffering. Jesus showed His concern for the happiness of people on earth when He said, "I am the door: by me if any man enter in, he shall be saved . . . I am come that they might have life, and that they might have it more abundantly" (John 10:9-10). He showed his concern for the welfare of humanity when He said, "But seek ye first the kingdom of God . . . and all these things shall be added unto you" (Matt. 6:33).

THE RENAISSANCE

Over a thousand years after its successful struggle against Gnosticism, Judeo-Christian culture faced the next challenge for its survival. This new challenge was part of the European Renaissance, one of the greatest movements in art and thought beginning in the fourteenth century. During the Renaissance, pagan beliefs such as astrology and the occult arts were married to secular humanist philosophy, which valued most pleasure, fame, and wealth.

Several of the Renaissance popes believed in and practice astrology. The highest level of Catholic leadership was enamored with and supported pagan culture. Much of the art commissioned by the Catholic Church during this period was dedicated to pagan themes. In political terms, the methods used by some of the Renaissance popes were the same as those used by secular princes: war, deceit, treachery, bribes. The authority of the pope, known as the papacy, was strengthened at this time but at the expense of weakening the average Christian's faith.

Prominent Christian voices as different as St. Catherine of Siena and the lowly monk Martin Luther personally witnessed and condemned the moral corruption in the Catholic Church. On a visit to the papal court in A.D. 1373, Catherine said she "could smell the odors of hell." Luther, who visited in A.D. 1511, said almost the same thing: "If there is a hell, then Rome is built upon it; and this I have heard in Rome itself."

In 1262, Etienne Tempier, the Catholic bishop of Paris, condemned the pagan beliefs that were spreading in the universities and were undermining the faith of their students. Bishop Tempier cataloged them as "the world is eternal . . . the soul is corrupted with the corruption of the body . . . God does not know individual events . . . human actions are not ruled by Divine Providence . . . creation is impossible . . . the Christian religion impedes learning . . . the words of theologians are founded on fables . . . happiness is obtained in this life, not another."[313]

Leonardo da Vinci, often used as the poster-boy of Renaissance greatness, showed his scorn for the importance of Jesus Christ in history, writing, "All the world is in mourning because one man died in the Orient . . . Those who have wished to worship men as gods have made a very grave error."[314] His secular attitude was widespread among the artists and writers of this period. The most famous Renaissance philosophers—Carlo Marsuppini, Poggio Bracciolini, Pietro Pomponazzi, Nicoletto Vernia, and Lorenzo Valla—all played a role in promoting secular humanism and neo-paganism.

Historian Will Durant's assessment of this period was that "Christianity, in both its theology and its ethics, had lost its hold on . . . a majority of the Italian humanists . . . the humanists, by and large, acted as if Christianity were a myth . . . not to be taken seriously by emancipated minds . . . Their lives reflected their actual creed; many of them accepted and practiced

---

313 Hans Thijssen, *Stanford Encyclopedia of Philosophy*, s.v. "Condemnation of 1277," January 30, 2003, https://plato.stanford.edu/entries/condemnation.

314 Jean-Paul Richter, *The Notebooks of Leonardo Davinci*, Vol. 2 (Mineola, New York: Dover Publications, 2016), 367.

the ethics of paganism."[315] By abandoning the Judeo-Christian tradition, the Renaissance was left morally rudderless. Skepticism produced disillusionment; disillusionment produced cynicism; and cynicism produced immorality. The Italian city-states of the Renaissance, like the ancient city-states of pagan Greece, found themselves perpetually at war. One of the most cynical political writers in history, Niccolò Machiavelli, stepped forth to end this chaos.

Like cynics and atheists throughout history, Machiavelli was quick to point out the hypocrisies and deep moral failings of the Catholic Church. "Had the religion of Christianity been preserved according to the ordinances of its founder . . . Christianity would have been far more united and happy . . . Nor can there be a greater proof of its decadence than the fact that the nearer people are to the Roman Church . . . the less religious are they.[316]

Machiavelli was stating the obvious, but unlike Catherine of Siena, Luther, and popes Pius II and Adrian VI, he was not genuinely concerned about the moral reform of the Church nor the spiritual renewal of the Christian faith. Durant writes of what was at the heart of Machiavelli's political philosophy, "What he rejects most decisively in Christianity is its ethic, its conception of goodness . . . its love of peace and its denunciation of war; its assumption that states as well as citizens, are bound by the one moral code."[317]

Machiavelli's goal, like his philosophy, was based upon pagan values and supported secular ends. He had a very flawed understanding of what Judeo-Christianity really teaches. Like other atheist political leaders/philosophers after him—such as Thomas Hobbes, Friedrich Nietzsche, and Vladimir Lenin—Machiavelli relied on a belief that "the end justifies the means." In essence, Machiavelli taught that a political leader could engage in any act of

315 Will Durant, *The Renaissance*, Vol. 5. *The Story of Civilization* (New York: Simon and Schuster, 2011), 84.
316 Niccolò Machiavelli, Chapter XII, in *Discourses on the First Ten Books of Titus Livius*, translated by Christian E. Detmold, 1882, https://www.marxists.org/reference/archive/machiavelli/works/discourses/index.htm.
317 Durant, 558.

immorality if it supports the success of his final goal. His goal was to use political power to create a preeminent Italian city-state that would be strong enough to dominate all the others militarily.

His now-famous book *The Prince* was a practical guide on political do's and don'ts on how to gain, maintain, and increase political control. It was a survival manual for a prince to follow in a dog-eat-dog world of perpetual war and intrigue. It is not by accident that many modern dictators like Hitler, Stalin, and Mussolini, all took the time to read and apply Machiavelli's insights. The mass murder of French Protestants by order of Catherine de' Medici, the starvation of millions of Ukrainians by Stalin, Hitler's Holocaust, and Mao's Cultural Revolution are all examples of where Machiavelli's philosophy of divorcing political power from morality leads.

Even putting the question of morality aside, "The end justifies the means" is often wrong in practical terms because no philosopher nor anyone else can accurately predict the outcome of any long-term strategy. The result of any process to change society is always conditioned by the means *used*, and means and ends are not so easily kept separate. What starts as a cause produces an effect that in turn becomes another cause. Hitler and Stalin did achieve "godlike" supremacy for a short time, but where is the "Thousand-Year Reich" or the Soviet Union now?

Machiavelli's statement that Christianity "makes us hold of small account the love of this world . . . has placed the supreme good in humility . . . and in contempt for worldly things"[318] accurately characterizes the medieval mind influenced by false teaching and not original Christianity.

The pagan Romans attacked Christians based upon the same false beliefs calling them "dregs of the people," "atheists," people who had a "hatred of the human race" and are "breaking up the home."

With the spread of the Renaissance to Northern Europe, Judeo-Christian culture reasserted itself. The best elements of Renaissance thought were

---

318 Machiavelli, 94.

co-opted into the defense of Judeo-Christianity. The belief that individual life is meaningful and that a good life requires freedom of thought became what people called "Christian Humanism."

———————◆———————◆———————

Francesco Petrarch, called the "Father of Humanism," took the noblest thinking from the classical Greco-Roman world and fused it with the Judeo-Christian tradition. He expressed his deepest values when he said, "I desire that death find me reading and writing, or, if it please Christ, praying and in tears."[319] It was with the Scientific Revolution and the intellectual movement it caused the Enlightenment, that secular humanism again took leadership on in the dance stage of European history. For a short period of time the Christian "Fundamentalism" of the Reformation placed a brake on Europe's slide into secularization, but the terrible wars of European religion, which followed in the wake of the Protestant Reformation, combined with major scientific discoveries produced a new, more popular, skepticism about religious faith.

By the seventeenth and eighteenth centuries, there was a growing middle-class of literate people who were susceptible to being influenced by a new group of secular-humanist writers and thinkers. The Enlightenment's emphasis on reason, tolerance, and human rights was a positive encouragement to the American Revolution; but in France, where these beliefs were corrupted by extreme, skepticism and atheism, it resulted in political radicalism, civil war, and widespread atrocities. The Enlightenment and the French Revolution linked together were now the next rehearsal for the fall of Judeo-Christian culture.

---

319 Francesco Petrarch, "I desire that death . . . ," QuoteFancy.com, https://quotefancy. com/quote/1365100/Petrarch-I-desire-that-death-find-me-ready-and-writing-or-if-it-please-Christ-praying-and.

CHAPTER FIFTEEN

THE DARKER SIDE OF ENLIGHTENMENT

THE ENLIGHTENMENT WAS AN INTELLECTUAL, cultural, and social movement that started in Europe during the 1600s and reached its peak influence in France and America during the late 1700s. Like its predecessor, the Renaissance, its main ideological thrust was secular humanism. Unlike the Renaissance, it included a much broader scope of interests and motivated a more general concern to bring about both political and social reforms.

The Renaissance had been about a talented few reaching their highest potential, but the Enlightenment was about raising the potential of the entire human race. During the Renaissance, the Englishman Sir Thomas More wrote a fantasy about a perfect society discovered on an island in the South Atlantic. He named this island "Utopia," a word he invented. But it was the Enlightenment writers who truly believed that utopian societies could be possible. For them, all good things were possible if religious faith were replaced by human reason guided by the Scientific Method.

Another significant difference between the Renaissance and the Enlightenment was the enormous influence that Enlightenment thinking had on the political landscape of the eighteenth and nineteenth centuries. Popular new theories and criticisms of traditional Judeo-Christian society led to major upheavals nationally and internationally. First in America and later in France, two of the most influential political revolutions in history took place.

In America, the high hopes of the Enlightenment which were reason, tolerance, and human rights were finally realized on earth. In France, what first appeared to be a repeat of the successful American Revolution soon degenerated into chaos, civil war, and eventually the dictatorship of Napoleon. Europeans and Americans who lived during this period and whose minds were influenced by the Enlightenment responded in one of two contradictory ways. They either enthusiastically embraced it as a much-needed remedy for the problems of the entire world or saw its ideas as the final program of the Antichrist. Both views were hotly expressed and acted upon during this period of history.

Two French writers of that period provided quotes that neatly summed up this dichotomy. Atheist author Denis Diderot said, "I would sacrifice my life . . . if I could annihilate forever the notion of God . . . The Christian religion is to my mind the most absurd and atrocious . . . the most unintelligible . . . the most mischievous . . . the most dreary . . . the most unsociable in it morality.[320] In opposition to this view, French literary critic Élie Fréron said, "Never was there an age more fertile than ours in seditious writers, who concentrate all their powers on attacking the Godhead. They call themselves apostles of humanity . . . They do not understand that they are upsetting the social order."[321]

Fréron was correct in two ways; there had never been a time in French history that so many intellectuals had openly criticized or doubted the core beliefs of the Judeo-Christianity. He was also correct that in time it would upset the social order. What he was wrong about was the intent of these writers. The writers and philosophers of the Enlightenment not only understood but fervently hoped for the destruction of both Church and State.

Any reasonable person who had eyes and a moral conscience knew that the French political system of absolute monarchy was an unjust, archaic system.

320 Denis Diderot, *Eighteenth Century France: 1700-1789*, ed. Paul Lacroix (New York: Ungar Publishing, 1963).
321 Ibid.

It had developed out of the Dark Ages when force and superstition were the rules. Like many societies before and after, the problem to be solved was not what needed to be changed but what would be the method of that change and what type of social/political system would take its replace. History has shown that when societies choose radical change over evolutionary reform, the results are usually catastrophic. In the history of the world, there have been countless revolutions and civil wars, but very few have achieved positive outcomes.

The avalanche of skeptical opinion and radical theory that swept over France as a result of the Enlightenment eventually produced the French Revolution in A.D. 1789. It was a revolution that began with high hopes and reasonable reforms but soon resulted in a civil war and political tyranny. At the peak of its anti-Christian fervor during the "Reign of Terror," mass murder included loading an entire village of believers on a barge and intentionally sinking it. This gruesome act was mockingly called "Revolutionary Baptism" by the atheists who performed it.[322]

But long before this horror occurred, the prerequisite undermining of religious faith and morality had already taken place. The attack on Judeo-Christianity had started in the 1600s and had continued to intensify before and during the French Revolution. Historians have identified several pre-Enlightenment sources which contributed to the anti-Christian mania that would later engulf France and infect the rest of Europe. These sources included the modern philosophy of Rene Descartes, Thomas Hobbes, Michel de Montaigne, and a group of English and German theologians that promoted a rationalistic version of Christianity called "deism."

Descartes (1596-1650) was a French mathematician, scientist, and philosopher. He, along with Thomas Hobbes, have received credit for being the first "modern philosophers." Descartes was a practicing Catholic, but his scientific belief in a totally material universe, functioning in a totally

---

322 "Dechristianization during the Reign of Terror (1793-1794)," Musee Protestant online, Accessed January 2, 2015, https://museeprotestant.org/en/notice/dechristianisation-during-the-reign-of-terror-1793-1794.

mechanical way, seemed to Christians living in the seventeenth and eighteenth centuries to do away with the need for a God. Descartes' theory made God seem like only a bystander in the universe and not an active participant.

Thomas Hobbes of England was also a well-known mathematician, scientist, and philosopher; but unlike Descartes, he was an intentional enemy of religious faith. His philosophy was materialism: "the doctrine that everything in the universe is reducible to matter and can be explained in terms of physical laws."[323] This was de facto atheism. Hobbes, like most atheists, had a cynical opinion of his fellow human beings. He described the natural condition of life as "solitary, poor, nasty, brutish, and short."[324] He believed that human beings lived in a constant state of fear and competition that resulted in a "war of all against all" and unless they lived under the control of an all-powerful dictatorial government, their selfish nature would prevent them from living in peace. For Hobbes, all rights and definitions of truth and morality were conditional and should be determined by an all-powerful sovereign.[325] In the political system, Hobbes advocated "absolute monarchy"; individual lives were no longer sacred or free.

Hobbes' philosophy was the English version of Niccolò Machiavelli's (see chapter 15). Thomas Hobbes, Machiavelli, and the French philosopher Michel de Montaigne anticipated the later writers of the Enlightenment by promoting the belief in moral relativism. To quote Montaigne on the topic:

> The laws of conscience, which we say are born from nature, are born of custom. Each man, holding in inward veneration the opinions and the behavior approved and accepted around him . . . We all huddled and concentrated in ourselves, and our vision is reduced to the length of our nose . . . a persuasion of certainty is manifest testimony of foolishness . . . The greatest part of what we know is the least part of what we know not.[326]

---

323   *Funk & Wagnalls Standard Dictionary*, s.v. "Materialism" (New York: Harper Paperbacks, 1993).
324   Thomas Hobbes, Chapter 20, in *Leviathan*, Vol. 8 (London: Penguin Classics, 2017), 64.
325   Ibid.
326   Michel Montaigne, *Montaigne Essays: "On Custom"* (Bristol: Penguin Classics, 1970), 117-19.

Montaigne was correct that a healthy level of skepticism should be applied to all beliefs and cultural norms. All belief systems must be analyzed and tested based on their practical effects and historical truth. But what Montaigne, Hobbes, Machiavelli, and the later Enlightenment writers did was direct all their intellectual fire against the fortress of Judeo-Christianity while giving pagan belief systems of the world a free pass.

In England, the revolutionary scientific discoveries of Sir Isaac Newton were a catalyst for the development of an alternative, quasi-religious belief system known as "deism." Deism, also known as "natural religion," is a watered-down, weak version of Christianity. Its believers accept most of the moral teachings of Christianity but dispense with the belief that God is supernaturally involved in the world. Deism teaches that God is the ultimate Source of reason that governs the operations of the natural world but only acts through the laws of nature.

The French political philosopher Montesquieu who visited England in the early 1700s, reported, "There is no religion in England . . . if religion is spoken of, everybody laughs."[327]

Charles Blount, one of the early deists, foreshadowed the devastating attack that would later be made as a result of Charles Darwin's theory of evolution. He wrote in his book *Anima Mundi*, "Some authors are of the opinion that man is nothing but an ape cultivated."[328] In fact, during this period of history, several Enlightenment writers promoted an early evolutionary view of life on earth. James Burnett, another early deist who was also and early anthropologist linked the development of human beings and chimps from common descent. Burnett wrote, "The orangutan . . . is a man who failed to develop."[329] Long before Charles Darwin's theory shocked religious opinion,

327 Steve Allen, "Montesquieu in England: his 'Notes on England,' with Commentary and Translation Commentary," (2017), Oxford University Comparative Law Forum, https://ouclf.law.ox.ac.uk/montesquieu-in-england-his-notes-on-england-with-commentary-and-translation-commentary.

328 Charles Blount, *Anima Mundi: A Short History of Free Thought*, Vol. 2, Ed. J.M. Robertson (New York: Russell & Russell, 1957).

329 James Burnett, *The Origin and Progress of Languages* (New York: Andesite Press, 2017).

his grandfather published a theory of evolution in 1802 entitled "The Temple of Nature."

As the Enlightenment movement advanced in the eighteenth century, skepticism and agnosticism became full-blown atheism. During the radical phase of the French Revolution, atheism became "evangelical atheism." This new type of atheism was not content with a status quo of "believe or not to believe" but was supportive of using force to compel others to become atheists. Without belief in absolute morality, which is anchored in the faith of an omnipotent God, both individuals and government leaders are, as the writer of Ephesians said, "tossed to and fro, and carried about with every wind of doctrine" (Eph. 4:14).

As the Enlightenment movement progressed, these evangelical atheists became the dominant voices among the leadership of the French Revolution. In an age without television, radio, computers, and smartphones, the printed word was essential in holding together and inspiring an international movement against religious faith. Before the French Revolution, it was the writings of Pierre Bayle which supplied this function.

Writing in the late 1600s, Bayle, who was called the "Father of the Enlightenment," initiated an unbroken line of vituperation and insult directed against the Judeo-Christian faith. His writings were republished in nine editions by 1750 and were a favorite in the private libraries of the educated, upper-class French. It was Bayle's writing which established the hostile tone that Denis Diderot and Jean d'Alembert continued into the later and more famous *French Encyclopedia of the Enlightenment*.

Bayle's anti Judeo-Christian writing included all the stock criticisms of religious faith that the later evangelical atheists of the Enlightenment and French Revolution would use. First, he attacked the Judeo-Christian faith by ridiculing the notion of a perfect God Who, out of benevolence, had created the natural world. "If man is the creature of one . . . perfectly good, most holy and omnipotent, how can he have so many bad inclinations? How can he commit so many crimes? Can perfect holiness produce a criminal creature? Can perfect goodness produce an unhappy creature?"[330] Bayle, like all cynics, was a moralist without religious faith. Doubters and atheists criticize God for allowing human beings the freedom to do wrong. What they fail to recognize is the fact that without freedom, human beings would not be human beings but only robots.

They also fail to recognize that without the Judeo-Christian Bible, there would be no perfect moral template for atheists to use as a standard to compare human behavior. The biblical history from Genesis through Revelations is a consistent message of God calling humanity to change from the path of doing wrong to the direction of doing right. Pierre Bayle's moral standard was nature itself. He expressed this when he wrote, "In sound philosophy Nature is nothing else than God Himself."[331] Nature by itself does reveal God's power and omniscience, but it does not show His moral goodness or surpassing love.

The "wild kingdom," with its primary law of "survival of the fittest," does not reveal that we should love our neighbor as ourselves or strive to bring about universal peace and justice in a broken world. Like all atheists and cynics, Bayle paints an extreme picture of human wickedness, ignoring the positive record of good people motivated by a sense of justice and compassion for others.

Influenced by Bayle, the most crucial name in atheistic writing during the Enlightenment period was the German Baron von Holbach. Holbach's book would strongly influence evangelical atheism during the French Revolution. He agreed with Bayle that a godless nature is all that exists. In his writing, we see the inevitable, dark pessimism which colors this type of thinking: "Man is the work of Nature . . . he is submitted to her laws. He cannot deliver himself from them . . . He is good or bad, happy or miserable, wise or foolish . . . without his will counting for anything . . . there is no such thing as real evil . . . The

330 Pierre Bayle, *Historical and Critical Dictionary*, s.v. "Adam" (Indianapolis: Hackett Publishing, 1991), 173.
331 Howard Robinson, *Bayle the Sceptic* (New York: Columbia University Press, 2020), 46.

friend of mankind cannot be a friend of God, who at all times has been a real scourge to the earth.[332]

Like the ancient pagans who said the fates or stars were in control of human life, these atheists of the Enlightenment reduced the dignity of man to a nature-controlled machine, blind to the causes of good and evil. They belittled the concept of "free will" and left humanity without a means of escaping enslavement from a cruel and uncaring nature. Once the belief in an absolute and universal God is dispensed with, a Pandora's Box of foolish and destructive, subjective opinion rules. Like all atheists, Bayle did not have an answer for dealing with life's problems. The acid of Bayle's quill fell not only religious faith but also on reason itself. He wrote, "Human reason is a principle of destruction and not of edification."[333]

Like many of the Enlightenment writers later to come—Jean-Jacques Rousseau, Johnathan Swift, and Denis Diderot—his philosophy was full of contradictions. It was closer to complete skepticism than to deism. Over time, the writers of the Enlightenment separated into two hostile camps: hopeful deists and hateful evangelical atheists. For this reason, the French Revolution started in hopefulness and ended in madness. Hopeful deists like Charles Blount marveled at the perfect order and reasonableness in nature, stating, "Whatever is against Nature is against Reason, and whatever is against Reason is absurd, and should be rejected."[334] But atheists like the French scientist La Mettrie rejected this view, writing,

"All reasoning based upon final causes is frivolous. It [nature] is blind when it gives life as it is innocent when it destroys it. Having, without seeing, made eyes that see, it has made, without thinking, a machine that thinks."[335]

332 Paul-Henry Thiery and Baron D'Holbach. "Nature and her Laws." In *The System of Nature*. Translated by Samuel Wilkinson. https://www.informationphilosopher. com/solutions/philosophers/dholbach/System_of_Nature.html#link2H_4_0008.
333 Charles Blount, "Miracles No Violations of the Laws of Nature," in *A Short History of Free Thought* (New York: Russell & Russell, 1957), 90.
334 Blount, 90.
335 Otis E. Fellows and Norman L. Torrey, *Diderot Studies* (Whitefish: Kissinger Publications, 2010), 307.

A member of the French Academy during this period, Jean Jacques Le Franc, wrote of the Enlightenment thinkers, "There is nothing sure in their principles, no consolation in their ethics, no rule for the present, no goal for the future.[336] But they did have one goal in common: the destruction of Church and State and replacing them with vague notions of human reason and the love of nature. Our modern world today inherited many of their pestiferous illusions, including:

1. The further we get from religious belief, the more progressive society becomes.
2. The end justifies the means.
3. Primitive societies are morally superior to civilizations.
4. There is no such thing as human nature.
5. Morality and truth are relative.
6. God is nature.
7. All evil is a product of ignorance.
8. Secular education is the cure for all societal problems.

One can see from this list the inconsistency and contradictoriness of Enlightenment thought.

Jean-Jacques Rousseau, one of the most famous and influential writers of this period, achieved his early fame based on his writings, which extolled nature as the only guide to living a virtuous and happy life. He created the myth of "the noble savage," writing, "Let us lay it down as an incontrovertible rule that the first impulses of nature are always right."[337] As the most contrary writer of the Enlightenment, he criticized civilization and reason as the sources of human injustice and suffering. He started as an anti-Enlightenment writer

---

336 Jean Jacques Le Franc, *The Religion of Rousseau*, ed. Pierre-Maurice-Masson (NSW: Generic, 2018), 762.
337 Robert Yennah, "Nature, Nurture, and the Mathematics of Culture in the Light of Selected Works of Voltaire and Rousseau," *Logon Journal of the Humanities*, Vol. 19, https://www.ajol.info/index.php/ljh/article/view/121519.

but, as time passed, advocated the creation of an all-powerful totalitarian state that would impose his beliefs on everyone else. He started as a vigorous champion of individual freedom and ended by stating, "Whoever refuses to obey the general will . . . will be forced to be free."[338]

His views on the social effects of Christianity were identical to Machiavelli's and the later German philosopher, Nietzsche. He wrote, "True Christians are made to be slaves."[339] Like Machiavelli, Nietzche, and the ancient pagan Romans, he criticized Christianity because he believed it produced passive individuals who lacked any social concern for the natural world. Like Hobbes and Machiavelli, he thought the only legitimate purpose of religious faith was to bolster state control over a new secular educational system. History has shown this belief to be one of the most enduring legacies of the Enlightenment. In the future, Nazis, Communists, Fascists, and radical Islamists all warped and exploited religious teaching to serve totalitarian purposes.

These Enlightenment illusions (or self-delusions) were combined in the bizarre political experiment known as the "radical phase of the French Revolution." The radical leaders of the revolution started with the atheist belief that the further humankind gets from religious belief, the more progressive society becomes. To accomplish this goal, these new evangelical atheists accepted Machiavelli's dictums that "the end justifies the means," and morality and truth are relative. From this starting point, they proceeded to create a new, radical educational system that ignored human nature and pinned all their hopes on creating a future utopia.

If all of this sounds familiar to modern America, it is because this was the eighteenth century version of political correctness, cancel culture, wokeness, and critical race theory. This was the first widespread attempt in modern times to socially engineer a new type of "Progressive," secular

338 Nicola Ann Hardwick, "Rousseau and the social contract tradition," E-International Relations, March 1, 2011, 34, https://www.e-ir.info/pdf/7356.
339 Jean Jacques Rousseau, *The Social Contract*, Vol. 4, No. 8, translated by H.J. Tozer (London: Swan Sonnenschein, 1895).

person. The Enlightenment writers and radicals of the French Revolution were the first political/social Progressives. They were the first in history to believe in the possibility of unlimited and universal progress based upon the application of science and secular reasoning. They were also the first to advocate the use of state power to transform society by means of mass-popular education.

The writings of the Enlightenment provide abundant evidence of this mindset. After Bayle's *Critical Dictionary*, the *French Encyclopedia* became the next literary weapon used to destroy Judeo-Christian culture and promote this original Progressive agenda.

The atheist writer Jean Claude Helvetius summed up this new Progressive creed: "destroy ignorance, and you will destroy all the seeds of moral evil . . . Education is capable of everything . . . The power of the priest depends upon the superstitions and stupid credulity of the people."[340]

On the continent of Europe, both Catholic and Protestant clergy had lost their faith and were seeking a new ideological footing. One of the earliest and angriest was the French Catholic priest Jean Meslier (1678-1733). He wrote a book-length essay, "My Testament," promoting atheism and a new secular educational system. Meslier stated the secular-humanist creed when he wrote, "To discern the true principles of morality men have no need of theology, or revelation, or of gods; they need but common sense. They have only to look within themselves, to reflect upon their own nature . . . Men are unhappy only because they are ignorant . . . they are wicked only because their reason is not sufficiently developed.[341]

It is ironic and prophetic to see where his common sense and secular reasoning led him. "Let the nation appropriate all property; let every man be put to moderate work; let the product be equally shared. Let men and women mate as they wish and part when they please,[sic] let their children be brought

340 David Wootton, "Helvetius: From Enlightenment to Revolution," *Political Theory* 28, No. 3 (June 2000): 307-336, https://www.jstor.org/stable/192208.
341 Jean Meslier, *My Testament* (Bellingham, WA: University Press of the Pacific, 2004), 42-43.

up together in communal schools. There would then be an end to domestic strife, to class war, to poverty."[342]

Around one hundred years after Meslier's death, Karl Marx published the *Communist Manifesto* in 1848. His manifesto promoted exactly the social program which Meslier had advocated. Even today, it is the same program that Black Lives Matter and other far-Left groups advocate. The Meslier/Marx plans combined the worst of secular humanism with the worst of neo-paganism. It was the fusion of evangelical atheism with pagan values.

After Meslier, three other Catholic clerics—Abbe de Saint-Pierre (1658-1743), Marquis de Condorcet (1743-1794), and Bonnot de Condillac (1718-1780)—all promoted the same secular-humanist belief in the perfectibility of humanity and unlimited human progress based upon science and reason.

Educated at a Jesuit College, Marquis de Condorcet (1743-1794) was a philosopher, mathematician, and political leader during the French Revolution. Like Saint-Pierre, he was most notable for his theory on the perfectibility of human society. He published his thesis under "Sketch for a Historical Picture of the Progress of the Human Mind." Wikipedia.org calls it "perhaps the most influential formulation of the idea of progress ever written." It made the idea of progress a central concern of Enlightenment thought. He argued that expanding knowledge in the natural and social sciences would lead to a just world of individual freedom, equality and material affluence. In Condorcet's own words, the day would come when "the sun would shine on earth of none but freemen, with no masters, save reason."[343]

Bonnot de Condillac developed a theory of psychology encouraging the belief that society could achieve perfection by radically changing the educational system. Condillac's psychological theory presented humanity as a malleable creature without a fixed human nature.[344] This view of

---

342 Ibid.
343 Marquis de Condorcet, "Outlines of an historical view of the progress of the human mind," *Sketch for a Historical Picture of the Progress of the Human Mind*, 1795, https://oll.libertyfund.org/title/condorcet-outlines-of-an-historical-view-of-the-progress-of-the-human-mind.
344 Durant, Vol. 10, 895.

human beings is the basis of all totalitarian educational systems. Call it brainwashing, social engineering, or re-education, its goal is always the same—shaping human thought to fulfill the dictates of some new ideology or philosophy.

The same loss of faith in orthodox Judeo-Christianity occurred in Protestant Switzerland and Germany. Jean D' Alembert, one of the editors of the *French Encyclopedia*, was enthusiastic about the change taking place among the Protestant pastors of Geneva, writing, "Several of them do not believe in the divinity of Jesus Christ . . . many . . . have no religion . . . rejecting all those things which are called mysteries and imagining that the first principle of a true religion is to propose nothing to belief which offends reason."[345]

The German Enlightenment (*Aufklarrung*) weakened people's Judeo-Christian faith in a more subtle and incremental way. Instead of the complete rejection of Christianity, it chose to promote its "death by a thousand cuts." Their method, known as the "higher criticism" of the Bible, focused on pointing out inconsistencies in the gospels, separating the theology of St. Paul from the original teachings of Jesus Christ or attempting to pit the Old Testament against the New Testament. This has been the standard method used by so-called Liberal Christianity in our on modern time.

Two of the greatest minds in German philosophy stand out in opposition to this rash, headlong plunge into secular humanism. Gottfried Wilhelm Leibniz and Emanuel Kant both deplored the spread of atheism in Germany. In 1700, Leibniz wrote of the coming dangers to society of abandoning the Judeo-Christian faith, "I know that excellent and well-meaning men maintain that these . . . opinions have less influence upon practice . . . but if they are ambitious . . . they will be capable, for pleasure or advancement, of setting on fire the four corners of the earth."[346]

---

345 D'Alembert, ibid.
346 Durant, ibid.

Modern theologians Reinhold Niebuhr and Paul Tillich both explained the inadequacies of secular-humanist philosophy to solve life's problems. Niebuhr wrote:

> The most persistent error of modern educators . . . is the assumption that our social difficulties are due to the failure of the social sciences . . . The invariable implication of this assumption is that, with a little more time, a little more . . . social pedagogy and a generally higher development of human intelligence, our social problems will approach solution . . . Modern educators are, like the rationalists of all ages, too enamored of the function of reason in life. The world of history . . . will never be conquered by reason . . . They do not see that the limitations of human imagination, the easy subservience of reason to prejudice and passion, and the consequent persistence of irrational egoism . . . make social conflict an inevitability in human history.[347]

Niebuhr went on to explain the intractable reasons why utopians societies are impossible:

> Pride, jealousy, disappointed love, hurt vanity, greed for greater treasures, lust for power . . . petty animosities . . . these all have been not the occasional but the perennially recurring causes and occasions of international conflict . . . The belief that the growth of human intelligence would automatically eliminate social injustice really dates from the 18th century and the Enlightenment . . . This faith of the Enlightenment is still the creed of the educators of our day and is shared more or less by . . . psychologists and social scientists.[348]

Paul Tillich agreed, writing:

---

347 Niebuhr, 16.
348 Ibid.

"Man's power of self-determination carries with it the possibility of a perverted, destructive self-determination."[349]

Tillich also wrote of the danger of utopianism:

"The amount of utopianism ... as in most countries after the First World War, is even greater than the amount of opportunism ... in the progressive mood of the 1920s, in the humanism and pacifism of the last decades, a disturbing number of illusions were cultivated and destroyed. Religion, perhaps, could have prevented these illusions ... about human nature and the nature of history."[350]

Secular humanists never tire of pointing out the dangers of religious extremism but fail to examine the extremism that is inherent in secular humanism. Its extremism comes from its overly optimistic faith in the goodness and wisdom of human beings. It bases its belief on two extreme leaps of faith. One leap requires us to believe that mankind is wise and good enough to create a utopian society. The second leap is based on its over-confidence that God does not exist and that human intelligence is the highest level of thought in the universe. The radical phase of the French Revolution proved that extremes in ideology will necessarily produce extremes in social/political systems and that extremes in social/political systems will produce extremes in violence and injustice.

In France, human reason was revered, and orthodox religious faith was demonized. By 1792, the French Revolution had been hijacked from its earlier moderate aims of reasonable reforms and constitutional government. The radical phase of the French Revolution led by the Jacobin Party was a struggle to remake French society in a secular-humanist image. All the Jacobins were

---

349 Paul Tillich, 165.
350 Ibid, 190.

enemies of orthodox Judeo-Christianity, but their own beliefs ranged from deism to evangelical atheism.

The men who gave the French Revolution its enduring motto of "Liberty, Equality, Fraternity" were the same people who, within a short time period, betrayed the Enlightenment cause and followed their emotions down the path of mass murder and tyranny. Camille Desmoulins, who some say invented the phrase "Liberty, Equality, Fraternity," lived just long enough to regret his murderous actions. He wrote to his wife from prison just before his execution, "I would never have believed that men could be so ferocious and unjust."[351] Yet here was the man who had become a famous revolutionary writer by urging and celebrating political violence. He was a favorite of the Paris mob that took a leading role in the most radical phase of the revolution. In 1793, when a less radical group of revolutionaries called the Girondists had rejected Desmoulins' blood thirsty policies, he cold-heartedly instigated their deaths.

Like all extremists, the radicals of the French Revolution were motivated by malicious intentions, which they attempted to hide behind a mask of idealism. These leaders were mostly middle to upper-class Frenchmen who had been deeply impressed with and inspired by the social/political writing of the Enlightenment. Desmoulins was a member of the far-Left subgroup of the Jacobins called the "Cordeliers," but even he was not the most radical. His execution was caused by his belated attempt to reduce the amount of unnecessary violence.

His former friend Maximilien Robespierre was the chief executive officer of the Committee of Public Safety. It was Robespierre who instituted the Reign of Terror to maintain the radical direction of the Revolution. Before Desmoulins' execution for treason, he wrote to Robespierre, asking him to "remember the lessons of history . . . love is stronger and more lasting than fear."[352] Desmoulins learned this lesson too late.

---

351 "Camille Desmoulins," Wikipedia Foundation, last modified October 22, 2022, https://en.wikipedia.org/wiki/Camille_Desmoulins.

352 Ibid.

Robespierre and the men who orchestrated the campaign for the dechristianization of France did not learn it at all. It is ironic that these radical haters of Judeo-Christianity took their political party's name from the old Catholic meeting house where they met. The Cordeliers met in a former convent that the Franciscans had used. A contemporary description of their meetings includes, "About three hundred persons of both sexes filled the place; their dress was so unkempt and so filthy that one would have taken them for a gathering of beggars. The Declaration of the Rights of Man was stuck on the wall, crowned by crossed daggers . . . Facing, behind . . . as supporters there appeared busts of . . . Helvetius (atheist writer) with Jean-Jacques Rousseau."[353]

Jean-Jacques Rousseau's myth of the "noble savage" was now in the radical stage of the French Revolution translated into the myth of the "wisdom of the common man." The Parisian mob now began to play a key role in French politics. History shows that the common man is no wiser than the un-common man if his mind is controlled by selfish appetites and superstitious belief.

The fingerprints of the Enlightenment writers are all over the policies advocated and carried out during the most radical phase of the revolution. Jean-Paul Marat (1743-1793) was a leading journalist who, like Camille Desmoulins, wrote furious articles calling for the use of violence against those who did not support his more radical goals for the revolution. The following is a typical excerpt of his literary style and thought: "five or six hundred heads cut off would have assured your repose, freedom and happiness."[354] Before the Revolution was finished, over forty thousand heads would roll, and over three hundred thousand people would be imprisoned, most without just cause.

Durant identified the Enlightenment writers who most influenced Marat as—Rousseau, Helvetius and Montesquieu. With no concern for justice or

---

353 "Cordeliers," Wikipedia Foundation, last modified July 8, 2022, https://en.wikipedia.org/wiki/Cordeliers.
354 Jean-Paul Marat, *Encyclopedia Britannica*, s.v. "Jean-Paul Marat," Accessed October 25, 2022, https://www.britannica.com/biography/Jean-Paul-Marat.

due process of law, Jean-Paul Marat created long lists of the names of people to be executed or imprisoned. Before the September Massacres of 1792, he had advocated that all prisoners should be burned alive. When the mobs finally followed his direction, twelve hundred prisoners were clubbed and hacked to death, including children as young as ten.

Marat missed seeing the full scope of the violence he had advocated. He was murdered by a lady seeking revenge for the people he had put to death. After his death, the popular culture of that day elevated him to cult status, calling him a hero of the revolution. How fitting in this upside-down world of morality, it was none other than the Marquis de Sade, who was a bisexual rapist later judged as insane, who delivered Marat's eulogy. "Like Jesus, Marat loved . . . the people . . . Like Jesus, Marat hated kings, and nobles, priest . . . Like Jesus, he never stopped fighting."[355] These radical, "atheist haters," tried to wrap their motives in the sanctity of Jesus while at the same time attempting to eradicate from the earth His moral and spiritual teachings.

The radicals of the French Revolution perpetrated the first Holocaust of modern history based upon ideology. And like the Nazis and Communists of a more modern period of history, the Committee of Public Safety called for a reign of terror to suppress all opposition to the revolutionary government's policies. Under the leadership of Maximilien Robespierre, the government warned those who were to carry out the policy of terror that they should not be moved by "false and mistaken humanity." This was the same message that Adolf Hitler and Heinrich Himmler gave to the members of the S.S. who ran the death camps during World War II. How ironic that secular-humanists who proclaim the supremacy of mankind, who are forever claiming to believe in humanity's innate goodness that requires no help from any Higher Power, were the ideological seedbed for these atrocious acts.

---

355 "Marat/Sade," Wikipedia Foundation, last modified June 2, 2022, https://en.wikipedia.org/wiki/Marat/Sade.

Ironic, indeed, that a philosophy which claimed to value humanity so much in practice valued human life so little. The original definition of secular humanism was established by the ancient Greeks thousands of years ago when they said, "Man is the measure of man" and "Man is the measure of all things." Based upon this starting point, one can see that there is little room for a concept of God, and without an infinite God, we are only left with an infinite measure of human pride.

Pierre Chaumette (1763-1794) was a principal leader of the radical movement called "dechristianization." The atheist writers Holbach and Diderot had a major influence on his hatred of Christianity. The following statements by Chaumette give us a sample of his reasons for desiring to wipe out Christianity in France: "[Christianity] . . . consist of ridiculous ideas . . . that have been very helpful to despotism . . . Church and counter revolution were one and the same . . . All Christians are enemies of reason . . . we now have open war between the rich and poor . . . Everyone knows that humans are nothing more than what education makes them."[356]

Chaumette was the first revolutionary leader to promote the formal worship of reason in Notre Dame Cathedral on November 10, 1793 (the cult of Reason). On November 23, 1793, the government of Paris gave out an order that all Christian churches in Paris had to be closed.[357] The revolutionary government had passed the "The Law of Suspects" in 1793, stating, "1. All priests and all persons protecting them are liable to death on the spot, 2. The destruction of all crosses, bells, and other external signs of worship, 3. The destruction of statues . . . and iconography from places

356 Charles A. Gliozzo, "The Philosophes and Religion: Intellectual Origins of the Dechristianization Movement in the French Revolution," Cambridge University Press, July 28, 2009, https://www.cambridge.org/core/services/aop-cambridge-core/content/view/A73FA2FF076104420E0404F42E46BA63/S0009640700026603a.pdf/the-philosophes-and-religion-intellectual-origins-of-the-dechristianization-movement-in-the-french-revolution.pdf.
357 Will and Ariel Durant, *The Age of Napoleon*, Vol. 11, *The Story of Civilization* (New York: Simon & Schuster, 2011), 73.

of worship.[358] In the early 1790s, French Revolutionary armies were sent to enforce the atheist policy of dechristianization in the provinces of France. In the region of Vendee, another 170,000 (primarily peasants) were killed by early 1794.

Another devotee of the use of terror and the dechristianization of France was Jean-Baptiste Carrier. He used the method of mass drownings of forty-six hundred people in the Loire River to force people to believe in atheism. Back in Paris during the same period, Robespierre's guillotine had executed seventeen thousand and left another ten thousand to die in prison.[359] History records that up to half a million lives had been lost, crosses and religious images smashed, and bonfires made of Bibles. Christian funerals were ended, and in the churches, pictures of Rousseau and Voltaire took the place of Jesus and the saints.

All the high-sounding early promises of the revolution, "Liberty, Equality, Fraternity" and the "Declaration of the Rights of Man," now dissolved in a class war, paranoia, and the egotistical lust for political power. The radical program of dechristianization was the first modern example of what people today call "cancel culture." It was the attempt to eradicate Christianity from historical memory. The revolutionary government decreed that the Catholic calendar should be replaced with a new calendar, where each month would be identified by a natural phenomenon that was part of the cycle of nature. Durant writes, "The Convention hoped that this Calendar would remind Frenchmen . . . of the earth . . . and Nature would replace God."[360]

The "evangelical atheists" had their day, and France was now a political and national basket case. France was now fighting both a civil and international war. The more the radicals pressed their case, the more bodies piled up, and the more the divisive hatred in French society grew. A French writer of that

358 Alberto M. Piedra, "The Dechristianization of France during the French Revolution," The Institute of World Politics, January 12, 2018, https://www.iwp.edu/articles/2018/01/12/the-dechristianization-of-france-during-during-the-french-revolution.

359 Setareh Janda, "The Darkest Moments of the French Revolutions," Ranker.com, June 17, 2020, https://www.ranker.com/list/french-revolution-bloodiest-moments/setareh-janda.

360 Durant, 48.

period, Nicolas Chamfort, summed up what the revolution had become; "Liberty, Equality, Fraternity" meant, "Be my brother or I'll kill you."[361] Jean-Baptiste Carrier had boasted that the revolutionaries would "make France a graveyard , rather than not regenerate it in our own way."[362] This statement encapsulates the general attitude of all political extremists in world history including: Hitler's Holocaust, Mao's Cultural revolution, Stalin's policy of Collectivization, and Pol Pot's killing fields in Cambodia.

It is interesting to note that Pol Pot as a young man went to school in France before returning to Cambodia to start his communist revolution. Historian Paul Johnson makes a strong case in his book *Intellectuals* that the mass murderer Pol Pot was strongly influenced by the writers of the Enlightenment and especially by Rousseau.[363] Johnson explains that when Pol Pot became the master of Cambodia and instituted a policy that all people living in cities had to return to the countryside to be peasant farmers, he was following the philosophy of Rousseau. The Enlightenment writer Rousseau developed a theory that the cause of human evil was civilization and included education and living in cities. Pol Pot policies included:

1. Closing schools
2. Closing hospitals
3. Closing factories
4. Abolishing banks
5. Outlawing religion
6. Confiscating private property
7. Relocating people from urban areas to collective farms[364]

361 Nicholas Chamfort, "Be My Brother . . . ,"Quotefancy.com, Accessed June 16, 2023, https://quotefancy.com/quote/1128581/Nicolas-Chamfort-Be-my-brother-or-I-will-kill-you.
362 *Encyclopedia Britannica*, s.v. "Jean-Baptiste Carrier: French Revolutionary," Accessed December 12, 2022, https://www.britannica.com/biography/Jean-Baptiste-Carrier.
363 *Intellectuals*, 25.
364 "Khmer Rouge: Cambodia's Years of Brutality," BBC News online, November 16, 2018, https://www.bbc.com/news/world-asia-pacific-10684399.

Pol Pot's policies resulted in 1.5 million deaths. He clearly outdid Chaumette, Carrier, and the other evangelical atheists of the French Revolution.

Proving the truth of Jesus' prophecy that those "that take the sword shall perish with the sword" (Matt. 26:52), the competing factions of hate and extremism turned on each other in France. Robespierre, more of a deist than an atheist, feared a backlash against the revolutionary government if the war on Christianity continued. Based on this fear, he and other members of the Committee of Public Safety ordered the arrests and execution of the evangelical atheists. Within a short period of time on July 27, 1794, a more general backlash known as the "Thermidorian Reaction" put Robespierre and the other Jacobin radicals who had instigated the reign of terror on the path that led to the guillotine.

The famous philosophers Voltaire and Rousseau eventually changed their minds about the adequacy of secular humanism as a replacement for religious faith. The old, religious skeptic Voltaire, close to the end of his life, wrote, "I die adoring God, loving my friends, not hating my enemies, and detesting persecution."[365] These are fine sentiments that any faithful Christian would be proud to write.

The Enlightenment and the French Revolution were the first modern rehearsal for the fall of Judeo-Christian culture. Others would come in the twentieth century with the rise of German Nazism and Russian communism; these great ideologies of hate were based upon ideas germinating during the Enlightenment and the French Revolution.

---

365 Durant, Vol. 9, 876.

CHAPTER SIXTEEN

MODERN PHILOSOPHY AND THE SEEDS OF TOTALITARIAN THOUGHT

BY 1799, THE RADICALS OF the French Revolution had either destroyed each other or had been eliminated by the people they had persecuted. The Revolution ended with the rise of a new military dictator, Napoleon Bonaparte. His strong dictatorship replaced the chaos of mob rule and the weak, alternating government based on factionalism. Due to his military genius and foreign conquest, Napoleon raised France to the height of glory but in the end reduced it to the ashes of defeat.

Napoleon (1769-1821) had grown up as a child of the Enlightenment and came to manhood under the last phase of the French Revolution. He shared its idealistic hopes for reasoned reform, but after many failures, he retreated into coldhearted cynicism. True to his Enlightenment education, he retained a skeptical mind between atheism and agnosticism. His greatest certainty of belief was in his ability to make France—and himself—distinguished. His creed was essentially the creed of pagan humanism, valuing knowledge and human achievements and, most of all, personal glory. In his own words, we find this candid confession:

> I love power . . . Power is my mistress . . . Death is nothing; but to live defeated and inglorious is to die daily . . . Friendship is but a name,[sic] I love nobody . . . I know very well that I have no true friends . . . My power depends upon my glory, and

my glory on my victories . . . Conquest has made me . . . and conquest alone can maintain me . . . I wish for the empire of the world . . . unlimited power was necessary to me . . . There is no immortality but the memory that is left in the minds of men . . . War justifies everything.[366]

From 1803 to 1815, a series of wars were fought that bear his name—the Napoleonic Wars. The Napoleonic Wars cost between 3.25 million to 6.5 million lives, including civilian deaths. For Napoleon "death was nothing" if someone else was doing the dying. His highest value was the satisfaction of his enormous ego. Napoleon's life is an object lesson on the limits and dangers of secular humanism as a philosophy by which to live. Theologian Reinhold Niebuhr described Napoleon's rule and his self-delusional thought this way: "He could bathe Europe in blood for the sake of gratifying his overweening lust for power as long as he could pose as the tool of French patriotism and as the instrument of revolutionary fervor . . . to create a tyranny more sanguinary and terrible than those which it sought ostensibly to destroy."[367]

In Napoleon's rule, we see all the evil methodology and mental traits later magnified in modern, totalitarian states. His disregard for the feelings and lives of ordinary people. "I like only people who are useful to me . . . The strong are good,[sic] the weak are wicked.[368] His use of secret police, mass incarceration, and propaganda to create a "cult of personality" were all employed by the totalitarian governments of the twentieth century. If you read about the life of Adolf Hitler, you find him admiringly referring to Napoleon, even to the point of saying that he always wanted to die on the same day Napoleon did.

The good news is that by 1815, Napoleon's plans for unlimited power and future conquest had been defeated. Not only had the map of Europe been

---

366 R.M. Johnston, *The Corsican, A Diary of Napoleon's Life In His Own Words* (Boston: Houghton Mifflin, 1910), 166.
367 Nieburhr, 17.
368 Napoleon Bonaparte and J.C. Herold, *The Mind of Napoleon* (New York: Columbia University Press), 172.

re-drawn, but a new cultural and intellectual movement had begun to replace the direction of the Enlightenment. This new movement was called the Romantic Movement—its philosophy known as Romanticism. Romanticism was a reaction (or overreaction) against the Enlightenment belief that only logic and science could reveal truth. One Romantic writer even characterized the Enlightenment as "an ugly skull without flesh and blood."

Science tells us that for "every action there is an equal and opposite reaction," and history tells us that political and cultural extremism will bring on an equal and opposite form of political and cultural extremism. The Romantics believed that all that is true, beautiful, and good couldn't be known through science under a microscope or at the far end of a telescope. The highly complex and varied experience of human life requires more than one way or method of understanding ourselves and the world in which we live. The Enlightenment was rationalism carried to an extreme, and the Romantic Movement was emotionalism taken to another extreme.

The "dance of history," at least in terms of culture and philosophy, was now being led by a new incarnation of neo-paganism in Romanticism. This period's novels, poems, music, and philosophy were all characterized by a new ideology that promoted mysticism and total personal freedom guided only by one's emotions. It was a philosophy that had seen its first primary literary expression in the writings of Rousseau. Now, it had become a fashionable belief system and the cultural mantra of a new generation. It was a philosophy that, in its way, was as unsettling as the Enlightenment and, in the long run, would produce its own social dysfunction.

The Romantics were the first "hippies." They were youthful enemies of traditional institutions and conventional morality. They believed nothing should come between a man and his freedom or pleasure. Though many of their ideas were diametrically opposed, the Enlightenment and Romanticism shared some fatally flawed beliefs. Both rejected the conventional morality of Judeo-Christianity, were impatient with slow reform, and supported radical, revolutionary change. Both also expressed a view of human nature, which was naively optimistic; they both believed it was possible to create a utopia on earth. It is worth noting that most of the Enlightenment and Romantic conceptions of utopia included a communist vision of the future.

The English Romantic poet Percy Bysshe Shelley started on the road of radicalism early. While at Oxford, he published *The Necessity of Atheism* in 1810. After being expelled from Oxford, he wrote and published *Queen Mab*, a poem that expressed his utopian views. *Queen Mab* expressed beliefs that fit well with today's modern, Progressive agenda of anti-capitalism, pro-atheism, free love, and even vegetarianism. Shelley believed that meat-eating was the cause of most wars. He wrote in the support of vegetarianism, "By all that is sacred in our hope for the human race, I conjure those who love happiness and truth to give fair trial to the vegetable system."[369]

Historian Paul Johnson writes of Shelley, "He loved humanity in general but was often cruel to human beings . . . He put ideas before people and his life is a testament to how heartless ideas can be." Like his friend Lord Byron, he believed in free love and "like Byron, always considered that he had a perpetual dispensation from normal rules of sexual behavior."[370]

Like his friend Shelley, Byron lost his religious faith early and did not waste any time attacking Judeo-Christianity. Like Bayle's irreverent critique of the story of the Garden of Eden, Byron wrote and published *Cain, A Mystery* in 1821 from a viewpoint sympathetic to Cain, the rebellious son who murders his brother and blames God for the act.[371]

Romanticism was, in essence, egocentrism on a grand scale. Judeo-Christianity was rejected and under attack because it placed moral limits on human behavior. The Romantics wanted to replace Judeo-Christianity with the worship of nature. The German poet Friedrich Schiller added one

---

369 Percy Shelley, *Vindication of a Natural Diet. Prose Works of the Romantic Period* (London: Penguin, 1956), 138.
370 Johnson, 31, 35-36.
371 Durant, Vol. 9, 617.

exception to this rule—poets, artists, and philosophers were superior beings capable of providing moral guidance. In his poem *The Gods of Greece*, Schiller argued that the world was better off before Christianity. In a letter to his fellow German poet Goethe, he wrote, "A healthy and beautiful nature-as yourself . . . requires no moral code, no law."[372]

Goethe expressed his life creed this way: "As a poet and artist I am a polytheist . . . while in my role as a scientist I incline to pantheism . . . For my own part I cling more or less to the teachings of Lucretius [an ancient Roman atheist] and confine myself and all my hopes to this life."[373]

Like many Enlightenment thinkers, the Romantics started as youthful radicals and ended their lives as pessimistic doubters—one of these being the famous Johann Wolfgang von Goethe. He expressed his final disillusionment by writing, "Viewed from the heights of reason, all life looks like some malignant disease . . . Men exist only to trouble and kill one another; so was it, so is it, so will it ever be."[374]

The young Goethe published one of his most famous novels in 1774, *The Sorrows of Young Werther*. The success of this novel made Goethe an international literary celebrity—even Napoleon read it. The plot of *The Sorrows of Young Werther* consists of a love triangle that ends in the protagonist's suicide. It was so popular among European youth that many started dressing like the main character.

On a darker note, the novel seems to have influenced some depressed young people to take their own lives. In Goethe's later novel *Faust*, his main character said, "Feeling is all." This summed up the Romantic Movement. Like the hippie motto of the 1960s, "If it feels good, do it," it provided an excuse for living an immoral life. Goethe revealed that he shared this same attitude

372 Friedrich Schiller, *Correspondence Between Schiller and Goethe from 1794 to 1805*, (New York: Wiley and Putnam, 1845), https://archive.org/details/correspondencebe01schi/page/n9/mode/2up.

373 Radoslav Andrea Tsanoff, "Goethe and philosophy," *Rice Institute Pamphlet—Rice University Studies* 19, No. 2 (1932), https://hdl.handle.net/1911/8553.

374 Egon Friedell, *Cultural History of the Modern Age* (New York: Alfred A. Knopf, 1954), 272.

when he wrote to a friend, "Your ideals shall not prevent me . . . from being genuine, and good and bad, like Nature."[375]

Romanticism was a philosophy that ignored short term and long-term consequences. The hopes and enthusiasms the Romantic writers attempted to instill in the young did not produce lasting happiness. Toward the end of Goethe's life, he predicted, "The incredible arrogance in which the young are growing up will show its results in a few years in the greatest follies."[376]

The Romantics saw the objectively true lessons of history, the slow accumulation of wisdom over thousands of years to be impediments to freedom and progress. In Romanticism, truth was subjective and had to come instantly as a blinding flash of intuition.

Besides the personally destructive practice of reducing all thought and action to an emotional impulse, the German philosophers and historians of this period promoted a dangerous new direction in political thought. Combining these thoughts would lead to the most remarkable social disasters of the twentieth century. If we wanted one quote from this period that explains the tragedies of the twentieth century, it would be from German novelist Wilhelm Heinse (1746-1803) who wrote, "What are millions of men- who all their lives have not had a single hour . . . compared with . . . one man of genius."[377] The hero in the novel expresses Heinse's philosophy when he says, "Crime is not crime, if it is brave; the only real crime is weakness; the truest virtues are strength and courage of body and will. Life is the manifestation of elemental instincts, and we miss the mark if we brand these as immoral."[378]

A little more than a hundred years later, Friedrich Nietzsche (1844-1900), another German philosopher, developed Heinse's quote into the full-fledged pagan philosophy of nihilism. Nihilism is defined as "a doctrine that denies

375 Emil Ludwig, "Das Gottliche," in *Goethe: The History of a Man, 1749-1832* (New York: G.P. Putnam's Sons, 1928), 3.

376 Thomas Mann, *Three Essays*, translated by H.T. Lowe-Porter (New York: Alfred A. Knopf, 1929), 64.

377 Wilhelm Heinse, *Ardinghello*, in *History of German Literature*, ed. Kuno Francke (New York: Henry Holt, 1910).

378 Ibid.

any basis for knowledge or truth . . . Total denial of all traditional principles, values . . . In politics . . . advocating the destruction of all political, economic, and social institutions."[379]

Like the earlier writers and philosophers of the Romantic period, Nietzsche greatly admired ancient pagan Greek culture. Like the ancient pagans, he ridiculed and disparaged Judeo-Christian culture as a philosophy of weaklings and losers. Nietzsche called Christian ethics "slave morality."[380] He viewed Christianity as a philosophy intended to emasculate and prevent the truly heroic and creative individuals from achieving their lofty plans and goals. His modern philosophy envisioned a "Superman" who transcended the moral responsibilities of the average person.

Nietzsche's disdain for the normal human being was expressed in his description of them as "bungled and botched."[381] The new superior person, according to Nietzsche, would live their lives *Beyond Good and Evil*, which was a title of one of his books. Although Nietzsche's philosophy was not based upon race, Hitler used it to support Nazism. Many of his ideas, like nihilism and pagan values, were interchangeable building blocks in Nazi thought. He died before the Nazi movement took power in Germany. Still, one of his statements can be read as a chilling prophecy of the future Holocaust. "The object is to attain that enormous energy of greatness which can model the man of the future by means of discipline and also by means of the annihilation of millions of the bungled and botched, and . . . avoid going to ruin at the sight of the suffering created thereby, the like of which has never been seen before."[382]

Nazism celebrated Germany's pagan past, and many Nazi leaders were devotees of occult practices and astrology. The Nazis especially extolled the

---

379 "Nihilism," Wikipedia Foundation, Accessed October 24, 2022, https://www.google. com/search?q=how+to+cite+wikipedia+in+chicago&rlz=1C1VDKB_enUS1011US1011& oq=how+to+cite+wikipe&aqs=chrome.1.0i512j0i20i263i512j69i57j0i512j0i20i263i512j0i51 2l5.4907j0j9&sourceid=chrome&ie=UTF-8.
380 Bertrand Russell, *The History of Western Philosophy* (New York: Simon & Schuster, 1972), 765.
381 Ibid, 762.
382 Ibid.

pagan values of heroic conquest and racial dominance. The Nazis appropriated Nietzsche's language of the "Superman." They proclaimed, as Wilhelm Heinse and Nietzsche had, that Judeo-Christian standards of morality could not be used to judge their behavior. Nietzsche explained the meaning of his famous proclamation, "God is dead" this way: "The belief in the Christian God has become unbelievable . . . everything that was built upon this faith . . . the whole of our European morality, is destined for collapse . . . The strongest and most evil spirits have hitherto advanced mankind the most: they have always rekindled the sleeping passions—all orderly arranged society lulls the passions to sleep."[383]

Nietzsche didn't believe in the possibility of universal morality that all peoples, races, and cultures could unite around. Nietzsche left to all people, including Hitler and Stalin, the right to develop their moral code. Hitler's version resulted in the Holocaust and Stalin's in the Gulag Archipelago.

———————◆———————

Nietzsche was the most famous philosopher to come out of the Romantic Movement, but earlier on, others had also contributed ideas embraced by future Totalitarian states. The German philosopher Johann Gottfried von Herder (1744-1803) was the earliest of these thinkers. The *Stanford Encyclopedia of Philosophy* describes Herder as "a philosopher of the first importance . . . relativism . . . is one of Herder's main contributions to moral philosophy."[384] Herder specialized in the study of languages and their relationship to thought. His studies concluded that all cultures were unique and their systems of morality were beyond outside criticism. Herder's moral relativism and his view of history as a progressive process would significantly influence a later and more famous German philosopher Georg Wilhelm Hegel (1770-1831).

---

383 Friedrich Nietzsche, *The Joyful Wisdom*, ed. Oscar Levy, translated by Paul Cohn, Thomas Common, and Maude Petre (London: Project Gutenberg, 2016), https://www.gutenberg.org/ebooks/52124.
384 *Stanford Encyclopedia of Philosophy*, s.v. "Johann Gottfried von Herder," October 23, 2001, https://plato.stanford.edu/entries/herder.

Other German Romantic philosophers who pushed the thesis of moral relativism to the breaking point included Johann Fichte (1762-1814) and Ludwig Tieck (1773-1853). In his "Essay toward a Critique of All Revelation," Fichte promoted the thesis that our ego is the only thing we can know for sure and even proclaimed, "The Universe is myself."[385] In 1807, Fichte gave a series of speeches entitled *Addresses to the German Nation*. These speeches promoted a thesis that anticipated Hitler's 150 years later.

Modern philosopher Bertrand Russell said these speeches claimed that the German person was "superior to all others."[386] Fichte called for a new system of education which would "mould[sic] the Germans into a corporate body."[387] He said the ultimate purpose of this new education system would be to "completely destroy the freedom of will."[388] Ludwig Tieck advanced this subjectivism and moral relativism to the outer limits of self-worship, stating, "All things exist only because I think them; virtue exists only because I think it."[389] In Fichte's and Tieck's philosophy, Herder's belief that each culture had its unique morality was reduced to every individual having his own unique morality.

We begin to see full scope and danger of these theories when we get to Hegel's philosophy. Hegel accepted the pagan view that the world is eternal and combined it with the Enlightenment belief in infinite historical progress guided by the "spirit of reason," which Hegel called the "absolute." Human rebellion and sin were necessary steps on the road to idealized perfection. For Hegel and later Karl Marx, the philosophy of history is all-important and individual lives pale in comparison to the macro-workings of a purposeful history. They rejected the Judeo-Christian view of history as a cosmic drama between good and evil that plays out in the hearts and minds of free individuals.

Hegel and Marx disagreed on the motive force that drove historical development, but they agreed on the minimized role of human freedom in that

---

385 Russell, 70.
386 Ibid, 71.
387 Ibid.
388 Ibid.
389 Durant, Vol. 10, 631.

process. For Hegel, the cause of historical change was the Zeitgeist, defined as the "spirit of reason" acting in time. For the atheist Karl Marx, the force behind history was Historical Materialism, defined as macro-economic and social laws that would determine the future of the world.[390] Human beings were mere pawns in the historical process. If human beings did not understand the process, they were merely swept along like floating debris in the river of historical change.

Hegel tried and failed to reconcile his philosophy with Christianity, but Karl Marx bluntly rejected the Judeo-Christian message, writing, "We [communists] have no compassion and we ask no compassion from you. When our turn comes, we shall not make excuses for the terror."[391] Both men believed in a progressive view of history, resulting in a utopia at the end of the process. Their problem was how one gets to the utopian finish line.

To get there, Hegel and Marx accepted the need for violence directed by an all-powerful government. Marx's view of the end of history was even more utopian. But Marx's theory required continuing class conflict and the penultimate stage called the "Dictatorship of the Proletariat" before the state (government) was no longer necessary.[392]

To Hegel, no guesswork is needed to understand his meaning of "the perfect embodiment of Spirit." He advocated the unification of Germany's independent states by force and promoted the Great Man theory of historical change: "The common multitude of the German people . . . must be gathered into one mass by the force of a conqueror."[393] The "Great Man" who he believed could fulfill this task was Napoleon, whom he described as "the emperor-that world soul . . . It is truly a wonderful sensation to see such an individual, concentrated here at a single point, astride a single horse, yet reaching across the world and ruling it."[394]

---

390 Russell, 733-34.
391 Johnson, 71.
392 Robert J. Fischer, "Dictatorship of the Proletariat," ScienceDirect, 2019, https://www.sciencedirect.com/topics/social-sciences/dictatorship-of-the-proletariat.
393 Durant, Vol. 11, 647.
394 Ibid, 607.

The theory of the Great Man of history who serves as the agent of progressive change would soon be subverted into the "cult of personality." Those who stopped worshiping God soon began to worship men. Motivations of self-worship and the hatred of others were now disguised as "progressive reform" and "social justice." They became reasons not just worth dying for but worth killing for.

In his book *The Powers of Evil*, Richard Cavendish links the German philosophy of the eighteenth and nineteenth centuries to the pagan philosophy of the ancient Greeks, "Hegel revived Heraclitan ideas of fate and fame . . . A Caesar, an Alexander, pursuing their own purposes, are in touch with the intentions of destiny and forward the plan of history. This is what makes them great men, and, as Hegel has frequently been quoted as saying, is what justifies their crime."[395]

Throughout nineteenth century philosophy, the pendulum of thought continued to swing between the extremes of neo-paganism and secular humanism. Some philosophers, like Baruch Spinoza, had the best of intentions and lived an impeccable life. But his philosophy undercut the belief in free will and a theistic faith in a personal God. Spinoza lived during the eighteenth century, but his philosophy had its most significant influence on the German philosophes of the nineteenth century. Nietzsche was very critical of Spinoza's philosophy in general but shared with him the belief that all human motives are self-seeking and that "joy consists in this, that one's power is increased."[396]

Arthur Schopenhauer (1788-1860), another Romantic Era, German philosopher who lived in the period just before Nietzsche and influenced Nietzsche's philosophy, combined German idealism with Hindu and Buddhist beliefs. In his most famous work, *The World as Will and Idea*, he describes the world as the product of "blind and insatiable will."[397] This "will" had no purpose other than the continuation of existence. For Schopenhauer, life was

---

395 Richard Cavendish, *The Powers of Evil* (New York: Dorset Press, 1993), 77.
396 Durant, Vol. 8, 345.
397 Russell, 755-56.

meaningless, and humanity's place in it was an exercise in pointless suffering. Nietzsche rejected Schopenhauer's philosophical pessimism but built his philosophy on the concept of an eternal, pagan "will" that animates the world.

Schopenhauer, influenced by the teaching of Buddha, recommended a passive withdrawal from the concerns of life, a kind of slow suicide.[398] Nietzsche accepted Schopenhauer's belief in a powerful cosmic "will" but said that this "will" had a purpose beyond mere existence. Nietzsche claimed that the purpose behind this eternal, cosmic will was the "Will to Power."[399]

Two other nineteenth century belief systems that significantly undermined traditional Judeo-Christian culture were Charles Darwin's theory of evolution and Sigmund Freud's theory of psychology. Both presented a view of humans as only animals and rejected any God-directed purpose in life.

Darwin viewed humanity as the byproduct of a long-term process called "natural selection." His theory was a biological version of Hegel's view of history. Animals evolved over a long period of time to a rational stage called human beings. Darwin's zoological research and tragic life experience of the early death of his daughter had brought him reluctantly to a position of agnosticism:

> For myself, I do not believe that there ever has been any revelation. As for a future life, every man must judge for himself between conflicting vague probabilities . . . In my most extreme fluctuations I have never been an atheist . . . I may say that the impossibility of conceiving that this grand and wondrous universe, with our conscious selves, arose through chance seems to me the chief argument for the existence of God.[400]

Unlike Darwin, Sigmund Freud (1856-1939) was a convinced atheist who intentionally used his psychological theory to discredit religious faith. In

---

398 Russell, 756-57.
399 Ibid, 760-64.
400 Nick Spencer, "Darwin's Complex Loss of Faith," The Guardian online, September 17, 2009, https://www.theguardian.com/commentisfree/belief/2009/sep/17/darwin-evolution-religion.

his own words, "I regard myself as one of the most dangerous enemies of religion."[401] Religious belief, according to Freud, was not only an illusion but also a form of collective mental illness. He said, "Religion is a universal obsessional neurosis."[402] It is well established that his theories were influenced by Darwin, Nietzsche, and Schopenhauer. He accepted Darwin's view that man was an evolved animal but cast serious doubts about him being both a rational animal and having free will. In philosopher Reuben Abel's book *Man Is the Measure,* he writes of Freud's theory, "Free will is an illusion; the psychical life is completely determined. Sexuality is the chief source of psychic energy."[403]

Theologian Paul Tillich wrote that both Darwin and Freud "on the ground of an evolutionary naturalism . . . have denied any objective validity to the voice of conscience."[404] Freud's theory of "psychosexual development" presents a picture of a human-animal whose thoughts and actions are primarily controlled by unknown subconscious thoughts. In an article by Professor C. Wayne Mayhall entitled "Sigmund Freud and the Problem of Guilt," he said of Freud's views, "Sigmund Freud despised religion, theism, and the Bible, and although his goal was to eradicate the problem of guilt, he is ultimately responsible for confusing it. His primary motivation for psychoanalysis was to transform guilt into neurosis and sin into sickness."[405]

In Freud's book *Totem and Taboo,* he described himself as "an author who is . . . completely estranged from the religion of his fathers—as well as from every other religion."[406] In his book *Obsessive Actions and Religious Practices,*

---

401 *Internet Encyclopedia of Philosophy,* s.v. "Sigmund Freud," Accessed October 30, 2022, https://iep.utm.edu/freud.
402 Ibid.
403 Reuben Abel, *Man is the Measure (Cordial Invitation to the Central Problems of Philosophy* (New York: The Free Press, 1976), 161.
404 Tillich, 147.
405 C. Wayne Mayhall, "Sigmund Freud and the Problem of Guilt," Accessed July 1, 2023, www.academia.edu/11346859/On_Sigmund_Freud_and_Guilt.
406 Sigmund Freud, *Totem and Taboo* (New York: Dodd, Mead & Company, 1918), Preface.

Freud wrote, "In the future science will go beyond religion and reason will replace faith in God."[407] It is unfortunate that a man as intelligent and well-read as Freud did not learn the lessons taught by the failures of the anti-religious Enlightenment and the radical stage of the French Revolution.

By undermining religious faith in general, instead of criticizing false beliefs, Freud undermined confidence in a universal morality that had received its utmost support from Judeo-Christianity. He focused his attention on ridding the world of "guilt complexes," instead of crediting the rational purpose of guilt as an early warning system against anti-social behaviors. It is also ironic that Freud, the founder of modern psychology, failed to defend the importance of a robust and moral conscience. Psychological studies have consistently shown that all psychopaths lack a conscience or a sense of guilt for their crimes. The theories of Darwin and Freud unintentionally contributed to the anarchy and lawlessness which would over-shadow the twentieth century.

The most important lesson that we can learn from the Romantic Movement is that human reason or emotions alone are not enough to ensure progress and human well-being. Respect for high moral standards, belief in a religion that teaches life is sacred, and that human beings are free moral agents are of critical importance to the well-being of the world. Wherever we see chaos and violence in the world, it is the absence of this Judeo-Christian message which proceeds it.

The two most systematically evil doctrines of the twentieth century, Nazism and communism, wholeheartedly embraced Darwin's theory of evolution. The communists used Herbert Spencer's version of Social Darwinism as a justification for the annihilation of an entire economic class

---

407 Sigmund Freud, *Obsessive Actions and Religious Practices: The Freud Reader* (New York: W.W. Norton Company, 1995).

of people. Hitler and the Nazis used Social Darwinism to justify eradicating a whole race of people. If humans are only animals struggling to survive in a long, violent, competitive chain of evolution, what would be the basis for any moral outrage over seeking to dominate others in that struggle?

Long before World War I and World War II, the cataclysmic events of the twentieth century, the ideological seeds of world conflict had already been planted. The modern philosophies of the eighteenth and nineteenth centuries fused with the theories of Freud and Darwin were the ideological mix that caused the greatest wars in human history.

CHAPTER SEVENTEEN

IDEOLOGIES OF HATE AND FALSE MESSIAHS

IN THE TWENTIETH CENTURY, WE saw the full horror of what secular humanism and neo-paganism led to. The twentieth century is responsible for more genocide and political murder than any other in history. The greatest civilizational and military struggle in history occurred between 1939 and 1945. Nazi Germany and Communist Russia were both responsible for the cause of World War II. This was the first bipolar war in history, the first war for global control by two competing extremist ideologies: Nazism and Communism.

A microcosm of this conflict had already played out in Germany before Hitler took complete power. Hitler had to destroy the Communist Party in Germany before his neo-pagan Nazi party could rule supreme. Hitler's party was never a majority, but like the Bolsheviks of Russia led by Lenin, he orchestrated a violent coup and overthrew a democracy.

The history of the Far East records the same bipolar struggle between the Communists of China and Japan's pagan "Empire of the Rising Sun." This war started earlier than Europe's but in time was inextricably linked to the struggle in the West. Before Nazi Germany and Soviet Russia were locked into a death match, they had been allies. In 1938, they signed a "non-aggression pact," which pledged them not to attack each other. What Nazis and Communists agreed on was their total disdain for the values of Western civilization, which were founded on the beliefs of Judeo-Christianity. The other two things they had in common were ferocious hate that permeated their ideologies and an insatiable desire for world conquest.

Studying the lives of Karl Marx, Adolf Hitler, Vladimir Lenin, and Joseph Stalin, we see these negative traits maximized to their fullest extent. Historian Paul Johnson described the father of modern communism, theorist Karl Marx, in this way: "He was filled with a burning desire to create a better world. Yet he ridiculed morality . . . he argued it was unscientific and could be an obstacle to the revolution . . . Like many self-centered individuals, he tended to think that moral laws did not apply to himself . . . The feelings and views of others were never of much interest or concern to him . . . He had no time or interest in democracy."[408]

A police report about Karl Marx said, "The dominating trait of his character is an unlimited ambition and love of power."[409] Fellow radical Mikhail Bukunin wrote, "Marx does not believe in God but he believes much in himself and makes everyone serve himself. His heart is not full of love but of bitterness and he has very little sympathy for the human race."[410]

Marx's great hatred of others and his disposition in favor of using violence is well-established in his writing. "There is only one way in which the murderous death agonies of the old society and the bloody birth throes of the new society can be shortened, simplified and concentrated, and that way is revolutionary terror . . . It is our interest and our task to make revolution permanent until . . . the proletariat has conquered state power . . . not only in one country but in all the leading countries of the world."[411] Furthermore, "Society is undergoing a . . . revolution, which must be submitted to, and which takes no more notice of human existences it breaks down than an earthquake regards the houses it subverts . . . The

---

408 Johnson, 72.
409 Ibid.
410 Ibid.
411 Karl Marx, "The Victory of the Counter-Revolution in Vienna," *Marx & Engels Collected Works*, Vol. 7. (London: Lawrence & Wishart, 2010), 145.

classes and the races, too weak to master the new conditions of life, must give way."[412]

Marx had no place in his theory for peaceful, progressive change by democratic means. He describes the true character of revolutionary change this way: "A revolution is certainly the most authoritarian thing there is; it is the act whereby one part of the population imposes its will upon the other part by means of rifles, bayonets, and cannon-authoritarian means . . . it must maintain this rule by means of the terror which its arms inspire."[413]

Showing his support for Darwin's theory of evolution and using it to support his brutal theory of historical change, he wrote: "The whole Darwinian theory of the struggle for existence is simply the transference from society to animate nature . . . Hobbes theory of the war of every man against every man . . . the same theories are next transferred back again from organic nature to history . . . as eternal laws of human society."[414]

In his book *Intellectuals*, historian Paul Johnson describes Marx's literary style. "Many passages give the impression that they have actually been written in a state of fury. In due course Lenin, Stalin and Mao Zedong practiced, on an enormous scale, the violence which Marx felt in his heart and which his works exude."[415] The modern English philosopher Bertrand Russell agreed by writing, "There is so much hate in Marx and in Communism that Communists can hardly be expected, when victorious to establish a regime affording no outlet for malevolence."[416] Henry Hazlitt provided this commonsense statement of the true meaning of Marx's theory: "The whole gospel of Karl Marx can be summed up in a single

412 David James, "Hegel and Marx on the Necessity of the Reign of Terror: Hegel Bulletin," *Hegel Bulletin* 41, No. 2 (October 26, 2017), https://www.cambridge.org/core/journals/hegel-bulletin/article/abs/hegel-and-marx-on-the-necessity-of-the-reign-of-terror/B1A4F597A9389D7846A37EB243694088.
413 Ibid.
414 Angus Taylor, "The Significance of Darwinian Theory for Marx and Engels," *Philosophy of the Social Sciences* 19, No. 4 (1989): https://doi.org/10.1177/004839318901900401.
415 Johnson, 54-55.
416 Russell, 84.

sentence: Hate the man who is better off than you are. Never under any circumstances admit that his success may be due to his own efforts, to the productive contribution he has made to the whole community. Always attribute his success to the exploitation, the cheating, the more or less open robbery of others."[417]

Other beliefs which are consistently expressed in his writings are the repudiation of representative democracy, economic freedom, and a belief in God. He and his confederate Friedrich Engels stated in *The Communist Manifesto*, "The first step in the revolution by the working class, is to raise the proletariat to the position of ruling class, to win the battle for democracy."[418]

Their theory does not start with democracy or with individual freedom. It begins with a violent revolution to overthrow existing governments—some of which were already democracies, such as the U.S. and Great Britain. Their concern was not with democracy in general but with the democracy of one class in society. Even after the success of a communist revolution, that class (the proletariat) was still under the dictatorial control of a small group, which Marx called the "dictatorship of the proletariat." The masses needed to continue waiting for freedom until Marx or the other communist elite decided they were ready for it. Marx called this unknown period "the period of the revolutionary transformation."[419]

If Marx hated anything more than liberalism or capitalism, it was religious faith or a belief in God. In this way, he was like Sigmund Freud. Both were Jews, but both were the most incredible modern opponents to traditional Judaism. Freud identified religious belief as a form of mental illness, and in Marx's own words, "'Religion is the sigh of the oppressed creature, the heart

---

417   Mark J. Perry, "Quotation of the Day on Marxism . . . ," American Enterprise Institute, Accessed October 27, 2022, https://www.aei.org/carpe-diem/quotation-of-the-day-on-marxism.

418   Karl Marx and Friedrich Engels, *The Communist Manifesto* (London: Workers Educational Association, 1848).

419   Karl Marx, "A Contribution to the Critique of Hegel's Philosophy of Right," in *Works of Karl Marx*, https://www.marxists.org/archive/marx/works/1843/critique-hpr/intro.htm, 1843-44.

of a heartless world, and the soul of soulless conditions. It is the opium of the people.'"[420]

Sounding like something which Hitler would later write, Marx published an essay entitled "On The Jewish Question" in 1844, writing, "Money is the zealous one God of Israel, beside which no other God may stand . . . What is the foundation of the Jew in our world? Practical necessity, private advantage. What is the object of the Jew's worship in this world? Money."[421]

Marx supplied the theory for modern communism, but Vladimir Lenin was the torch-bearer who, in 1917, made it a reality in Russia. Lenin was true to all of Marx's main objectives. His Bolshevik government ended parliamentary democracy, established a one-party state, and began the widespread use of terror to control the opposition. His government began the re-education of the masses to create a new atheistic "Socialist Man."

Lenin showed his cold, brutal nature before the Russian Revolution. During a great famine in Russia in 1891-1892, he expressed that "famines are inevitable; they can be abolished only by the abolition of this order of society . . . famine today performs a progressive function . . . this talk of feeding the starving . . . is nothing but an expression of the usual sugary sentimentality so characteristic of our intelligentsia.[422] This famine cost between 375,000 to five hundred thousand lives.

After overthrowing the elected government of Russia, his communist government's policies caused another famine in Ukraine during 1921-1923. Lenin's cruel pride prevented him from asking foreign governments for help. This time, the death toll reached five million people.

He showed the same callous attitude toward the suffering of the Russian people when they were losing World War I to the Germans. His only focus

---

420 "Marxism and Religion," In Defense of Marxism, Accessed July 1, 2023, https://www.marxist.com/theory-marxism-and-religion.htm.
421 United States Congress House on Committee on Un-American Activities, *Facts on Communism: the Soviet Union, from Lenin to Khrushchev*, Vol. 1 (Washington, D.C.: U.S. G.P.O., 1961), 17.
422 Ibid.

was on how this disaster would help the communists come to power. His response to the millions of Russians who died fighting was, "Only after we have overthrown . . . the bourgeoisie of the whole world, and not only of one country, will wars become impossible."[423]

During the earlier Russo-Japanese war of 1904-1905, his Communist Party promoted defeatism. He expressed his dream of the future: "Life is marching, through the defeat of Russia, to a revolution in Russia, and through that revolution . . . to civil war in Europe."[424] For Lenin, the ten million who would die in the First World War was only a prelude to the global violence he wanted to see.

In 1917, Lenin wrote a book entitled *The State and Revolution.* In this book, he expressed that all governments are organized to carry out violence against their oppressed subjects. For him, the communist state would be no different. The "dictatorship of the proletariat would rule it." He justified this dictatorship by writing, "The proletariat needs state power, the centralized organization of force, the organization of violence, for the purpose of crushing the resistance of the exploiters."[425]

As Lenin's government took over, they ended freedom of the press and began to have their political opponents arrested. Lenin believed that only a dictatorship would be successful:

> We Bolsheviks are for stern rule . . . history has shown that in the history of revolutionary movements, the dictatorship of individual persons was very often the vehicle, the channel of the dictatorship of the revolutionary classes . . . When people talk to us about morality we say: For Communist, morality consists entirely of . . . united discipline and . . . mass struggle . . . We do not believe in eternal morality . . . We say that our morality is entirely subordinated to the interests of the class struggle."[426]

---

423 Ibid, 33.
424 Ibid, Vol. 2, 17, https://archive.org/details/factsoncommunism195902unit.
425 Ibid, 45.
426 Ibid, 78-79.

Martin Latsis, who served as the head of Communist Russia's first secret police (the Cheka), openly expressed the amoral method of how it would function:

> [The Cheka] . . . is not an investigating commission and not a court . . . It is a fighting organ . . . it does not forgive, it rather reduces to ashes everyone who stands . . . on the other side of the barricade . . . Do not ask for incriminating evidence to prove that the prisoner opposed the Soviets . . . Your first question is to ask him what class he belongs to, what are his origin, education and profession . . . This is the meaning and essence of the red terror.[427]

In 1922, Lenin instructed the People's Commissar of Justice that "the court must not eliminate terror . . . it must explain and legalize it in principle."[428] His justification for this policy had already been explained in his book, *The Immediate Tasks of the Soviet Government*. "The misfortune of previous revolutions has been that the revolutionary enthusiasm of the masse . . . which . . . gave them the strength ruthlessly to suppress the elements of disintegration, did not last long."[429]

Lenin was at the top of the power "food chain," but all the other communists agreed with using terror to impose their one-party rule. The commander of the Red Army, Leon Trotsky, stated, "As for us, we were never concerned with the . . . Vegetarian-Quaker prattle about the 'sacredness of human life' . . . To make the individual sacred we must destroy the social order . . . and this problem can only be solved by blood and iron."[430]

Alexander Potresov, one of Lenin's early associates, wrote, "Lenin knew only two categories of people . . . his own and the strangers . . . relationships

---

427 Ibid, 107.
428 Ibid, 106.
429 Ibid, 104.
430 Tyler Bonin, "Red October Happened 100 Years Ago, but Soviet Ideology Lives On," *The Federalist*, October 26, 2017, https://thefederalist.com/2017/10/26/red-october-happened-100-years-ago-soviet-ideology-lives.

between these opposite-poles-between the comrade friend and the heretical enemy-did not exist."[431]

Objective truth—as most people use the word—meant nothing to Lenin. Victory over his enemies was all that mattered. He explained the purpose of communist propaganda, saying, "The wording (of our press campaign) is calculated to provoke in the reader hatred, disgust, contempt . . . The phrasing must be calculated not to convince but to destroy . . . not to correct the adversary's mistake, but to annihilate."[432]

Lenin took power in 1917. By the time he died in 1924, he was responsible for the deaths of three million people. The terror regime he initiated exponentially increased under the next communist dictator, Joseph Stalin. The eighty-four prison/labor camps under Lenin's rule grew to thirty thousand under Stalin. The three million murdered under Lenin were quickly surpassed by Stalin's nine million. Stalin competed with Hitler for the world's greatest mass murderer until Chairman Mao of China surpassed both, killing at least forty-five million people; some historians say seventy million. Indirectly, Stalin could still get credit for being the greatest mass murderer in history. With the aid and inspiration of the Soviet Union, other communist states—China, North Korea, Vietnam, and Cuba—were born. Stalin truly believed in the last part of his statement: "One man's death is a tragedy, but a million deaths is a statistic."

Evil leaders throughout history have been responsible for millions of deaths (Genghis Khan, Attila the Hun, Tamerlane); but what is different with the modern ideologies of hate, such as communism and Nazism, are their leaders often killed more of their people than outsiders.

If there is such a thing as higher and lower categories of evil, Stalin and Hitler would undoubtedly be in the highest. Dr. David J. Dallin, an expert on

---

431 Ibid, 15.
432 Monica Showalter, "Six Principles of Propaganda Lenin Used to Consolidate Power," Investor's Business Daily online, September 20, 2013, https://www.investors.com/politics/commentary/lenin-used-six-principles-of-propaganda-to-consolidate-control.

the cruel workings of the Soviet Union from 1917-1953, was the author of *Fact On Communism*. His report was the official document that described "The Soviet Union, From Lenin To Khrushchev." Dallin describes Stalin's rule this way:

> As a totalitarian dictator he wielded greater power than did his contemporaries Hitler and Mussolini. In the early 1930's he reached the summit of his power. Few Russian autocrats . . . had been . . . as ruthless in their actions. Amoral, vengeful, suspicious, contemptuous of human life, conceited and egotistical, Stalin triumphed mainly because in his personal traits of character he embodied the main elements of communism-belligerency, lack of humaneness, a taste for oppressing and belief in a police state."[433]

Other communist leaders of that time, most of whom Stalin later killed, confirm Dallin's later assessment. Nikolai Bukharin, a prominent early Bolshevik leader, described Stalin as having an "implacable jealousy of anyone who knows more or does things better than he . . . He is eaten up with vain desire . . . Stalin knows only vengeance . . . the dagger in the back."[434] Stalin himself confirmed this in 1923 when he described the pleasure that revenge gave him: "To choose one's victim, to prepare one's plans minutely, to slake an implacable vengeance and then go to bed."[435]

Lenin had no problem using terror against non-communists, but he saw too late that Stalin was a danger not only to non-Communists but also to the Communist Party itself. Lenin, sick from several cerebral strokes, began to warn the party about Stalin, writing in his *Last Testament*: "Stalin is too rude . . . Therefore, I propose to the comrades to find a way to remove Stalin . . . and appoint . . . another man who in all respects differs from Stalin . . . namely, more patient, more loyal, more polite and attentive to other comrades."[436]

---

433 *Facts on Communism*, Vol. 2.
434 Ibid, 153.
435 Ibid.
436 Ibid, 145.

Lenin's effort was too little, too late. Stalin survived, but many other prominent communists did not. Documents taken from the meeting of the Seventeenth Communist Party Congress show that seventy percent of the elected members of the Central Committee were arrested and shot under Stalin's dictatorship. In 1935, Stalin began the Great Purge of the Communist Party. Dallin writes, "The purge operation actually lasted for almost four years and resulted in thousands of arrests, trials, and executions . . . Stalin's mania grandiose . . . grew beyond all limits . . . No public speech, on whatever subject, could be made that did not mention the 'genius' Stalin; no important newspaper article could omit quotations from the infallible Stalin."[437] "At least 750,000 people were killed during the Great Purge."[438] It was after this "Great Purge" of the Communist Party that Dallin says of Stalin:

> Thought that now he could decide all things alone and all he needed were people to fill the stage; he treated all others in such a way that they could only listen to and praise him . . . A servile attitude towards Stalin became obligatory and universal. Stalin had to be acknowledged as the genius in politics, sociology, Marxism . . . military affairs, science and linguistics. He was deified; he could commit no error."[439]

One of the great lessons that the history of totalitarian governments teaches is that atheism does not do away with the act of worship. It only transfers to unworthy human beings. When people stop worshiping the true God, they begin to worship anyone else, such as political leaders, sports stars, music and movie stars, and other celebrities. As the poet T.S. Eliot pointed out, "If you will not have God . . . then you should pay your respects to Hitler or Stalin."

The following quotes by Stalin show that he took pride in his sinful, cruel nature:

437 Ibid.
438 "Great Terror," History.com, Updated October 4, 2022, https://www.history.com/topics/russia/great-purge.
439 United States Congress, 156.

- "Gratitude is a sickness suffered by dogs."
- "Everyone imposes his own system as far as his army can reach."
- "By May 1st, 1937, there should not be one single church left within the borders of Soviet Russia, and the idea of God will have been banished from the Soviet Union."
- "A man's eyes should be torn out if he can only see the past."
- "You do not lament the loss of hair of one who has been beheaded."
- "In the future, there will be fewer but better Russians."
- "You know, they are fooling us,[sic] there is no God."
- "Death is the solution to all problems. No man—no problem."
- "I believe in only one thing, the power of human will."[440]

All communists were evangelical atheists, but Stalin did the most of anyone in history to physically and mentally destroy Judeo-Christian culture in Russia. The Soviet Union was the first nation to openly declare itself an atheist state. Acting on Karl Marx's statement that "communism begins where atheism begins," Stalin, from 1928 to the German invasion of Russia in 1941, directed a campaign against religious belief in the Soviet Union.

Lenin began the anti-religious campaign ten years earlier, but Stalin launched the first Godless Five-Year Plan in 1928, and again in 1932, Stalin declared another Five-Year Plan of atheism. The effect of these plans was almost the totally destruction of organized religion in the Soviet Union. Borrowing from the tactics used by the "evangelical atheists" of the French Revolution, the Soviets did away with the old religious calendar and replaced it with a new Soviet one. The Soviet calendar had only five days in a week thus eliminating days for worship.

New laws on religious associations were adopted in 1929, which "forbade all forms of public, social, communal, educational, publishing or missionary

440 "Joseph Stalin>Quotes," Goodreads, Accessed October 27, 2022, https://www.goodreads.com/author/quotes/138332.Joseph_Stalin.

activities for religious believers."[441] Parents were not allowed to teach their children at home. Those who continued to practice their religious faith were sent to labor camps. In the 1950s, the Soviets would use government psychiatrists to declare people of religious belief to be mentally ill and imprisoned them in state hospitals.

Throughout the Soviet Union, local communist groups called "League of Militant Atheists" helped the government by informing on people of religious faith.[442] In 1927, there were 29,584 Orthodox churches in Russia, but by 1940, there were only five hundred left. All private education became outlawed, and the new communist educational system started a program of anti-religious education in the first grade. During Stalin's purges from 1937 to 1938, 168,300 Russian clergies were arrested, and 106,300 were killed.[443]

During this same period of Russian history, Stalin pursued his policies of "forced collectivization" and "rapid industrialization." His policies resulted in the great famine of 1933. Five-and-a-half million people would die because Stalin, like Lenin, refused to accept foreign aid from the West. Dallin explained Stalin's refusal. "A request by Stalin for food would have destroyed his boastful claim of miraculous achievements in the socialized economy. He preferred to sacrifice millions of lives rather than Soviet prestige . . . It was during this period (1929-34) that the system of . . . Corrective labor Camps was established . . . Hundreds of thousands, probably millions, of persons were shipped to the newly opened camps.[444]

The Soviet economist Sergei Prokopovich wrote of this period, "One thing remains clear beyond any doubt: in the Union of Soviet Socialist Republics, we have a class of slaves of many millions, whose living and

---

441 "Persecution of Christians in the Soviet Union," Wikipedia Foundation, last edited on November 2, 2022, https://en.wikipedia.org/wiki/Persecution_of_Christians_in_the_Soviet_Union.

442 "League of Militant Atheists," Wikipedia Foundation, Last edited on January 10, 2023, https://en.wikipedia.org/wiki/League_of_Militant_Atheists.

443 "Great Purge," Wikipedia Foundation, Last updated January 12, 2023, https://en.wikipedia.org/wiki/Great_Purge.

444 United States Congress, 166.

working condition are infinitely worse than those of the American negroes in the Southern states." Out of a population of 150 million people, up to fourteen million were prisoners.[445]

Stalin was anti-Semitic, like Hitler. In his book *Facts On Communism*, Dallin described Stalin's plan by saying, "The main novelty of the new purge was the fact that it was coupled with an anti-Semitic drive . . . Stalin's anti-Semitic orientation had been strengthened when postwar developments proved the sympathy of many Soviet Jews with the pro-Western culture and way of life . . . The desire of thousands of Soviet Jews to emigrate from 'Socialist' Russia to a capitalist country."[446]

Before his death in 1953, Stalin was still planning another purge. Stalin's "Final Solution" called for all Soviet Jews to be moved thirty-eight hundred miles from Moscow to a Siberian concentration camp. Stalin's sudden death was the only thing that saved the Soviet Jews from this terrible fate.[447]

In 1933, Adolf Hitler came to power in Germany. Hitler was a right-wing extremist who hated the communists and the Slavic people of the Soviet Union but admired Stalin's brutal use of power. Inspired by Stalin's vast prison/labor camps network, Hitler would soon copy him, creating more than one thousand concentration camps. In 1917, when Stalin was helping Lenin to overthrow the elected government in Russia, Hitler served in the First World War as a message-runner between the different sectors of the battlefield. Just before the end of the war, Hitler was temporarily blinded by a British gas attack.

To understand Hitler, one must understand the effect Germany's loss in World War I had on him. When Germany lost the war, he was emotionally devastated and suffered a momentary relapse into blindness. Hitler later wrote of this experience, "When I was confined to bed, the idea came to me that I would liberate Germany, that I would make it great."[448]

---

445 Ibid, 186.
446 Ibid, 274.
447 Ibid, 276.
448 Walter C. Langer, *The Mind of Adolf Hitler: The Secret Wartime Report* (New York: Basic Books, Inc, 1972), 42.

Just as the Communist revolution in Russia presented a purpose for Stalin to fulfill, it was the same for Hitler in becoming the savior of Germany. Like Stalin, Hitler was a man whose mind was primarily characterized by what he hated, and anti-Semitism was at the top of his list. His attack on Germany's Jews started in the same way it did under Stalin in Russia: professional Jews lost their right to practice their professions and were later arrested, tortured, and killed.

Hitler also shared Stalin's hatred of Judeo-Christian moral/spiritual teachings. He wrote:

> Christianity is the prototype of Bolshevism: the mobilization by the Jew of the masses of slaves with the object of undermining society . . . Taken to its logical extreme, Christianity would mean the systematic cultivation of human failure . . . the teachings of Christianity are a rebellion against the natural law of selection by struggle and survival of fittest . . . The heaviest blow that ever-struck humanity was the coming of Christianity.[449]

In this one statement, we can see the influence that came from the neo-pagan philosophies of the Romantic period and the theory of "Social Darwinism." Like Nietzsche, Hitler saw Judeo-Christianity as a "slave morality," a belief system that limits the naturally superior person and prevents his great achievements from taking place. When he said, "The teachings of Christianity are a rebellion against the natural law of selection by struggle and survival of the fittest," he was endorsing Darwin's Theory of Natural Selection. Hitler's fundamental rejection of Judeo-Christian beliefs is well documented in numerous statements:

- If you tell a big enough lie and tell it frequently enough, it will be believed.
- It is not truth that matters, but victory.
- Humanitarianism is the expression of stupidity and cowardice.

449 Helga Zepp-LaRouche, *The Hitler Book* (New York: New Benjamin Franklin House, 1984), 42.

- The very first essential for success is a perpetually constant and regular employment of violence.
- Those who want to live, let them fight, and those who do not want to fight in this world of eternal struggle do not deserve to live.
- Kill, destroy, sack. Lie as much you want, after victory nobody asks why.
- The great strength of the totalitarian state is that it forces those who fear it to imitate it.

Hitler's worldview was a version of Social Darwinism. Social Darwinism was not a theory endorsed by Charles Darwin but the product of another nineteenth-century philosopher, Herbert Spencer (1820-1903). Spencer's theory was published before Darwin's theory and was based upon an earlier theory of evolution by Jean-Baptiste Lamarck. Social Darwinism took the concept of the "survival of the fittest" and applied it to human society.

The danger of this kind of thinking is evident when you read Spencer's book *Social Statics,* published in 1850. In this work, he advanced an argument in favor of imperialism, writing, "The forces which are working out the great scheme of perfect happiness, taking no account of incidental suffering, exterminate such sections of mankind as stand in their way . . . Be he human or be he brute—the hindrance must be got rid of."[450]

Spencer, an atheist, adapted part of Darwin's Theory of Natural Selection to create Social Darwinism, and Hitler adapted part of Spencer's theory to create Nazism. What Hitler added to Darwinism was borrowed from an earlier race theorist, Houston Stewart Chamberlain (1855-1927). Chamberlain's philosophy was expressed in his book *The Foundations of the Nineteenth Century,* where he writes:

> Certain anthropologists would . . . teach us that all races are equally gifted; we point to history and answer: that is a lie! . . . the

---

450 Harry Barows Acton, *Encyclopedia Britannica,* s.v. "Herbert Spencer," Accessed October 27, 2022. https://www.britannica.com/biography/Herbert-Spencer.

Germanic races belong to the most highly gifted group, the group usually termed Aryan . . . Physically and mentally the Aryans are pre-eminent among all peoples; for that reason they are by right . . . the lords of the world . . . the men who founded Judaism were impelled on . . . by a demoniacal power . . . Not only the Jew, but also all that is derived from the Jewish mind, corrodes and disintegrates what is best in us.[451]

Hitler also studied the lives of Napoleon, Frederick the Great, and Peter the Great of Russia. He commented on their successes and failures, but mostly, he admired them for their autocracy and military conquests. Hitler accepted a progressive view of history like Hegel and saw himself as one of the great men of history who would make that change possible. Historian Werner Maser wrote, "Hitler . . . was convinced that he had discovered and grasped . . . the 'eternal course of history' . . . he came to see himself as . . . someone who had lifted the veil of history and discovered the final truth."[452]

Hitler often talked about "providence" and his "mission." But this providence was not the Judeo-Christian concept of Providence. When describing God, Hitler used words like "Christianity" and "Almighty" but rejected the Judeo-Christian essentials of love, forgiveness, and humility. He viewed nature and man's place in it as a wild, cruel struggle for dominance. For him, his providence and mission were directed by a pagan, magical force that animated all of life. His view was like Schopenhauer's "The World as Will" and closest to Nietzsche's "Will to Power." No theistic God was necessary for his plans. Hitler only needed to align himself with this dominating natural force and make decisions that put the German people ahead of all others. Hitler may have believed in a Higher Power, but it was not the Judeo-Christian Higher Power. If he believed in a Higher Power, it had to be one that agreed with his racist views and served his selfish purposes. He was, in effect, his own god.

451 *Encyclopedia Britannica*, s.v. "Houston Stewart Chamberlain," Accessed October 27, 2022, https://www.britannica.com/biography/Houston-Stewart-Chamberlain.
452 Werner Maser, *Hitler: Legend, Myth & Reality* (New York: Harper & Row, 1971).

The core values of Nazism were neo-pagan: the glorification of the conquering hero, belief in demigods (Supermen); the ranking of human life in a caste system; and seeking fame, pleasure, and wealth at the cruel expense of others. The pagan Greeks, Romans, Aztecs, Assyrians, and many other pagan cultures would have been right at home with Nazism.

Historians today continue to debate whether Hitler was an atheist. Did neo-paganism and the occult beliefs strongly influence him? Was he plain evil or insane? The answer is that his mind was a constant battlefield that revealed signs of all the above. His only fixed point in thought was his great hatred of all others who did not share his beliefs or did not worship at the altar of "Heil Hitler." Historians like John Toland documented that beyond his belief in an amoral force in nature promoting dominance, Hitler was a very superstitious man. Other historians and biographers, such as Trevor Ravenscroft, Jacques Bergier, Dusty Sklar, and Louis Pauwel, all say that there was a strong connection between Hitler and occultism.

In an essay entitled "Hitler and the Occult: The Magical Thinking of Adolf Hitler," Professor Raymond L. Sickinger of Providence College presents a middle ground position, "There is little doubt that Hitler's personality was one prone to 'believing in magic' . . . a form of magical thinking in which the world is thought to be manipulated by will . . . he trusted inspiration more than he did thought . . . In his early life, Hitler indeed thought and acted in a magical way and his experiences taught him to trust, rather than to discredit, this magical approach to life."[453]

Sickinger's thesis is that Hitler's thinking was based upon a fundamental of all forms of paganism or occultism: the belief that certain special people had magical powers. Many other top Nazis like Heinrich Himmler, Rudolph Hess, Alfred Rosenburg, Dietrich Eckhart, and Karl Maria Wiligut were

---

453 Raymond L. Sickinger, "Hitler and the Occult: The Magical Thinking of Adolf Hitler," *The Journal of Popular Culture* 34, No. 2 (March, 2004): 107-225, https://www. researchgate.net/publication/229795572_Hitler_and_the_Occult_The_Magical_ Thinking_of_Adolf_Hitler.

dedicated practitioners of occultism.[454] Hitler's ego did not allow him to be part of any group of which he was not the author. His underlings could dabble in the black arts, but he had to stand alone on the mountain top dispensing unquestionable commands like Zeus. Hitler said of himself, "Geniuses of the extraordinary type, can show no consideration for normal humanity."[455] Nazi "Brown shirt" leader Ernst Roehm, whom Hitler later murdered, saw the same characteristic in Hitler: "What he wants is to sit on the hilltop and pretend he's God . . . He wants to let things run their course. He expects a miracle."[456]

A friend of Hitler's from the earliest days, Ernst Hanfstaengl, said that Hitler "was to all intents and purposes an atheist." The majority view expressed by historians is that, from an early age, he lost faith in Christianity and became very hostile to it as a belief system. Historian Laurence Rees wrote that he found no evidence that "Hitler, in his personal life, ever expressed belief in the basic tenets of the Christian Church."[457]

After he came to power in 1933, his high-ranking Nazis colleagues who knew him best recorded in unguarded moments his honest thoughts. Hitler's private secretary Martin Bormann kept a record of his informal statements:

- When understanding of the universe has become widespread, when the majority of men know that the stars are not sources of light but worlds, perhaps inhabited worlds like ours, then the Christian doctrine will be convicted of absurdity.

454 Nicholas Goodrick-Clarke, *Occult Roots of Nazism: Secret Aryan Cults and Their Influence on Nazi Ideology* (New York: New York University Press, 1993).

455 "A Psychological Analysis of Adolph Hitler His life and Legend-Psychological Analysis and Reconstruction," Jewish Virtual Library, Accessed October 27, 2022, https://www.jewishvirtuallibrary.org/a-psychological-analysis-of-adolph-hitler-his-life-and-legend-psychological-analysis-and-reconstruction.

456 *Encyclopedia Britannica*, s.v. "Ernst Röhm," Accessed October 27, 2022, https://www.britannica.com/biography/Ernst-Rohm.

457 "Religious Views of Adolf Hitler," Wikipedia Foundation, Last edited January 3, 2023, https://en.wikipedia.org/wiki/Religious_views_of_Adolf_Hitler.

- Once I have settled my other problem [World War II], I'll have my reckoning with the Church. I'll have it reeling on the ropes.
- I shall never come to terms with the Christian lie . . . Our epoch will certainly see the end of the disease Christianity.
- "It's certain that Jesus was not a Jew . . . The decisive falsification of Jesus' doctrine was the work of St. Paul.[458]

Joseph Goebbels was Hitler's leading propagandist for the Nazi Party from 1933-1945. Goebbels and his entire family died with Hitler in the Fuhrerbunker. He recorded these statements about Hitler:

- "He hates Christianity, because it has crippled all that is noble in humanity . . . The Fuhrer is deeply religious, though completely anti-Christian. He views Christianity as a symptom of decay . . . it is a branch of the Jewish race."
- "Hitler was a fierce opponent of Christianity."[459]

Albert Speer, who was the Minister of Armaments for Germany during World War II and a close confidant of Hitler recorded these statements:

- "You see, it's been our misfortune to have the wrong religion. Why didn't we have the religion of the Japanese [pagan], who regard sacrifice for the fatherland as the highest good?
- "Amid his political associates in Berlin, Hitler made harsh pronouncements against the Church."[460]

458 Martin Bormann, *Hitler's Table Talk*, Ed. Hugh Trevor-Roper editor (New York: Enigma Books, 2000).
459 Joseph Goebbels, "Joseph Goebbels›Quotes," Goodreads.com, https://www.goodreads.com/author/quotes/281832.Joseph_Goebbels
460 Albert Speer, "Religious Views of Adolf Hitler," Wikipedia Foundation, Accessed June 18, 2023, https://en.wikipedia.org/wiki/Religious_views_of_Adolf_Hitler.

According to Goebbels, Hitler believed the highest point in history was during the pagan Augustan age of the Roman empire. Goebbels said Hitler thought Christianity had "corrupted and infected the entire world of antiquity."[461]

But more important than these recorded statements are the anti-Christian policies the Nazis government implemented once in power. The following report entitled "The Nazi Master Plan: The Persecution of the Christian Churches" was entered into evidence for the Nuremberg Trials at the end of the war:

> Throughout the period of National Socialist rule, religious liberties in Germany and in the occupied areas were seriously impaired. The various Christian Churches were systematically cut off from effective communication with the people. They were confined as far as possible to the performance of narrowly religious functions, and even within this narrow sphere were subjected to as many hindrances as the Nazis dared to impose. These results were accomplished partly by legal and partly by illegal and terroristic means.[462]

Heinrich Himmler, the head of the Nazi S.S., wrote the following comments about Christianity in 1937:

> We live in an era of the ultimate conflict with Christianity. It is part of the mission of the SS to give the German people in the next half century the non-Christian ideological foundations on which to lead and shape their lives. This task does not consist solely in overcoming an ideological opponent but must be accompanied at every step by a positive impetus: in this case that means the

461 Goebbels, ibid.
462 Joe Sharkey, "Word for Word/the Case Against the Nazis; How Hitler's Forces Planned to Destroy German Christianity," The New York Times online, January 13, 2002, https://www.nytimes.com/2002/01/13/weekinreview/word-for-word-case-against-nazis-hitler-s-forces-planned-destroy-german.html.

reconstruction of the German heritage in the widest and most comprehensive sense.[463]

"Himmler saw the main task of his . . . organization to be that of 'acting as the vanguard in overcoming Christianity and restoring a 'Germanic' way of living . . . He set about making his SS the focus of a 'cult of the Teutons.'"[464]

A list of some of the Nazi actions taken against religious churches includes:

1. Clergy were sent to concentration camps.
2. Religious youth organizations closed.
3. Church properties were converted into cinemas and brothels.
4. The suppression of monasteries and expulsion of religious orders.
5. Goebbels banned all Church media.
6. The removal of crucifixes in religious schools. In Nazi schools, Christian prayers were replaced with sun-worship and Teutonic rituals.
7. Catholic welfare programs were restricted.
8. All unions were liquidated.
9. The murder of invalids.[465]

A pastoral letter of German bishops in 1942 stated, "For years a war has raged in our Fatherland against Christianity and the Church . . . We demand juridical proof of all sentences and release of all fellow citizens who have been deprived of their liberty without proof . . . We . . . shall not

463 Christopher Tatara, "Hitler, Himmler, and Christianity in the Early Third Reich," *Constructing the Past* 14, No. 1, (April 2013): https://digitalcommons.iwu.edu/cgi/viewcontent.cgi?article= &context=constructing.
464 "Nazi Persecution of the Catholic Church in Germany," Wikipedia Foundation, August 26, 2022, https://en.wikipedia.org/wiki/Nazi_persecution_of_the_Catholic_Church_ in_Germany.
465 "Catholic Church and Nazi Germany," Wikipedia Foundation, last edited September 11, 2022, https://en.wikipedia.org/wiki/Catholic_Church_and_Nazi_Germany.

cease to protest against the killing of innocent persons."[466] According to evidence presented at the Nuremberg Trials, the Nazi Master Plan was the work of Alfred Rosenberg, a neo-pagan philosopher who was influenced by Gnostic philosophy and whom Hitler appointed head of educational and cultural affairs within the Third Reich. Rosenberg's thirty-point plan included these acts:

1. The National Reich's Church (Nazi) . . . is determined to exterminate . . . by every means the strange and foreign Christian faiths imported into Germany.
2. The National Reich's Church has no scribes, pastors, chaplains or priests, but National Reich orators are to speak in them.
3. The National Reich's Church demands immediate cessation of the publication and dissemination of the Bible in Germany as well as the publication of Sunday papers, pamphlets, publications and books of a religious nature.
4. The National Reich's Church has to take severe measures in order to prevent the Bible and other Christian publications being imported into Germany.
5. The National Reich's Church . . . has decided the Fuhrer's 'Mein Kampf' is the greatest of all documents.
6. The National Reich's Church will clear away from its altars all crucifixes . . . Bibles and pictures of Saints.
7. On the altars there must be nothing but 'Mein Kampf' . . . to God the most sacred book.
8. The National Reich's Church does not acknowledge forgiveness of sins . . . a sin once committed will be ruthlessly punished.

"Catholic Bishops in Nazi Germany," Wikipedia Foundation, last edited July 18, 2022, https://en.wikipedia.org/wiki/Catholic_bishops_in_Nazi_Germany.

9. The National Reich's abolishes confirmation and religious education as well as communion.

10. On the day of its foundation the Christian cross must be removed from all churches . . . it must be superseded by the only unconquerable symbol of Germany the "Haken Krevz [swastika].[467]

The philosophy behind these actions was based upon Rosenberg's book *The Myth of the Twentieth Century*. Like Hitler, Rosenberg's philosophy was strongly influenced by Houston Stewart Chamberlain, Friedrich Nietzsche, Arthur Schopenhauer, and Meister Eckhart. Rosenberg's main contribution to Nazi thought was his development of the racial theme in Nazi philosophy and the belief that God had not created only one human race. He believed "each biological race possesses a . . . unique soul . . . Germanic Nordics . . . composing its vanguard elite . . . qualitatively superior."[468] In Rosenberg's own insane language we find the purpose behind Nazism: "under the sign of the swastika unchains the racial world-revolution. It is the awakening of the race-soul, which after long sleep victoriously ends the race chaos."[469]

As a result of Germany and Russia substituting either secular humanism or neo-paganism for the moral/spiritual values of Judeo-Christianity, the world experienced the most destructive war in human history.

> Some 75 million people died in World War II, including about 20 million military personnel and 40 million civilians, many of whom died because of deliberate genocide and starvation . . . Nazi Germany, as part of a deliberate program of extermination killed over 11 million people including 6 million Jews . . . the Soviet gulags (labor camps) led to the deaths of 3.6 million

---

467 Andrew Othuke Akpeli, "Alfred Rosenberg's 30-Point Church Plan for the National Reich Church," Dutable, March 29, 2019, https://dutable.com/2012/03/16/alfred-rosenbergs-30-point-church-plan.

468 Volkischer Beobachter, "Myth of the Twentieth Century," in *Nazi Paper*, Edited by Alfred Rosenberg (Berlin: 1930).

469 Ibid.

civilians . . . In Asia and the Pacific . . . more than 10 million civilians, mostly Chinese . . . were killed by the Japanese occupation forces.[470]

The social history of America, England, Russia, and Germany after the First World War reveals two countertrends at work in the 1920s. One trend was increasing interest and practice of occultism (neo-paganism). The other trend was the movement away from traditional religious faith to a more secular belief. The one exception in America was the increase in fundamentalism in rural America. Both trends weakened the traditional influence of Judeo-Christianity in these societies.

America and the United Kingdom stayed on the right side of history because they were victors in the war. Their economies were growing, and they both had a long tradition of human rights and democratic rule. In the case of Germany and Russia, the opposite was true. Russia and Germany experienced revolution, civil war, economic crisis, and deprivation. Russia and Germany had a long history of authoritarianism and only a short history of national democratic rule. Having cut themselves free from the strong mooring of absolute truth and universal morality, Germany and Russia drifted into a moral abyss that resulted in World War II.

Nazism and communism were the two most destructive mythological systems in modern history. They were the fanciful ideologies of evil men who had rejected Judeo-Christian culture. Theologian Paul Tillich, who lived through this period of history, provides us with a cogent analysis of the nature of ideologies and their ongoing danger to the world: "The creation of . . . ideologies-religiously speaking, idols-representing man's will to power, occurs unconsciously. It is not a conscious falsification or a political lie. If this were the case, ideologies would not be very dangerous.

---

470 John McLean, "History of Western Civilization II," ER Services, Accessed October 27, 2022, https://courses.lumenlearning.com/suny-hccc-worldhistory2/chapter/casualties-of-world-war-ii.

But are dangerous precisely because they are unconscious and are therefore objects of belief and fanaticism.[471]

In other words, the evangelical atheists of the French Revolution, the German philosophers of the Romantic period, and the Nazis and communists of modern history were all true believers. They were true believers willing to die and kill for their ideologies.

In this dangerous modern world where false ideologies are constantly being born or re-born, Tillich offers Judeo-Christianity as a necessary prescription for the well-being of humanity:

> To reveal these . . . ideologies is one of the most important functions of the Protestant principle, just as it was one of the main points in the attack of the prophets (Jewish) on the religious and social order of their time. Theology . . . must provide general insight into human nature, into its distorted character and its proneness to create ideologies . . . Man does not have to deceive himself about himself, because he is accepted as he is . . . But being accepted by God means also being transformed by God.[472]

This is the view of a person that Wikipedia describes "as one of the most influential theologians of the twentieth century."[473] One of the most famous modern philosophers of the twentieth century, Lord Bertrand Russel, an atheist, agreed with this view. In one of his essays on fascism, he wrote, "Modern democracy has derived strength from the moral ideals of Christianity, and has done much to divert governments from exclusive pre-occupation with the interest of the rich and powerful. Fascism is, in this respect, a return to what was worst in ancient paganism . . . the influence of skepticism . . . made it seem hopeless to discover truth, but very profitable to assert falsehood."[474]

---

471 Tillich, 170.
472 Ibid, 170-71.
473 "Paul Tillich," Wikipedia Foundation, Last updated June 15, 2023, https://en.wikipedia.org/wiki/Paul_Tillich.
474 Russell, 86.

Judaism and Christianity both believe in a universal and impersonal standard of truth. Russell concludes his essay on fascism, stating these beliefs are "of supreme importance to the well-being of the human species."[475] Nazism and communism, like radical Islam today, were attempts at "social engineering." The Nazis wanted to create a perfect Aryan man, the Communists a perfect Socialist man; and ISIS today seeks to create perfect Muslims who will rule over an ideal Islamic caliphate. Historian Paul Johnson identifies this tendency in totalitarian societies: "social engineering has been the salient delusion and the greatest curse of the modern age. In the twentieth century it has killed scores of millions of innocent people, in Soviet Russia, Nazi Germany, Communist China . . . it is the last thing which Western democracies, with all their faults, have ever espoused . . . It is the birthright of the totalitarian tradition. It was pioneered by Rousseau."[476]

Johnson was correct in his critique up until very recent times. Today, modern Leftists and neo-pagans have established a new plan for social engineering: CRT, cancel culture, and political correctness. The philosopher Bertrand Russell was not a man of religious faith, but he understood the need for a positive system of belief that could counter the human heart's weaknesses and evil tendencies. His answer was to promote philosophy: "finding pleasure in thought rather than in action is a safeguard against un-wisdom and excessive love of power, a means of preserving serenity in misfortune and peace of mind among worries."[477] The problem with this solution was that only a small group of people have either the ability or interest to become a philosopher.

The world's problems are too large, and Russell's remedy is too small. His secular-humanist answer of each person becoming his own philosopher-king (a term created by Plato) provides no guarantee that the philosophy they come up with would be benevolent or wise. Of the twenty most influential

---

475 Ibid, 56.
476 Johnson, 261.
477 Russell, 34-35.

philosophers of the nineteenth century which led up to World War I, at least fourteen were atheists and only two were Christians. Russell did, however, provide a good description of the problem of living without purpose: "For those to whom . . . religion can no longer bring comfort, there is need of some substitute, if life is not to become dusty and harsh and filled with trivial self-assertion. The world at present (1930's) [sic] is full of angry self-centered groups, each incapable of viewing human life as a whole, each willing to destroy civilization rather than yield an inch."[478]

The answer to the problem of human sin, which causes human suffering, cannot only be an intellectual answer. The strings of the human heart must be moved for people to care, and it must be a rational belief system, accessible to all, and of maximum practical benefit. No tipped intellectualism can resist cruel fanaticism. No tipped intellectualism can inspire people to fight and die for a just cause. It takes a solid, positive faith system to withstand a strong negative one. In the modern history of the world, the most outstanding contribution made by those nations whose cultures were based upon the values and spiritual beliefs of Judeo-Christian culture was their successful leadership in defeating the evil forces that caused World War II.

---

478 Ibid, 36.

CHAPTER EIGHTEEN

THE TRIUMPH OF NEO-PAGANISM IN AMERICA

SINCE THE HEROIC DEFEAT OF the totalitarian governments of the 1930s to 1940s, the average citizen of America plodded along, not realizing the cultural rot beneath the surface of our society. This was the cultural rot that the great conservative writer William F. Buckley, Jr, warned us about in his famous first book *God and Man at Yale*:

> I believe that the duel between Christianity and atheism is the most important in the world. I further believe that the struggle between individualism and collectivism is the same struggle reproduced on another level . . . Students who come to college with strong religious convictions . . . will unconsciously look to see what the authorities judge to be important. If religion is relegated to the role of a not-too-important sideshow, if its part in our intellectual and emotional tradition is ignored . . . students will go their way, troubled . . . and . . . uneasy . . . upon the assumption that religion does not matter.[479]

With *God and Man at Yale*, Mr. Buckley not only launched his career as a great conservative journalist but sounded, as Thomas Jefferson once said, "a fire bell in the night." The average American citizen awoke from slumber to realize that America's colleges and universities were becoming captives of

---

479 William Buckley Jr., *God and Man at Yale* (New York: Simon and Schuster, 1951).

Left-wing, secular-humanist faculties and administrations. His publication of *GAMAY* in 1951 has proven prophetic. What was once only the problem of certain very liberal private universities is now a K-12 public school problem. What Mr. Buckley understood was this was not just a problem of an elite American university indoctrinating only their students, but also the problem of successive generations of teachers, professors, journalists, screenwriters, playwrights, novelists, lawyers, and our future political leaders. These leaders would eventually make our laws, judge our Supreme Court cases, and eventually serve as our presidents. This was the stacking of America's cultural deck, setting the agenda for America's pagan future. From this liberal/Left educational base in both America and Europe, the art and literature of Modernism emerged.

> Some of Modernism's most famous authors included Ernest Hemingway, Virginia Woolf, James Joyce, Ezra Pound, William Faulkner, T.S. Eliot, Gertrude Stein, and F. Scott Fitzgerald . . . Modernism was a response to the influx of the revolutionary ideas of thinkers such as Darwin, Freud, and Nietzsche. Altogether these individual presented ideas that deconstructed important traditional foundations of society, such as religion, ethics, sexuality.[480]

Hemingway was an atheist; Virginia Woolf was an atheist; and James Joyce once wrote, "My mind rejects the whole present social order and Christianity." These and many atheist and agnostic writers, filmmakers, artists, critics, journalists, and intellectuals of all stripes have been the dominant voices since the 1960s.

Before William F. Buckley, another famous Catholic had already sounded the alarm in 1947. Archbishop Fulton Sheen wrote:

> We are at the end of Christendom . . . Christendom is economic, political, social life as inspired by Christian principals. That is

---

480 "Modernism," Enotes.com, Accessed October 30, 2022, https://www.enotes.com/ homework-help/what-themes-characteristics-modernism-743192.

ending . . . Look at the symptoms: the breakup of the family, divorce, abortion, immorality, general dishonesty . . . Only those who live by faith really know what is happening in the world. The great masses without faith are unconscious of the destructive processes going on.[481]

There were even earlier conservative voices calling out Liberal/Left tendencies in American culture. In the 1880s, Anthony Comstock, who worked for the YMCA, wrote "Traps for the Young" and "Frauds Exposed . . . and Youth Corrupted." He described a dangerous new view of sexual morality called "Free Love" or "marriage is bondage; love is lust, celibacy is suicide; while fidelity to marriage vows is a relic of barbarism. All restraints which keep boys and girls . . . pure and chaste . . . are not to be tolerated by them."[482]

Fifty-four years later, in 1934, a freelance writer named Malcolm Cowley wrote essays critical of this alternative lifestyle being promoted and settling in Greenwich Village, New York. "Greenwich Village was not only a place, a mood, a way of life . . . it was a doctrine . . . By 1920, it had become a system of ideas that could roughly be summarized as . . . Each of us at birth has special potentialities which are slowly crushed and destroyed by a standardized society . . . the world will be saved by this new, free generation."[483]

Sheen and Buckley were modern prophets "crying in the wilderness." They were challenging the new norm of the majority opinion among the elites in academia and those that control our news media and mass-popular culture. This was the same creeping, moral darkness that motivated a gifted, young Baptist evangelist from North Carolina to begin the first of his 417 crusades in 1947: Billy Graham.

---

481 Joseph Pronechen, "Archbishop Sheen's Warning of a Crisis in Christendom," National Catholic Register, Accessed October 30, 2022, https://www.ncregister.com/blog/archbishop-sheen-s-warning-of-a-crisis-in-christendom.

482 Robert C. Bannister and Anthony Comstock, "Free Love Traps," In *American Values in Transition; a Reader* (New York: Harcourt Brace Jovanovich, 1972), 29.

483 Ibid, "War in Bohemia," 33.

The trend in atheistic and agnostic philosophy that started with the Enlightenment has continued to the present. A 2014 survey conducted by David Chalmers, Professor of Philosophy at New York University, found that, of one thousand current professional philosophers, 72.8 percent consider themselves atheists. The other gurus of modern culture—professors of psychology—also score very low on the scale of religious belief: fifty percent are atheists, and eleven percent agnostic.[484]

We can also add to these social sciences the atheist founder of sociology, Auguste Comte and the atheist Emile Durkheim, who established it as an academic discipline. For the last sixty years, America has entrusted the education of its young to a group of academics whose views were not only outside of but also enemies of the mainstream of Judeo-Christian culture.

Only two percent of America's population in 2014 could be identified as atheist, but a survey published as "The Religiosity of American College and University Professors" found that "nearly 37 percent of professors at elite schools like Harvard are atheist or agnostic."[485]

A study conducted in 1999 by Rothman, Lichter, and Nevitte found that "72% of U.S. professors identify themselves as left of center politically." A more recent national survey by Neil Gross and Solon Simmons found "atheists professors of psychology . . . lead the pact with 50 percent . . . Amongst biologists 33.3 percent were agnostic and 27.5 percent were atheist . . . professors in the social sciences and humanities are more than twice as likely to identify themselves as religiously progress (liberal) . . . 51.5 percent of professors say they believe in God but of these 31.2 percent claim to have no religious affiliation."[486]

---

484 Epiphenom, "Psychologists Are the Least Religious of American Professors," Patheos.com, May 30, 2009, https://www.patheos.com/blogs/epiphenom/2009/05/psychologists-are-least-religious-of.html.

485 *Sociology of Religion*, Vol. 70, No. 3, JSTOR (Oxford: Oxford University Press, 2009), https://www.jstor.org/stable/i40016531.

486 Stanley Rothman, S. Robert Lichter, Neil Nevitter, "Politics and Professional Advancement Among College Faculty," *The Forum* 3, No. 1 (Toronto: University of Toronto, 2005), https://studentsforacademicfreedom.org/wp-content/uploads/2020/05/Politics_Faculty.pdf.

From a list of the fifty most influential philosophers of today, a few examples of their views on religious faith can provide us with a sample of academic thought at the doctoral level:

- "[Human beings are] lumbering robots controlled by our selfish genes" (Richard Dawkins).
- "When you look at the vast size of the universe, and how accidental and insignificant human life is in it . . . the existence of God seems implausible" (Stephen Hawking).
- "Forget Jesus. The stars died so you could be born" (Lawrence Krauss).
- "Evolution is the greatest engine of atheism ever invented" (William B. Provine).
- "Science flies you to the Moon. Religion flies you into buildings" (Victor Stenger).
- "[The human condition is] . . . frailty, futility, and finally death" (Philip Roth).
- "I think in Europe, we have outgrown [religion]. We've waited it out and its[sic] gone" (Martin Amis).
- "Religion remains the last great prop and stay of arbitrary injustices and the coercion which backs them up" (Ophelia Benson).
- "Evolution sets the brain's style of drives and emotions. Experience in culture shapes the style into specific habits and preferences using the reward system" (Patricia Churchland).
- "Religion is an insult to human dignity" (Steven Weinberg).
- "Religion has to be explained as a material process" (Edward O. Wilson).
- "My object is to show that atheism is a rational position and that belief in God is not" (Michael Martin).
- "The notion that human life is sacred just because it is human life is medieval" (Peter Singer).[487]

---

487 "50 Most Influential Living Philosophers," TheBestSchools.org, August 12, 2022, https://thebestschools.org/magazine/most-influential-living-philosophers.

The changes in our mass-popular culture over the last sixty years have done the most to undermine religious faith and promote neo-pagan values. Still, it was the changes in our educational system that trained the minds of those who create and control that mass-popular culture. The most up-to-date social research about changes in worldwide religious faith reveals the twin trends of increasing secularization and neo-pagan belief. In 2018, Pew Research identified North America and Europe as places where "young adults are more likely to be religiously unaffiliated . . . This is especially true in North America, where in both the U.S. and Canada younger people are less likely to claim a religious identity . . . The gap is also prevalent in Europe . . . and in Latin America."[488]

When asked in the same survey "Is religious faith very important in your life?" there is a seventeen percent difference between those under age forty and those forty and above. The same study showed that "Young adults are less likely to pray . . . in all countries surveyed in Latin America, in both the U.S. and Canada, and in 27 out of 35 European countries . . . the trends are clear-the U.S. is steadily becoming less Christian and less religiously observant as the share of adults who are not religious grows. From 2009 to 2018, the number of religiously unaffiliated in America grew almost 30 million."[489]

The "General Social Survey" funded by the National Institutes of Science found the same changes in America. "By 2014 . . . fewer Americans participated in religious activities or embraced religious beliefs, with especially striking declines . . . among 18-to 29 year-olds[sic] . . . Nearly a third of Millennials were secular . . . Eight times more 18-to 29 year-olds never prayed in 2014 versus the early 1980's[sic] . . . Most studies agree that religious affiliation has declined in the United States since the 1970's[sic]."[490]

488 "Importance of religion in one's life,," Pew Research Center, June 13, 2022, https://www.pewresearch.org/religion/religious-landscape-study/importance-of-religion-in-ones-life.

489 Ibid.

490 René Bautista and Michael Davern, "General Social Survey (GSS)," (Chicago: NORC at the University of Chicago), Accessed October 30, 2022, https://www.norc.org/Research/Projects/Pages/general-social-survey.aspx.

The problem is not just confined to the drop in the absolute numbers of those who self-identify as Christians. There has also been a sharp drop in the personal religious commitment of many of the same people who still call themselves Christians. Pew Research identified several key measures proving young adults are less religious than older self-identified Christians. They attend church less, pray less, and say religion is not as crucial to their lives.

Beyond the finding that American society is more secular, we must ask, what alternative religious beliefs are attracting the young's attention and claiming their allegiance? The answers are neo-paganism with paranormal and other fantasy beliefs mixed in. Parallel with the decline of faith in Judeo-Christian beliefs has been the increasing acceptance of pagan morality and occult supernatural beliefs.

What is happening in America and Western civilization, in general, has occurred many times in history. Periods of rapid cultural change or civilization crisis have often increased the appetite for magical and occult answers. In Western civilization, we see this happening as far back as the Hellenistic age (323 B.C.-138 A.D.). The upper classes of this period, influenced by the new philosophies and science, became disillusioned with their traditional religious beliefs. Among the elite group of educated people, there was a major decline in religious faith. At the other end of the social spectrum, ordinary people shifted their faith to more occult forms of religious practice. "Throughout the Hellenistic world, people would consult oracles, and use charms and figurines to deter misfortune or to cast spells . . . Also developed in this era was the complex system of astrology."[491]

This last statement perfectly describes what is currently taking place in America and Western civilization in general. Historically, the same process took place in Great Britain from 1880-1929, in Russia from 1890-1927, in America and Western Europe during the 1920s and 60s, and later in Russia after the fall

---

491 "Hellenistic Period," Wikipedia Foundation, last edited October 24, 2022, https://en.wikipedia.org/wiki/Hellenistic_period.

of the Soviet Union: "occult and magical ideas . . . marked by the emergence of new-formed societies dedicated to the exploration of the occult."[492]

What is happening in America and Europe is the confluence of Left-wing/Progressive political ideology and religious occultism. An online article by Christina Rees and Neil Fauerso entitled "The Occult is So Hot Right Now!" discusses the emergence of this alliance and its connection to the arts. Neil Fauerso begins the conversation, saying, "You sent me this excellent article, 'The Rise of Progressive Occultism' by Tara Isabella Burton that, to summarize, posits that a variety of new age, pagan, and occult cultures and practices . . . witchcraft . . . goddess worship, etc. are on the rise, especially among millennials, who are wanting to create a political identity in opposition to the evangelical white nationalism of current conservatism.[493]

Christina Rees, a more practical-minded, Left-wing neo-pagan, responded, "I think this trend is . . . depressing and even dangerous . . . Old white Republican men cannot be 'hexed' out of office. Glaciers cannot be 'voodooded' into not melting. You realize believing in astrology and voting are not mutually exclusive."[494]

Neil Fauerso wrote:

> I am a bit more sympathetic than you . . . occultism is a cyclical phenomenon . . . the counterculture of the 1960's [sic] with the invention of Wicca, interest in meditation and eastern religion, and astrology . . . periods of occultism happen every few decades . . . I would note that probably half of my millennial friends are at least kind of into astrology . . . Aesthetically, I'm basically unreservedly pro-occult. I love horror movies, folkloric mythology . . . even the imagery of healing crystals.[495]

492 Michael Hagemeister and Birgit Menzel, *The New Age of Russia. Occult and Esoteric Dimensions* (Bern: Peter Lang International Academic Publishers, 2021), https://library.oapen.org/handle/20.500.12657/26681.

493 Christine Rees and Neil Fauerso, "The Occult Is So Hot Right Now!," Glasstire, June 29, 2019, https://glasstire.com/2019/06/29/the-occult-is-so-hot-right-now.

494 Ibid.

495 Ibid.

The original article by Tara Isabella Burton, which they were discussing, contains more insights into America's neo-pagan world:

> Progressive New York Representative Alexandria Ocasio-Cortez shared her birth-time with a self-described psychic and astrologer . . . who in turn shared her entire birth chart with what can only be described as Astrology Twitter . . . Twenty-nine percent of Americans say they believe in astrology . . . while just 22 percent of Americans call themselves mainline Protestants . . . progressive millennials have appropriated the rhetoric, imagery, and rituals of what was once called the "New Age"—from astrology to witchcraft—as both a political and spiritual statement of identity . . . an increasing number of left-leaning millennials more and more of whom do not belong to any organized religion . . . the language of witches and demons, of spells and sage, or cleansing and bad energy, of star and signs-has become the de facto religion of millennial progressive.[496]

The most up-to-date research on the growth of neo-pagan and other fantasy beliefs among young adults supports Tara Burton's view. Young adults make up the largest part of the group who identify as religiously "nothing in particular." Among that group, sixty-one percent believe in animism; fifty-two percent believe in psychics; fifty-one percent believe in reincarnation; and forty-seven percent believe in astrology.[497]

On the darker end of the New Age spectrum, *Newsweek* reported in 2018, "Number of witches rises dramatically across U.S. as Millennials reject Christianity . . . pagan religious practices increased in the U.S. over the past few decades . . . Millennials turning to alternatives . . . astrology and tarot

---

496 Tara Isabella Burton, "The Rise of Progressive Occultism," The American Interest, August 12, 2019, https://www.the-american-interest.com/2019/06/07/the-rise-of-progressive-occultism.

497 A.W. Geiger, "17 Striking Findings from 2017," Pew Research Center, December 26, 2017, https://www.pewresearch.org/fact-tank/2017/12/26/17-striking-findings-from-2017.

cards . . . 1.5 million witches across the country . . . there were 8,000 wiccans in 1990 . . . there were about 340,000 in 2008."[498]

The 1.5 million estimate is based on the Pew Research report in 2014. The religious trend toward neo-pagan/occult practice has strengthened since 2014, so the number now would be much higher.

This strong correlation between the changing religious beliefs of young people and the New Age phenomenon is also mirrored in their attachment to other paranormal beliefs, such as the existence of ghosts and aliens visiting the earth. Sixty percent of young Americans believe in extraterrestrials. Author Daniel Kolitz quotes several professors of comparative religion/philosophy on the topic.[499]

Diana Walsh Pasulka, professor of philosophy and religion, University of North Carolina Wilmington wrote:

> For most people in the Western tradition, religion is something that follows a set form of patterns. There is a God . . . non-Western . . . indigenous cultures do not think of religion in this way . . . In many indigenous spiritualities . . . extraterrestrials are often called "star people," . . . and are even ancestors of certain tribes on Earth . . . Buddhism also references the existence of other worlds . . . What is new, however, is that there are "UFO religions," or religions today that incorporate ideas that extraterrestials are here for various reasons.[500]

Karen Pechilis, professor of comparative religions at Drew University said, "I think Buddhism is a good candidate for being the religion most friendly to the idea of life existing on other planets . . . some Buddhist texts describe various regions, not all of them earthly."[501]

498 Benjamin Fearnow, "Number of Witches Rises Dramatically across U.S. As Millenials Reject Christianity," Newsweek online, March 25, 2020, https://www.newsweek.com/witchcraft-wiccans-mysticism-astrology-witches-millennials-pagans-religion-1221019.
499 Daniel Kolitz, "Which Religion Is Friendliest to the Idea of Aliens?," Gizmodo, January 27, 2020, https://gizmodo.com/which-religion-is-friendliest-to-the-idea-of-aliens-1841241730.
500 Ibid.
501 Ibid.

Liz Wilson, professor of comparative religion at the Miami University of Ohio, says, "Buddhism, hands down. No religion offers as vivid a depiction of what life is like on planets far from ours."[502]

Douglas Vakoch, president of Messaging Extraterrestrial Intelligence, a non-profit research organization said, "Numerous schools of Buddhism and Hinduism posit countless celestial realms, populated by beings more or less spiritually advanced than humans."[503]

Christian Weidemann, a lecturer of Protestant theology at the University of Muenster explained, "Every major religion on Earth could easily accommodate the discovery of . . . alien life with the one exception, Christianity."[504]

In the 1990s, a Gallup poll found that twenty-seven percent of Americans believed that aliens had visited the Earth. Another Gallup poll in 2014 found that fifty-four percent of Americans believe in aliens. In 2019, another poll showed that majorities in Britain, the U.S, and Germany believe in extraterrestrials.[505] Recent Pew Research and Gallup surveys show a sharp increase in Americans and Europeans who now believe in ghosts. University of California professor Claude Fischer wrote, "Young Americans are about twice as likely to say they believe in ghosts . . . than older Americans."[506]

As Jolie Roys wrote in *The Christian Post*, "The rejection of Christianity has left a void that people . . . will seek to fill."[507] In America and Europe, where declining Judeo-Christian belief is taking place, there are rising neo-pagan and paranormal beliefs filling that void. Shadi Hamid described this radical change in America's religious belief in an essay published in *The Atlantic* in 2021:

502 Ibid.
503 Ibid.
504 Ibid.
505 Lydia Saad, "Do American Believe in UFOs?," Gallup, Inc. August 20, 2021, https://news.gallup.com/poll/350096/americans-believe-ufos.aspx.
506 Claude S. Fischer, "Spooked: Who still believes in ghosts?," Cal Alumni Association, October 31, 2013, https://alumni.berkeley.edu/california-magazine/online/spooked-who-still-believes-ghosts.
507 Brandon Showalter, "Witches Outnumber Presbyterians in the US; Wicca, Paganism Growing 'Astronomically,'" *The Christian Post*, October 10, 2018, https://www.christianpost.com/news/witches-outnumber-presbyterians-in-the-us-wicca-paganism-growing-astronomically.html.

The United States had long been a holdout among Western democracies . . . uniquely . . . devout. From 1937 to 1998, church membership remained relatively constant, hovering at about 70 percent. Then something happened. Over the past two decades, that number has dropped to less than 50 percent, the sharpest recorded decline in American history . . . the atheists, agnostics, and those claiming no religion—have grown rapidly.[508]

According to Hamid, there has been a dangerous substitution of political extremism for traditional religious belief systems. What is missing from Hamid's analysis is the substitution of a fast-growing neo-pagan values system for what had been the traditional values of Judeo-Christianity. This is the ideological tail that wags the cultural dog, "Culture is king." It always has been and always will be.

The disaffection of young adults from traditional Judeo-Christian culture and their increasing attachment to either secular humanism or neo-paganism or some confused mixture of both spells doom for American civilization. Without a solid Judeo-Christian foundation, American society will sink into a quicksand of moral relativism and pagan foolishness and untruth. These two trends in our communities today are increasing sexual immorality and violence. They have been strengthening over the last sixty years. If this process continues, it will eventually make traditional American culture unrecognizable. Anyone who grew up during the existence of the "Greatest Generation" will become part of the new "Lost Generation." The moral majority of the past will shrink into oblivion.

It is not the practice of the occult that will cause the most significant harm. Witchcraft and astrology will not capture and destroy the lives of most people. The increasing secularization of our society will serve as a counterbalance to any large-scale acceptance of the occult. The greatest harm of both secular humanism and neo-paganism will be their combined weakening of people's

508 Shadi Hamid, "America Without God," RealClearPolicy, March 11, 2021, https://www. realclearpolicy.com/2021/03/11/america_without_god_767624.html#.

faith in the moral/spiritual values of Judeo-Christianity. Without the large-scale acceptance and practice of those values, human emotion and appetites will rule the day. Contemporary sociological/psychological statistics show that, out of this "witches brew" of increasing violence and the low level of sexual morality, American society is being wrecked.

To appreciate how far and fast this transformation has taken place, consider the following examples. In 1970, student radical and homosexual Carl Wittman published *A Gay Manifesto*. The initial response by heterosexual radicals to its publication was generally hostile. Still, within a short period of time, it was used by the Gay Liberation Front as a new guide for homosexual activism. Wittman expressed the following views:

> "The bulk of the social work/psychiatric field looks upon homosexuality as a problem,and treats us as sick . . . (In 1973, the American Psychological Association finally gave in and removed homosexuality from its lists of mental illnesses.) . . . Traditional marriage is a rotten, oppressive institution . . . marriage is a contract which smothers both people, denies needs, and places impossible demands on both people . . . Nature leaves undefined the object of sexual desire. The gender of that object is imposed socially . . . Kids can take care of themselves and are sexual beings . . . Those of us who began cruising in early adolescence know this . . . We can make a direct appeal to young people, who are not so up-tight about homosexuality . . . We have to define for ourselves a new pluralistic, role-free social structure for ourselves . . . It must contain . . . the freedom . . . to live alone, live together for a while . . . either as couples, or in larger numbers; and the ability to flow easily from one of these states to another as our needs change. Free the homosexual in everyone.[509]

Wittman was also a forerunner of the radical environmental movement. He moved to Oregon in the early 1970s, lived in a commune until 1986, and

509 Victor Salvo, "Carl Wittman – Nominee," The Legacy Project, Accessed October 30, 2022, https://legacyprojectchicago.org/person/carl-wittman.

in the last stage of HIV infection, committed suicide. Thirty-four years after his death, a Gallup poll in 2023 found, "One of the main reasons LGBT identification has been increasing . . . is that younger generations are far more likely to consider themselves to be something other than heterosexual . . . about one in six adult members of Generation Z (those aged 18 to 23)."[510]

Who would have believed that Carl Wittman's *A Gay Manifesto* would have survived the world of fringe thought to become the accepted wisdom of today's young? In an attempt to appear sophisticated and ultra-tolerant, young Americans are mimicking current cultural celebrities who are also attempting to appear sophisticated and ultra-tolerant in supporting LGBTQ rights. "Genderfluid" and "pansexual" are coveted terms young people use to identify their sexual orientation. Only sixty-six percent of the younger generation identify themselves as heterosexual. Identity confusion, like moral confusion, has always been the friend of the pagan world. For these advanced thinkers, to call oneself heterosexual is too limiting, too judgmental. Actress Bella Thorne explained, "I'm actually pansexual, and I didn't know that. Somebody explained to me . . . You like beings,[sic] you like what you like. Doesn't have to be a girl or a guy or a he or she or they or this or that. It's literally you like personality. You just like being."[511]

An ordinary person would ask, "Can you like things without being sexually excited by them?" There are many types of beings in the world that normal people are not sexually excited by—rocks, trees, animals, parents, brothers, sisters, relatives, friends, etc. What is particularly worrisome about the high number of young adults who claim to be something other than heterosexual is the implication that many people who were born normal— heterosexual—are intentionally experimenting with homosexual behavior to prove how broad-minded and stylish they are.

---

510   Jeffrey M. Jones, "U.S. LGBT Identification Steady at 7.2%," Gallup, Inc., February 22, 2023, https://news.gallup.com/poll/470708/lgbt-identification-steady.aspx.

511   Lisa Respers France, "Bella Thorne Says She's Actually Pansexual, Not Bisexual," Cable News Network, July 23, 2019, https://edition.cnn.com/2019/07/23/entertainment/bella-thorne-pansexual-trnd/index.html.

Across the Atlantic Ocean, in the early 1960s, another angry young misfit, Kenneth Tynan, was busy rocking the boat in the United Kingdom and proving how fashionable he was. In school debates, he shocked or entertained others by advocating the repeal of laws against homosexuality, abortion, and the practice of masturbation. Having achieved adulthood, Tynan continued to surprise by promoting and practicing sadomasochism. He eventually gained fame as a literary journalist and producer of plays. Historian Paul Johnson wrote of him, "He became a power in the London theatre . . . in the 1960's he probably had more influence than anyone else in world theatre . . . No one in Britain played a bigger role in destroying the old system of censorship."[512] His main achievements were introducing four-letter words and nudity into British theater and on television. Tynan was certainly true to his motto, "Write heresy, pure heresy."

In less than fifty years, this cultural agitation in favor of homosexual rights and a more permissive society has brought the United Kingdom to what Jibran Khan described as the "War on Religion in Great Britain." Khan wrote:

> Secularism is being imposed on religious schools in England . . . The Office of Standards in Education . . . waged a war against religious schools of all denominations . . . in the name of "British values" . . . faith schools must promote homosexual relationships . . . a private Jewish institution . . . failed a third . . . inspection in a row . . . The school did not teach pupils about gender reassignment . . . this restricted their cultural development . . . rendering them unfit for present day society.[513]

Amanda Spielman, who was the chief regulator of British schools, said in defense of this policy, "It is right that we use compulsory education to make sure children acquire a deep understanding of and respect for the

---

512 Johnson, 326-27.
513 Jibran Khan, "Amanda Spielman's War on Religion in Great Britain," National Review online, January 28, 2019. https://www.nationalreview.com/2019/01/amanda-spielman-religious-schools-england-secularism.

British values even if they are in tension with parental wishes or community norms."[514] In other words, Spielman said that secular-humanists in positions of political power know what is best for other people's children, including even children in private, religious schools paid for by their parents. Liberals and secular humanists make a big deal out of the importance of multiculturalism and tolerance, but it seems that when they achieve power in government, they soon develop moral amnesia. They believe they have a right to raise all children according to their values.

It would be impossible to trace all the thoughts and actions of the millions of individual people who have contributed to the decline and fall of Judeo-Christian culture in America. What the life of any person or any civilization comes down to are the values they live by and the parenting which instills those values. If we were to choose two lives that illustrate the essential failure of following secularism and neo-paganism, it would be in the lives of the perpetrators of the Columbine massacre. The writer Wendy Murray Zoba summed it up well when she wrote in *Christianity Today*, "Eric and Dylan told us why they did what they did . . . They were acting on the laws they had been taught by their culture. There is no God. You are your own god. There is no eternal law. You make your own law. The material world is all there is . . . Something has gone terribly wrong in this culture . . . there were big spiritual questions raised at Columbine and they will not go away.[515]

The statements below by Eric Harris and Dylan Klebold are only a less intellectual expression of Friedrich Nietzsche's philosophy. They wanted to be their version of supermen, transcending the average standard of morality and, like Nietzsche, going "beyond good and evil." They were beyond good, but they became the essence of evil. Like Nietzsche, they expressed a profound hatred of Judeo-Christianity.

---

514   Ibid.
515   Wendy Murray Zoba, "'Do You Believe in God?," ChristianityToday online, October 4, 1999, https://www.christianitytoday.com/ct/1999/october4/columbine-shooting-do-you-believe-in-god.html.

Eric Harris wrote on his website, "Jesus is dead . . . the Bible is just a freaking book . . . God is egotistical."[516] Like Nietzsche, he questioned, "Why should morals apply to everyone? Who cares what you think?" Klebold agreed, stating, "We're going to have followers because we're so . . . god like."[517]

For Harris and Klebold, the sacredness of human life did not exist. Human beings were soulless. Without the belief in the sacredness of human life, Harris invented his creed: "My belief is that if I say something, it goes. I am the law,[sic] if you don't like it, you die . . . If I don't like . . . what you want me to do, you die."[518]

An analysis of the mass shootings which have taken place in the last few years revealed "the non-religious make up 22.8 percent (now higher) of our population and committed 83 percent of the crimes . . . someone with no religion in this country is 60 times more likely to be a mass shooter than a corresponding Christian . . . Christian influence clearly . . . reduces the chance of someone becoming a mass shooter."[519]

Without a new spiritual Great Awakening based upon the values of Judeo-Christianity, American society will continue to sink further into a pit of self-destruction.

---

516 Ibid.
517 Ibid.
518 Ibid.
519 "Mass Shootings and Religion: A Hard Look at the Numbers," National Gun Network, Accessed May 30, 2018, https://www.nationalgunnetwork.com/mass-shootings-and-religion-a-hard-look-at-the-numbers.

CONCLUSION

CANDLES IN THE DARKNESS

HAVING CONCLUDED THAT AMERICA'S CULTURE is no longer predominantly Judeo-Christian, the question becomes, what can we do about it?

The current sociological trends indicate increasing secularization and neo-paganism. Most likely, some strange hybrid of the two will eventually hold sway for a considerable period of time. The vast majority of Americans and the rest of the world will continue to believe in something. The question is what will they believe, and what affect will those beliefs have upon the earth? Scientific knowledge is helpful for both the planning and development of a future life, but as this book has proven, it is inadequate for supplying meaning and purpose to that life.

The long history of the world shows human nature to be problematic. Crime, inter-personal conflict, and war are universal and constant. Presently, there are more than forty conflicts taking place in the world.[520] "Live and let live" sounds nice but in reality, without a high level of morality supported by religious inspiration, it is merely a pleasant thought. Human nature is characterized by being restless and rarely satisfied. People desire an answer to the riddle of human existence. Most of the world's people will not "live by bread alone"; they will require an answer in a philosophy, a religion, or a cult. Simply imagining a better world like John Lennon, will not get us there.

---

520 Mark Prigg, "US Military Reveals $65m Funding for 'Matrix' Projects to Plug Human Brains Directly Into a Computer," Daily Mail Online, July 10, 2017, https://www.dailymail.co.uk/sciencetech/article-4683264/US-military-reveals-funding-Matrix-projects.html.

Islam is the fastest growing religion in the world with 1.8 billion followers.[521] Islam cannot lead the world to peace and unity. It was a religion born out of conflict. Its self-styled prophet relied on the arts of war to bring it into existence and spread it by military conquest. Harvard political science professor Samuel Huntington wrote in 1993, "In Eurasia the great . . . fault lines between civilizations are once more aflame. This is particularly true along the boundaries of the . . . Islamic bloc of nations from the bulge of Africa and central Asia."[522] By 2016, the problem was even worse. *World Watch Monitor* reported, "Most wars across the world are taking place in majority-Muslim countries, with Muslims mainly fighting each other."[523]

The division between the Sunni and Shia Muslim sects is fueling conflicts across the Middle East and in Africa. In the twenty-first century, more Muslims have been killed by other Muslims than in any war with outsiders.[524] No religion that justifies using force to maintain or spread its beliefs can bring peace to the world. Such a belief system can only be a source of universal conflict and human suffering. In the history of the world, Muslims themselves have suffered the most under the effects of their faith system. Not just Muslim women but any Muslim who desires to think freely or practice religious freedom is in jeopardy of punishment or death for the crime of apostasy (i.e. choosing not to be a Muslim).

Pew Research found "laws restricting apostasy and blasphemy are most common in the Middle East and North Africa, where 18 of the region's 20 counties (90%) criminalize blasphemy and . . . (70%) criminalize apostasy . . . By far the most countries with anti-apostasy measures were in the Middle East-North

---

521   Michael Lipka and Conrad Hackett, "Why Muslims Are the World's Fastest-Growing Religious Group," Pew Research Center, April 6, 2017, https://www.pewresearch.org/fact-tank/2017/04/06/why-muslims-are-the-worlds-fastest-growing-religious-group.

522   Samuel P. Huntington, "The Clash of Civilizations?," Foreign Affairs, Summer 1993, https://www.foreignaffairs.com/articles/united-states/1993-06-01/clash-civilizations.

523   Nils Petter Gleditsch and Ida Rudolfsen, "Are Muslim Countries More Violent?," The Washington Post online, May 16, 2016, https://www.washingtonpost.com/news/monkey-cage/wp/2016/05/16/are-muslim-countries-more-violent.

524   Ibid.

Africa region (14-20)."[525] Of course, moderate, non-terrorist Muslims have also been the principal victims of Islamic extremists. Those moderate Muslims are often people who live in the West (Europe or America) and have accepted Western civilization's values of religious tolerance and religious freedom.

The Quran is a book with many wise and true statements in it. Those who have read it know it contains not only Mohammed's thoughts based upon his self-described visions but also many Jewish and Christian writings. The problem with Islam is the mythology that Mohammed created based on his supposed visions. Islam contains both pagan and non-pagan elements. Its view of Heaven is more mundane than spiritual, more like a Viking view than a Christian view. It describes a male-centric paradise consisting of physical pleasures like food, sex, and other sensual delights, but women's happiness is an after-thought.

Islamic extremism is not in decline as the recent fall of Afghanistan to the Taliban shows. Islam is particularly dangerous because it mimics Judeo-Christian teaching and leads people to believe that there are no significant differences between it and Judeo-Christianity. While most people living in Western civilization are becoming more secular or indifferent about religious issues, radical Islam is spreading in Africa, the Middle East, and Central and Southeast Asia.[526] Over time, more and more innocent lives will be brought under radical Islam's ruthless control.

This threat to the peace and freedom of the world is matched or even exceeded by the growing power of Communist China. The present world is caught between the vise grip of expanding radical Islam and Communist China. Approximately 3.3 billion of the earth's people are living under Islamic or Communist rule. A survey of those countries where it is most dangerous to express the Gospel of Jesus Christ finds the same dual-threat. Open Doors,

525   Virginia Villa, "Four-in-Ten Countries and Territories Worldwide Had Blasphemy Laws in 2019," Pew Research Center, Accessed January 25, 2022, https://www.pewresearch.org/fact-tank/2022/01/25/four-in-ten-countries-and-territories-worldwide-had-blasphemy-laws-in-2019-2.
526   Lipka, ibid.

which monitors the worldwide persecution of Christians, found, "Islamic extremism remains the global, dominant driver of persecution, responsible for initiating oppression and conflict in 35 of the 50 countries on the list."[527]

Communist North Korea had held the number one spot for the persecution of Christians for twenty years but now shares that place with Afghanistan. Communist Vietnam is number eighteen, and Communist China is number forty-three on that same list.[528] Modern liberals who preach tolerance and often criticize Christians for being judgmental would be shocked to find Buddhist Myanmar, Hindu India, and Sri Lanka are on the same list (numbers twenty-four, twenty-five, and forty-four respectively).[529]

In 1964, President Lyndon Johnson spoke of the necessity of winning the "Hearts and Minds" of the people in Vietnam to resist the communist take-over of their country. The failures in Afghanistan and Vietnam prove that there are limits to what military power alone can accomplish. The Judeo-Christian view is expressed in Ephesians 6:12: "For we wrestle not against flesh and blood, but against powers, against the rulers of the darkness of this world, against spiritual wickedness in high places."

Many in our modern world scoff at the practice of evangelism and especially the efforts of sending missionaries to foreign lands, but only by promoting the saving power of God's Word can the world's hearts and minds be changed. The good news is that this is taking place now. The New Testament Bible makes clear "there is no respect of persons with God" (Rom. 2:11).

The unstoppable and eternal truth is that Jesus Christ is the Lord and Savior of the world; He is "the way, the truth, and the life" (John 14:6). What He said about human nature will always be true. What He said about escaping the problem of sin will always be true. Jesus Christ provides the world the only

527   Lindy Lowry, "'We need to pay attention'—Islamic extremists kill 100+ Congolese in 15 days," Open Doors USA, January 26, 2021, https://cdn.opendoors.ph/en/2021/01/29798.
528   "The 50 Countries Where It's Most Dangerous to Follow Jesus in 2021," Christianity Today online, January 13, 2021, https://www.christianitytoday.com/news/2021/january/christian-persecution-2021-countries-open-doors-watch-list.html.
529   Ibid.

durable solution to life's problems, the only lasting escape from restless striving and continual conflict. Jesus told the world thousands of years ago, "For unto whomever much is given, of him shall be much required" (Luke 12:48).

No country in world history has had more natural, cultural, or political advantages than the United States of America. What has happened in America over the last sixty years also took place thousands of years ago to the nation of Israel. The ancient Jewish prophets spent most of their time decrying Israel's apostasy and warning them of future punishment. In A.D. 70, the Romans conquered the Jewish state and turned the Jewish people into slaves or vagabonds. The apostle Paul used their example to warn the early Christians. He wrote in Romans 11:21, "For if God spared not the natural branches, take heed lest He also spare not thee."

The victory of Jesus Christ in the world is not the victory of any race, culture, or nation. The victory of Jesus Christ is a victory that can only be measured by changing hearts and minds, by increasing good and diminishing evil. There is no such thing as a Christian nation. There are only nations that have been more or less influenced by Judeo-Christian teaching. Over the last fifteen hundred years, those nations or cultures most affected by Judeo-Christianity are those located in what is called Western civilization.

Present evidence does not show the decline and fall of Christianity but only its decline in the West. Globally, Christianity is very much alive and well. What the most up-to-date statistics on religious growth show is a reversal of the earlier historical pattern; those areas of the world where Christianity is having phenomenal growth now are the same areas in the past that were the most resistant to that growth—Africa, Asia, Oceania, and Latin America. *The Washington Post* took note of this change in an article published in 2015 entitled "Think Christianity Is Dying? No, Christianity Is Shifting Dramatically."[530]

---

530 Wes Granberg-Michaelson, "Think Christianity Is Dying? No, Christianity Is Shifting Dramatically," The Washington Post online, May 20, 2015, https://www.washingtonpost. com/news/acts-of-faith/wp/2015/05/20/think-christianity-is-dying-no-christianity-is-shifting-dramatically.

According to 2021 Pew Research, there are 516 million Christians in Sub-Saharan Africa and 285 million in the Asia-Pacific region. There are more practicing Christians in Africa and Asia than in the United States and Europe. Pew Research projects that by 2050, there will be 1.1 billion Christians in Africa, which will be thirty-eight percent of the world's Christian population. On the African continent alone, it has been estimated that over 2.1 million followers of Islam have converted to Christianity.[531]

Another candle in the darkness is the fact that Communist China, is the country where Christianity is growing the fastest. More Christians are worshipping in China on any given Sunday than in Europe.[532] This growth is taking place despite ongoing persecution by the communist government. In 2018, research by Gordon Theological Seminary showed that the second most Christian people in the world live in Latin America (601 million).[533] By 2050, Christianity will remain the majority religion on five of the world's seven continents.[534]

One of the greatest proofs of the vitality and truth of the Christian message is its continuous growth in hostile environments. This characteristic of Christianity has been with it from the beginning. When Christianity began its first remarkable explosive growth during the Roman Empire, it was but a few believers in an enormous pagan world. Jesus Christ prophesied this tremendous growth in his Parable of the Muster Seed. In Matthew 13:31-32, He said, "The kingdom of heaven is like to a grain of mustard seed . . . Which indeed is least of all seeds but when it is grown, it is the greatest among

531 "The Future of World Religions: Population Growth Projections, 2010-2050," Pew Research Center, Accessed April 28, 2022, https://www.pewresearch.org/religion/2015/04/02/religious-projections-2010-2050.
532 Michael J. O'Loughlin, "'More Chinese at Church on a Sunday Than in the Whole of Europe,'" America Magazine online, September 14, 2011, https://www.americamagazine.org/content/all-things/more-chinese-church-sunday-whole-europe-0.
533 Dr. Gina A. Zurlo, "Who Owns Global Christianity?," Gordon Conwell Theological Seminary, September 27, 2019, https://www.gordonconwell.edu/blog/who-owns-global-christianity.
534 "The Future of World Religions," ibid. https://www.pewresearch.org/religion/2015/04/02/religious-projections-2010-2050.

herbs, and becometh a tree, so that the birds of the air come and lodge in the branches thereof."

Today's Christians in China, North Korea, India, and the Islamic world suffer constant harassment and death. The laws of the state are against them. Popular opinion is against them. Custom and tradition are against them, but they have sincere and passionate love and faith in Jesus Christ. If humanity ever needed proof that faith and love are the most tremendous motivating forces in this world, they have it in the survival and growth of Christianity in both the ancient and modern world. The survival and re-establishment of the Jewish state is another example of the same.

Jesus' message of love and faith is out of the bottle and cannot be put back. Christianity will not come to an end until the problem of human sin comes to an end. The challenging but hopeful message for America and Europe is, as moral disobedience and faithlessness increases, human suffering will also increase and with it, the human desire to escape that suffering. Pagan values and secular-humanistic philosophy will only increase the speed and spread of that suffering. When the modern world finally hits bottom, Jesus and His hopeful message will be there to offer a helping hand up. It is hard to imagine a world culture more sexually depraved than ancient Rome's, but during that most decadent stage of history, Christianity grew at its fastest pace.

Another sign to give hope but that will confound modern liberals is the fact that it is in the most conservative Christian churches where the greatest growth is taking place.[535] Those churches that think they must compromise or accommodate themselves with modern culture to grow are mistaken. The inspiration of Christianity lies in the powerful certainty of Christ's basic teachings. Those churches which have tried to be all things to all people and have watered down the Gospel message turning it into a purely "Social Gospel" are the same churches that are now dying.

---

535 Aaron Earls, "7 Surprising Trends in Global Christianity in 2019," Lifeway Research, June 11, 2019, https://research.lifeway.com/2019/06/11/7-surprising-trends-in-global-christianity-in-2019.

In the end, the survival and success of Christianity can only be judged by the life and teaching of one man—Jesus Christ. Those who would see Christianity defeated can only do so by removing faith in the life of that one man who claimed to be "the way, the truth and the life" (John 14:6). There is no evidence that when Jesus' life and teachings have been accurately presented to the world that it has produced anything less than wonder, admiration, and love. This fact is what Jesus was referring to when, in John 12:32, He said, "If I be lifted up from the earth, will draw all men unto me."

Jesus knew that not everyone would accept Him as the Son of God or become a Christian. His statement was about the enduring power of His example of perfect love. He was stating His lasting legacy to the entire world. His perfect life and love would always have the ability to captivate and motivate imperfect human beings to emulate his example. Christ can only be judged by his life and teachings, and individual Christians can only be judged by how well they follow his example.

Jesus never claimed that most of the world's inhabitants would follow His example. In fact, He said the opposite in Matthew 7:13-14: "Enter ye in at the strait gate: for wide is the gate, and broad is the way, that leadeth to destruction . . . Strait is the gate, and narrow is the way which leadeth unto life, and few there be that find it."

The final good news is that God "will have all men to be saved, and to come unto the knowledge of the truth" (1 Tim. 2:4). A necessary part of that good news is we are all free to choose. True Christianity is the most accessible of all religions. The only barrier to faith in Jesus Christ is a person's unwillingness to believe. Christianity has a long record of success. Over thousands of years, billions of people have found the answers to life's problems in its teaching. They have seen in the person of Jesus Christ a faithful Friend. The ultimate proof that Christianity is true is the joy and peace that it brings to the life of every believer who accepts it. Christian faith is not built on the end of the world or the continuation of the world. It is built on the present joy and peace that Christians experience each day by knowing and loving Jesus. Christians have placed their future in the strong hands of an eternal, loving God.

The final words on this topic must come from an ancient Christian named John. He was punished for his faith by being exiled to live a lonely life on an island called Patmos. "And let him that is athirst come. And whoever will, let him take the water of life freely . . . The grace of our Lord Jesus Christ be with you all. Amen" (Rev. 22:17-21).

BIBLIOGRAPHY

"10 Most Anti-Christian Movies of All Time." Vulture online. December 7, 2007. https://www.vulture.com/2007/12/list_antireligious_movies.html.

"2010 Overview." United States Census Bureau. 2010, https://www.census.gov/history/www/through_the_decades/overview/2010_overview_1.html.

"50 Countries Where It's Most Dangerous to Follow Jesus in 2021, The." Christianity Today online. January 13, 2021. https://www.christianitytoday.com/news/2021/january/christian-persecution-2021-countries-open-doors-watch-list.html.

"50 Most Influential Living Philosophers." TheBestSchools.org. August 12, 2022. https://thebestschools.org/magazine/most-influential-living-philosophers.

Abbott, Geoffrey. *Encyclopedia Britannica*. s.v. "Flagellation." Accessed October 18, 2022. https://www.britannica.com/topic/flagellation.

Abel, Reuben. *Man is the Measure (Cordial Invitation to the Central Problems of Philosophy*. New York: The Free Press, 1976.

Abramowitz, Michael J. "Democracy in Crisis." Freedom House.org. 2018. https://freedomhouse.org/report/freedom-world/2018/democracy-crisis.

Acton, Harry Barows. *Encyclopedia Britannica*. s.v. "Herbert Spencer." Accessed October 27, 2022. https://www.britannica.com/biography/Herbert-Spencer.

Akpeli, Andrew Othuke. "Alfred Rosenberg's 30-Point Church Plan for the National Reich Church." Dutable. March 29, 2019. https://dutable.com/2012/03/16/alfred-rosenbergs-30-point-church-plan.

Allen, Steve. "Montesquieu in England: his 'Notes on England,' with Commentary and Translation Commentary." 2017. Oxford University Comparative Law Forum. https://ouclf.law.ox.ac.uk/montesquieu-in-england-his-notes-on-england-with-commentary-and-translation-commentary.

Allison, Simon. "Conflict is still Africa's biggest challenge." Reliefweb.int. January 6, 2020. https://reliefweb.int/report/world/conflict-still-africa-s-biggest-challenge-2020.

Alper, Becka A. and Alan Cooperman. "10 Key Findings about Jewish Americans." Pew Research Center. May 11, 2021. https://www.pewresearch.org/fact-tank/2021/05/11/10-key-findings-about-jewish-americans.

Augustine—Letter 93 to Vincentius (*Cogite Intrare*)." Early Church Texts. Accessed October 20, 2022. https://www.earlychurchtexts.com/main/augustine/letter_93_to_vincentius_cogite_intrare.shtml.

Bagchi, Suvojit. "Christian, Muslim Households Top in Donation for Charity." THG publishing PVT, Ltd. July 15, 2017. https://www.thehindu.com/news/national/christian-muslim-households-top-in-donations-for-charity/article19285920.ece.

Ballie, R. "Study Shows a Significant Increase in Sexual Content on TV." *American Psychological Association* 32. No. 5. May 2001. https://www.apa.org/monitor/may01/sexualtv.

Bancroft, George. "The Office of the People in Art, Government, and Religion." In *American Values in Transition; A Reader.* Harcourt Brace Jovanovich, 1972.

Bannister, Robert C. and Anthony Comstock. "Free Love Traps." In *American Values in Transition; a Reader.* New York: Harcourt Brace Jovanovich, 1972.

"Bathhouse War, The." The Washington Post online. April 19, 1984. https://www.washingtonpost.com/archive/lifestyle/1984/04/19/the-bathhouse-war/5c864455-2310-4f9e-ac70-e0f57083a511.

Bautista, René and Michael Davern. "General Social Survey (GSS)." Chicago: NORC at the University of Chicago. Accessed October 30, 2022. https://www.norc.org/Research/Projects/Pages/general-social-survey.aspx.

Bayle, Pierre. *Historical and Critical Dictionary.* s.v. "Adam." Indianapolis: Hackett Publishing, 1991.

Benson, Jay, Matthew Frank, et al. "Annual Risk of Coup Report-2019. Vienna: One Earth Future 2019. https://oneearthfuture.org/publication/annual-risk-coup-report-2019.

Beobachter, Volkischer. "Myth of the Twentieth Century." *Nazi Paper.* Ed. Alfred Rosenberg. Berlin: 1930.

Berlin, Isaiah. "Two Concepts of Liberty." In *Freedom: Its History, Nature , and Varieties.* By James A. Gould and Robert E. Dewey. London: MacMillian,1970.

"Bill Gates, in Communist newspaper, urges more in China to help poor." Reuters.com. April 28, 2014. https://www.reuters.com/article/us-china-philanthropy-gates/bill-gates-in-communist-newspaper-urges-more-in-china-to-help-poor-idUKKBN0DE0QY20140428.

Bleakley, Amy. "Trends of Sexual and Violent Content by Gender in Top-Grossing U.S. Films, 1950-2006." *The Journal of Adolescent Health* 51. No. 1. July 2021: 73-9. https://pubmed.ncbi.nlm.nih.gov/22727080.

Blount, Charles. "Miracles No Violations of the Laws of Nature." In *A Short History of Free Thought*. New York: Russell & Russell. 1957.

Blount, Charles. *Anima Mundi: A Short History of Free Thought*. Vol. 2. Ed. J.M. Robertson. New York: Russell & Russell, 1957.

Blumenfeld, Yorick. "Tribalism and Nationalism in Africa." *CQ Researcher* online. November 2, 1960. https://library.cqpress.com/cqresearcher/document.php?id=cqresrre1960110208.

Bonaparte, Napoleon and J.C. Herold. *The Mind of Napoleon*. New York: Columbia University Press.

Bonin, Tyler. "Red October Happened 100 Years Ago, but Soviet Ideology Lives On." The Federalist. October 26, 2017. https://thefederalist.com/2017/10/26/red-october-happened-100-years-ago-but-soviet-ideology-lives.

Bons, Eberhard. "Marriage and Family in Flavius Josephus's Contra Apionem (II, § 199–206) Against Its Hellenistic Background." In *Family and Kinship in the Deuterocanonical and Cognate Literature*. By De Gruyter. Accessed December 12, 2013. https://www.degruyter.com/document/doi/10.1515/9783110310436.455/html.

Bormann, Martin. *Hitler's Table Talk*. Ed. Hugh Trevor-Roper. New York: Enigma Books, 2000.

Brown, Elizabeth Nolan. "What Americans Think About Prostitution Laws." Reason.com, February 6, 2020, https://reason.com/2020/02/06/what-americans-think-about-prostitution-laws.

Buckley, William Jr. *God and Man at Yale*. New York: Simon and Schuster, 1951.

Burnett, James. *The Origin and Progress of Languages*. New York: Andesite Press, 2017.

Burton, Tara Isabella. "The Rise of Progressive Occultism." The American Interest. August 12, 2019. https://www.the-american-interest.com/2019/06/07/the-rise-of-progressive-occultism.

Byers, Melissa. "The Father Absence Crisis in America [Infographic]." National Fatherhood Initiative. Accessed October 22, 2022. https://www.fatherhood.org/championing-fatherhood/the-father-absence-crisis-in-america.

"Camille Desmoulins." Wikipedia Foundation. Last modified October 22, 2022. https://en.wikipedia.org/wiki/Camille_Desmoulins.

"Catholic Bishops in Nazi Germany." Wikipedia Foundation. Last edited July 18, 2022. https://en.wikipedia.org/wiki/Catholic_bishops_in_Nazi_Germany.

"Catholic Church and Nazi Germany." Wikipedia Foundation. Last edited September 11, 2022. https://en.wikipedia.org/wiki/Catholic_Church_and_Nazi_Germany.

Cavendish, Richard. *The Powers of Evil.* New York: Dorset Press, 1993.

Chamfort, Nicholas. "Be My Brother . . . " Quotefancy.com. Accessed June 16, 2023. https://quotefancy.com/quote/1128581/Nicolas-Chamfort-Be-my-brother-or-I-will-kill-you.

"Chapter 2: Culture Counts: The Influence of Culture and Society on Mental Health." In *Mental Health: Culture, Race, and Ethnicity: A Supplement to Mental Health: A Report of the Surgeon General*. Rockville: Substance Abuse and Mental Health Services Administration, 2001. https://www.ncbi.nlm.nih.gov/books/NBK44249.

Charities Aid Foundation. "CAF World Giving Index, 2021." London: CAF Publications, 2021. https://www.cafonline.org/docs/default-source/about-us-research/cafworldgivingindex2021_report_web2_100621.pdf.

Cheatham, Amelia and Diana Roy. "Central America's Turbulent Northern Triangle." Council on Foreign Relations. June 22, 2022. https://www.cfr.org/backgrounder/central-americas-turbulent-northern-triangle.

"Child Prostitution and Pedophiles in Thailand." Facts and Details. Accessed October 22, 2022. https://factsanddetails.com/southeast-asia/Thailand/sub5_8d/entry-3247.html.

Christie, William. "Child Sacrifice in North America, With a Note on Suttee." *The Journal de la société des américanistes* 23. No. 1. Société des Américanistes, 1931. https://www.jstor.org/stable/24601335.

Collins, Rebecca L., Marc N. Elliott, et al. "Does Watching Sex on Television Influence Teens' Sexual Activity?," RAND Corporation, January 1, 2004, https://www.rand.org/pubs/research_briefs/RB9068.html.

"Cordeliers." Wikipedia Foundation. Last modified July 8, 2022. https://en.wikipedia.org/wiki/Cordeliers.

Coulacoglou, Carina and Donald H. Saflofske. "Advances in Theoretical, Developmental, and Cross-Culture Perspectives of Psychopathology." *Psychometrics and Psychological Assessment*. Cambridge: Academic Press, 2018.

Cranney, Stephen and Aleksander Stulhofer. "'Whosoever Looketh on a Person to Lust After Them': Religiosity, the Use of Mainstream and Nonmainstream Sexually Explicit Material, and Sexual Satisfaction in Heterosexual Men and Women." *Journal of Sex* 54. No. 6. 694–705, https://doi.org/10.1080/00224499.2016.1216068.

Dailey, Timothy J. "Comparing the Lifestyles of Homosexual Couples to Married Couples." United Productions. Accessed January 1, 2023. https://unite-production.s3.amazonaws.com/tenants/mtcalvaryhuron/attachments/75957/Comparing_the_Lifestyles_of_Homosexual_Couples_to_Married_Couples.pdf.

Dailey, Timothy J. "Homesexual Parenting: Placing Children at Risk." Family Research Council. 2007. https://ac21doj.org/contents/homosexuality/homosexualParentingPlacingChildrenAtRisk-Part2.html.

Danzi, Patricia. "ICRC Action in Africa - Interview of Patricia Danzi." International Committee of the Red Cross. July 11, 2018. YouTube video. 2:49. https://www.youtube.com/watch?v=JKWj0_LUFdE&t=1s.

Davis, Patricia. "100,000,000 The race to save children behind the staggering number." Missing Kids.org. December 1, 2021. https://www.missingkids.org/blog/2021/100,000,000-the-race-to-save-children-behind-the-staggering-number.

De Condorcet, Marquis. "Outlines of an historical view of the progress of the human mind." *Sketch for a Historical Picture of the Progress of the Human Mind.* 1795.   https://oll.libertyfund.org/title/condorcet-outlines-of-an-historical-view-of-the-progress-of-the-human-mind.

"Dechristianization during the Reign of Terror (1793-1794)." Musee Protestant online. Accessed January 2, 2015. https://museeprotestant.org/en/notice/dechristianisation-during-the-reign-of-terror-1793-1794.

Dein, Simon. "Religion, Spirituality, and Mental Health." Psychiatric Times online. January 10, 2010. https://www.psychiatrictimes.com/view/religion-spirituality-and-mental-health.

Delusional Disorder: Causes, Symptoms, Types & Treatment." Cleveland Clinic online. Accessed October 18, 2022. https://my.clevelandclinic.org/health/diseases/9599-delusional-disorder.

Dewey, Robert E., James A. Gould, and H.J. Pos. "Unesco Report on the Investigation Concerning Freedom." In *Freedom: Its History, Nature and Varieties.* London: Macmillan, 1970.

Dewey, Robert E., James A. Gould, and Lord Acton. "The History of Freedom in Ancient and Modern Europe." In *Freedom: Its History, Nature and Varieties.* London: Macmillan, 1970.

DeYoung, Mary. "The World According to NAMBLA: Accounting for Deviance." *Journal of Sociology & Social Welfare* 16. No. 1. (1989). https://scholarworks.wmich.edu/jssw/vol16/iss1/9.

Diamant, Jeff. "Half of U.S. Christians Say Casual Sex between Consenting Adults Is Sometimes or Always Acceptable." Pew Research Center. August 31, 2020. https://www.pewresearch.org/fact-tank/2020/08/31/half-of-u-s-christians-say-casual-sex-between-consenting-adults-is-sometimes-or-always-acceptable.

DiBenedetto, Katelyn. "Analyzing Tophets: Did the Phoenicians Practice Child Sacrifice?" Honors Thesis. University at Albany, 2012. https://scholarsarchive.library.albany.edu/honorscollege_anthro/5.

Diderot, Denis. *Eighteenth Century France: 1700-1789.* Ed. Paul Lacroix. New York: Ungar Publishing, 1963.

Disparities in Suicide." Centers for Disease Control and Prevention. Accessed October 22, 2022. https://www.cdc.gov/suicide/facts/disparities-in-suicide.html.

Dix, Dorothea. Wikimedia Foundation. Last modified December 5, 2022. https://en.wikipedia.org/wiki/Dorothea_Dix.

Domestic Violence and the LGBTQ Community." National Coalition Against Domestic Violence. June 6, 2018. https://ncadv.org/blog/posts/domestic-violence-and-the-lgbtq-community.

Doychinov, Nikolay. "The Global Health Observatory, HIV/AIDS." World Health Organization. 2022. https://www.who.int/data/gho/data/themes/hiv-aids.

Durant, Will and Ariel. *Age of Louis XIV*, The. Vol. 8. *The Story of Civilization*. New York: Simon and Schuster, 2011.

Durant, Will and Ariel. *Age of Napoleon, The*. Vol. 11. *The Story of Civilization*. New York: Simon & Schuster, 2011.

Durant, Will and Ariel. *Age of Voltaire*, The. Vol. 9. *The Story of Civilization*. New York: Simon and Schuster, 1975.

Durant, Will and Ariel. *Rousseau and Revolution*. Vol. 10. *The Story of Civilization*. New York: Simon & Schuster, 1972.

Durant, Will. *Age of Faith, The*. Vol. 4. *The Story of Civilization*. New York: Simon and Schuster, 1950.

Durant, Will. *Ancient World, The*. Vol. 1. *The Story of Civilization*. New York: Simon and Schuster, 1976.

Durant, Will. *Caesar and Christ*. Vol. 3. *The Story of Civilization*. New York: Simon & Schuster, 1972.

Durant, Will. *Life of Greece, The*. Vol. 2. *The Story of Civilization*. New York: Simon and Schuster, 1939.

Durant, Will. *Reformation, The*. Vol. 6. *The Story of Civilization*. New York: Simon and Schuster, 2011.

Durant, Will. *Renaissance, The*. Vol. 5. *The Story of Civilization*. New York: Simon and Schuster, 2011.

Dyson, R.W. *St. Thomas Aquinas: Political Writings*. Cambridge: Cambridge University Press, 2002.

Earls, Aaron. "7 Surprising Trends in Global Christianity in 2019." Lifeway Research. June 11, 2019. https://research.lifeway.com/2019/06/11/7-surprising-trends-in-global-christianity-in-2019.

Effects of Religious Practice on Crime Rates." Marripedia.com. Accessed July 1, 2023. https://www.marripedia.org/effects_of_religious_practice_on_crime_rates.

Encyclopedia Britannica. s.v. "Ernst Röhm." Accessed October 27, 2022. https://www.britannica.com/biography/Ernst-Rohm.

Encyclopedia Britannica. s.v. "Houston Stewart Chamberlain." Accessed October 27, 2022. https://www.britannica.com/biography/Houston-Stewart-Chamberlain.

Encyclopedia Britannica. s.v. "Jean-Baptiste Carrier: French Revolutionary." Accessed December 12, 2022. https://www.britannica.com/biography/Jean-Baptiste-Carrier.

Encyclopedia Britannica. s.v. "Totemism." Accessed October 18, 2022. https://www.britannica.com/topic/totemism-religion.

Epiphenom. "Psychologists Are the Least Religious of American Professors." Patheos.com. May 30, 2009. https://www.patheos.com/blogs/epiphenom/2009/05/psychologists-are-least-religious-of.html.

Erman, Adolf. *Life in Ancient Egypt.* New York: Dover Publications, 1971.

Ettinger, Zoe. "After a Historic Vote, Vladimir Putin Could Remain in Power in Russia Until 2036. Here Are 15 of the World's Longest Serving Leaders." BusinessInsider online. July 2, 2020. https://africa.businessinsider.com/strategy/after-a-historic-vote-vladimir-putin-could-remain-in-power-in-russia-until-2036-here/122yjbz.amp.

Evans, Jonathan and Chris Baronavski. "How Do European Countries Differ in Religious Commitment? Use Our Interactive Map to Find Out." Pew Research Center. December 5, 2018. https://www.pewresearch.org/fact-tank/2018/12/05/how-do-european-countries-differ-in-religious-commitment.

"Facts about Suicide." Centers for Disease Control and Prevention. Last revised October 24, 2022. https://www.cdc.gov/suicide/facts/index.html.

Famakinwa, J.O. "Is the Unexamined Life Worth Living or Not?" *Think* 11. No. 31. (2012): 97-103. https://doi.org/10.1017/S1477175612000073.

"Families Unmarried." Max-Planck-Gesellschaft online. April 21, 2016. https://www.mpg.de/10451277/unmarried-families.

Fearnow, Benjamin. "Number of Witches Rises Dramatically across U.S. As Millenials Reject Christianity." Newsweek online. March 25, 2020. https://www.newsweek.com/witchcraft-wiccans-mysticism-astrology-witches-millennials-pagans-religion-1221019.

Felix, Marcus Minucius. *A Source Book of Theological and Historical Passages, The Faith of the Early Fathers.* Vol. 1. Ed. William A. Jurgens. Collegeville: Liturgical Press, 1970.

Fellows, Otis E. and Norman L. Torrey. *Diderot Studies.* Whitefish: Kissinger Publications, 2010.

Felsenstein, Kenneth Michael. "Scarification harmful cultural practice or vehicle to higher being?" *Hektoen International Journal.* February 28, 2017. https://hekint.org/2017/01/27/scarification-harmful-cultural-practice-or-vehicle-to-higher-being.

Fischer, Claude S. "Spooked: Who still believes in ghosts?" Cal Alumni Association. October 31, 2013. https://alumni.berkeley.edu/california-magazine/online/spooked-who-still-believes-ghosts.

Fischer, Robert J. "Dictatorship of the Proletariat." ScienceDirect. 2019. https://www.sciencedirect.com/topics/social-sciences/dictatorship-of-the-proletariat.

Flood, Michael. "Pornography Has Deeply Troubling Effects on Young People, but There Are Ways We Can Minimise the Harm." The Conversation.com. January 5, 2020. https://theconversation.com/pornography-has-deeply-troubling-effects-on-young-people-but-there-are-ways-we-can-minimise-the-harm-127319.

"Foreword to the Second Edition of the Quotations of Chairman Mao, 1966." USC US China Institute. December 16, 1966. https://china.usc.edu/foreword-second-edition-quotations-chairman-mao-1966.

France, Lisa Respers. "Bella Thorne Says She's Actually Pansexual, Not Bisexual." Cable News Network. July 23, 2019. https://edition.cnn.com/2019/07/23/entertainment/bella-thorne-pansexual-trnd/index.html.

Frazer, James George. *The Golden Bough: A Study in Magic and Religion.* London: Penguin Books, 1996.

Freud, Sigmund. *Obsessive Actions and Religious Practices: The Freud Reader.* New York: W.W. Norton Company, 1995.

Freud, Sigmund. *Totem and Taboo.* New York: Dodd, Mead & Company, 1918.

Friedell, Egon. *Cultural History of the Modern Age.* New York: Alfred A. Knopf, 1954.

Funk & Wagnalls Standard Dictionary. s.v. "Materialism." New York: Harper Paperbacks, 1993.

"Future of World Religions: Population Growth Projections, 2010-2050, The." Pew Research Center. Accessed April 28, 2022. https://www.pewresearch.org/religion/2015/04/02/religious-projections-2010-2050.

Garcia-Navarro, Lulu. "All Across Latin America, Unwed Mothers Are Now the Norm." NPR online. December 14, 2015. https://www.npr.org/sections/parallels/2015/12/14/459098779/all-across-latin-america-unwed-mothers-are-now-the-norm.

Geiger, A.W. "17 Striking Findings from 2017." Pew Research Center, December 26, 2017, https://www.pewresearch.org/fact-tank/2017/12/26/17-striking-findings-from-2017.

Gettleman, Jeffrey. "Africa's Forever Wars: Why the continent's conflicts never end." Foreign Policy online. February 11, 2010. https://foreignpolicy.com/2010/02/11/africas-forever-wars/

"Giving USA: Total U.S, charitable giving remained strong in 2021, reaching $484.85 billion." Lilly Family School of Philanthropy. June 21, 2022. https://philanthropy.iupui.edu/news-events/news-item/giving-usa:--total-u.s.-charitable-giving-remained-strong-in-2021,-reaching-$484.85-billion.html?id=392#:~:text=Giving%20USA%3A%20Total%20U.S.%20charitable,in%202021%2C%20reaching%20%24484.85%20billion&text=Giving%20USA%202022%3A%20The%20Annual,to%20U.S.%20charities%20in%202021.

Gleditsch, Nils Petter and Ida Rudolfsen. "Are Muslim Countries More Violent?" The Washington Post online. May 16, 2016. https://www.washingtonpost.com/news/monkey-cage/wp/2016/05/16/are-muslim-countries-more-violent.

Gliozzo, Charles A. "The Philosophes and Religion: Intellectual Origins of the Dechristianization Movement in the French Revolution." Cambridge University Press. July 28, 2009. https://www.cambridge.org/core/services/aop-cambridge-core/content/view/A73FA2FF076104420E0404F42E46BA63/S0009640700026603a.pdf/the-philosophes-and-religion-intellectual-origins-of-the-dechristianization-movement-in-the-french-revolution.pdf.

Global Estimates of Modern Slavery: Forced Labour and Forced Marriage." International Labour Organization. September 19, 2017. https://www.ilo.org/global/publications/books/WCMS_575479/lang--en/index.htm.

Global Slavery Index. Minderoo Foundation. Accessed June 29, 2023, https://www.walkfree.org/global-slavery-index.

Goebbels, Joseph. "Joseph Goebbels›Quotes." Goodreads.com. https://www.goodreads.com/author/quotes/281832.Joseph_Goebbels.

Goodrick-Clarke, Nicholas. Occult Roots of Nazism: Secret Aryan Cults and Their Influence on Nazi Ideology. New York: New York University Press, 1993.

Graham, Darin. "Only 19 countries are still full democracies, report suggests." Indy100.com. February 2, 2018. https://www.indy100.com/news/democracy-index-economist-intelligence-unit-map-data-report-norway-democratic-united-states-8191501.

Granberg-Michaelson, Wes. "Think Christianity Is Dying? No, Christianity Is Shifting Dramatically." The Washington Post online. May 20, 2015. https://www.washingtonpost.com/news/acts-of-faith/wp/2015/05/20/think-christianity-is-dying-no-christianity-is-shifting-dramatically.

Grandoni, Dino. "92% Of Top Ten Billboard Songs Are about Sex." Atlantic Media Company. September 30, 2011. https://www.theatlantic.com/culture/archive/2011/09/92-top-ten-billboard-songs-are-about-sex/337242.

"Great Purge." Wikipedia Foundation. Last updated January 12, 2023. https://en.wikipedia.org/wiki/Great_Purge.

"Great Terror." History.com. Updated October 4, 2022. https://www.history.com/topics/russia/great-purge.

Grimes, William. "George Weinberg Dies at 87; Coined 'Homophobia' after Seeing Fear of Gays." The New York Times online. March 22, 2017. https://www.nytimes.com/2017/03/22/us/george-weinberg-dead-coined-homophobia.html.

\Hagemeister, Michael and Birgit Menzel. *The New Age of Russia. Occult and Esoteric Dimensions.* Bern: Peter Lang International Academic Publishers, 2021. https://library.oapen.org/handle/20.500.12657/26681.

Hamid, Shadi. "America Without God." RealClearPolicy. March 11, 2021. https://www.realclearpolicy.com/2021/03/11/america_without_god_767624.html#.

Hamilton, Edith. *The Greek Way.* New York: Discus/Avon, 1973.

Hardwick, Nicola Ann. "Rousseau and the social contract tradition." E-International Relations. March 1, 2011. https://www.e-ir.info/pdf/7356.

Harner, Michael. "The Enigma of Aztec Sacrifice." *Natural History* 86. No. 4. April, 1977. https://www.latinamericanstudies.org/aztecs/sacrifice.htm.

Harsanyi, David. "Americans are more generous than Europeans—by a large margin." New York Post online. October 23, 2021. https://nypost.com/2021/10/23/americans-are-more-generous-than-europeans-by-a-large-margin.

Hedegaard, Holly, Sally Curtin, and Margaret Warner. "Suicide Mortality in the United States, 1999-2017." NCHS Data Brief. No. 330. Hyattsville: National Center for Health Statistics. 2018. https://www.cdc.gov/nchs/products/databriefs/db330.htm.

Hedlin, Simon. "Why Legalizing Prostitution May Not Work." Forbes online. October 17, 2016. https://www.forbes.com/sites/realspin/2016/10/17/why-legalizing-prostitution-may-not-work.

Heinse, Wilhelm. *Ardinghello.* In *History of German Literature.* Ed. Kuno Francke. New York: Henry Holt, 1910.

"Hel (The Underworld)." Daniel McCoy. https://norse-mythology.org/cosmology/the-nine-worlds/helheim.

Hellenistic Period." Wikipedia Foundation. Last edited October 24, 2022. https://en.wikipedia.org/wiki/Hellenistic_period.

Herman, Arthur. *How the Scots Invented the Modern World.* New York: Three Rivers Press, 2001.

Hesiod. *The Homeric Hymns and Homerica.* Vol. 57. Translated by Hugh G. Evelyn-White. London: William Heinermann, 1914.

Hesiod. *Theogony.* Trans. Martin L. West. Oxford: Clarendon Press, 1966.

History of Modern Paganism." BBC online. Last updated October 2, 2002. https://www.bbc.co.uk/religion/religions/paganism/history/modern_1.shtml.

Hobbes, Thomas. *Leviathan.* Vol. 8. London: Penguin Classics, 2017.

Home, the Most Dangerous Place for Women, with Majority of Female Homicide Victims Worldwide Killed by Partners or Family, UNODC Study Says." United Nations: Office on Drugs and Crime. Accessed October 27, 2022.   https://www.unodc.org/unodc/en/press/releases/2018/November/home--the-most-dangerous-place-for-women--with-majority-of-female-homicide-victims-worldwide-killed-by-partners-or-family--unodc-study-says.html.

Homer. "Book 24." In *The Iliad.* Trans. Barry B. Powell. New York: Oxford University Press, 2014.

How Much Has the Catholic Church Paid to Abuse Victims." Massey Law Firm. December 13, 2021. https://dmasseylaw.com/how-much-catholic-church-paid-abuse-victims.

Hsuan, Fu. "Woman Song." Third Century China. Public Domain.

Huntington, Samuel P. "The Clash of Civilizations?" Foreign Affairs. Summer 1993. https://www.foreignaffairs.com/articles/united-states/1993-06-01/clash-civilizations.

Hurlbut, Jesse Lyman. "Preface." In *The Story of the Christian Church.* Grand Rapids: Zondervan, 1970.

Importance of religion in one's life." Pew Research Center. June 13, 2022. https://www.pewresearch.org/religion/religious-landscape-study/importance-of-religion-in-ones-life.

Internet Encyclopedia of Philosophy, s.v. "Sigmund Freud," Accessed October 30, 2022, https://iep.utm.edu/freud.

Internet Encyclopedia of Philosophy. s.v. "Gnosticism." Accessed October 24, 2022. https://iep.utm.edu/gnostic.

Issues in Jewish Ethics: 'Kosher' Sex." Jewish Virtual Library. Accessed October 22, 2022. https://www.jewishvirtuallibrary.org/quot-kosher-quot-sex.

James, David. "Hegel and Marx on the Necessity of the Reign of Terror: Hegel Bulletin." *Hegel Bulletin* 41. No. 2. (October 26, 2017). https://www.cambridge.org/core/journals/hegel-bulletin/article/abs/hegel-and-marx-on-the-necessity-of-the-reign-of-terror/B1A4F597A9389D7846A37EB243694088.

Janda, Setareh. "The Darkest Moments of the French Revolutions." Ranker.com. June 17, 2020. https://www.ranker.com/list/french-revolution-bloodiest-moments/setareh-janda.

Jay, Karla. *The Gay Report: Lesbians and Gay Men Speak Out About Sexual Experiences and Lifestyles*. Mandaluyong: Summit Books, 1979.

Johnson, Paul. *A History of the American People*. New York: HarperCollins, 1997.

Johnston, R.M. *The Corsican, A Diary of Napoleon's Life In His Own Words*. Boston: Houghton Mifflin, 1910.

Jones, Jeffrey M. "U.S. LGBT Identification Steady at 7.2%." Gallup, Inc. February 22, 2023. https://news.gallup.com/poll/470708/lgbt-identification-steady.aspx.

"Joseph Stalin>Quotes." Goodreads. Accessed October 27, 2022. https://www.goodreads.com/author/quotes/138332.Joseph_Stalin.

"Judaism and Sexuality." My Jewish Learning. Accessed October 22, 2021. https://www.myjewishlearning.com/article/judaism-and-sexuality.

Juma, Calestous. "Viewpoint: How tribalism stunts African democracy." BBC.com. November 27, 2012. https://www.bbc.com/news/world-africa-20465752.

Jurgens, W.A. "Bishop Theophilus of Antioch, 'Letter to Autolycus.'" In *The Faith of the Early Fathers*. Vol. 1. Collegeville: Liturgical Press, 1970.

Kelland, Kate. "Nearly 40 per Cent of Europeans Suffer Mental Illness." Thomson Reuters. September 6, 2011. https://www.reuters.com/article/uk-europe-mental-illness-idUKTRE7832KL20110905.

Kesten, Dr. Joanna. "Drug Use in Street Sex Workers: The DUSSK Study." ARC West. Accessed January 11, 2021. https://arc-w.nihr.ac.uk/research/projects/reducing-drug-use-female-street-sex-workers-feasibility-study.

Khan, Jibran. "Amanda Spielman's War on Religion in Great Britain." National Review online. January 28, 2019. https://www.nationalreview.com/2019/01/amanda-spielman-religious-schools-england-secularism.

Khmer Rouge: Cambodia's Years of Brutality." BBC News online. November 16, 2018. https://www.bbc.com/news/world-asia-pacific-10684399.

Kibiswa, Naupess K. "Local Populations at Risk of Violence in the Democratic Republic of Congo," United States Holocaust Memorial Museum, July 19, 2021, https://www.ushmm.org/genocide-prevention/blog/local-populations-at-risk-of-violence-in-the-democratic-republic-of-congo.

Kilday, Gregg. "Hollywood Out of Step with American Morals: Poll." Reuters.com. November 17, 2008. https://www.reuters.com/article/us-poll-idUSTRE4AG0VK20081117.

Kolitz, Daniel. "Which Religion Is Friendliest to the Idea of Aliens?" Gizmodo. January 27, 2020. https://gizmodo.com/which-religion-is-friendliest-to-the-idea-of-aliens-1841241730.

Kort, Joe. "Monogamy: It's Not What You Think." Psychology Today online. 2018. https://www.psychologytoday.com/us/blog/understanding-the-erotic-code/201809/monogamy-it-s-not-what-you-think.

Koskenniemi, Erkki. "How did Judaism and early Church face contemporary sexual morality?" Translated by Elina Salminen. Lutheran Evangelical Association of Finland. Accessed October 22, 2022. https://www.bibletoolbox.net/en/bible/sexual-morality.

Kost, Ryan. "Bathhouse Ban Revoked: Amid One Pandemic, SF Confronts Legacy of Another." San Francisco Chronicle online. September 14, 2020. https://www.sfchronicle.com/bayarea/article/Bathhouse-ban-revoked-Amid-one-pandemic-San-15558609.php.

Koval, Peter, Elise Holland, and Michelle Stratemeyer. "Sexually Objectifying Women Leads Women to Objectify Themselves, and Harms Emotional Well-Being." The Conversation online. July 23, 2019. https://theconversation.com/sexually-objectifying-women-leads-women-to-objectify-themselves-and-harms-emotional-well-being-120762.

Kramer, Stephanie. "U.S. Has World's Highest Rate of Children Living in Single-Parent Households." Pew Research Center. May 28, 2021. https://www.pewresearch.org/fact-tank/2019/12/12/u-s-children-more-likely-than-children-in-other-countries-to-live-with-just-one-parent.

Krishnamurti, J. "Be a Light unto Yourself." Awakin.org. Accessed October 18, 2022. https://www.awakin.org/v2/read/view.php?tid=183.

Lambert, Ken. "The Link Between Atheists, Agnostics and Mass Shooters." Catholic Business Journal online. 2018. https://www.catholicbusinessjournal.com/voices/contributors/ken-lambert/the-link-between-atheists-agnostics-and-mass-shooters.

Langer, Walter C. The Mind of Adolf Hitler: The Secret Wartime Report. New York: Basic Books, Inc, 1972.

Laski, Harold J. "The Changing Content of Freedom in History." In Freedom: Its History, Nature and Varieties. Eds. James A. Gould and Robert E. Dewey. London: Macmillan Company, 1970.

Le Franc, Jean Jacques. The Religion of Rousseau. Ed. Pierre-Maurice-Masson. NSW: Generic, 2018.

"League of Militant Atheists." Wikipedia Foundation. Last edited on January 10, 2023. https://en.wikipedia.org/wiki/League_of_Militant_Atheists.

Lipka, Michael and Conrad Hackett. "Why Muslims Are the World's Fastest-Growing Religious Group." Pew Research Center. April 6, 2017. https://www.pewresearch.org/fact-tank/2017/04/06/why-muslims-are-the-worlds-fastest-growing-religious-group.

"List of Apologies Made by Pope John Paul II." Wikipedia Foundation. Last modified June 26, 2022. https://en.wikipedia.org/wiki/List_of_apologies_made_by_Pope_John_Paul_II.

"List of Dramatic Television Series with LGBT Characters: 1960s-2000s." Wikipedia Foundation. Last edited December 25, 2022, https://en.wikipedia.org/wiki/List_of_dramatic_television_series_with_LGBT_characters:_1960s%E2%80%932000s.

Livingston, Gretchen. "The Changing Profile of Unmarried Parents." Pew Research Center. April 25, 2018. https://www.pewresearch.org/social-trends/2018/04/25/the-changing-profile-of-unmarried-parents.

Loader, William. "'Not as the Gentiles': Sexual Issues at the Interface between Judaism and Its Greco-Roman World." Multidisciplinary Digital Publishing Institute. August 28, 2018. https://www.mdpi.com/2077-1444/9/9/258.

Loconte, Joseph. "Martin Luther and the Long March to Freedom of Conscience." National Geographic online. October 27, 2017. https://www.nationalgeographic.com/history/article/martin-luther-freedom-protestant-reformation-500.

Lowry, Brian. "Sexual Content Becomes More Prevalent on TV, Study Finds." Los Angeles Times online. February 7, 2001. https://www.latimes.com/archives/la-xpm-2001-feb-07-ca-21942-story.html.

Lowry, Lindy. "'We need to pay attention'—Islamic extremists kill 100+ Congolese in 15 days." Open Doors USA. January 26, 2021. https://cdn.opendoors.ph/en/2021/01/29798.

"Lucretius." Quoteslyfe. Accessed October 26, 2022. https://www.quoteslyfe.com/quote/Fear-is-the-mother-of-all-gods-830238.

Ludwig, Emil. "Das Gottliche." In *Goethe: The History of a Man*, 1749-1832. New York: G.P. Putnam's Sons, 1928.

Luther, Martin. "On the Liberty of a Christian Man." In *Freedom: Its History, Nature and Varieties*. Eds. James A. Gould and Robert E. Dewey. London: Macmillan, 1970.

Ly, Laura. "Boy Scouts of America files for bankruptcy. Hundreds of sexual abuse lawsuits are now on hold." Cable News Network online. February 18, 2020. https://www.cnn.com/2020/02/18/us/boy-scouts-bankruptcy/index.html.

Machiavelli, Niccolò. Chapter XII. In *Discourses on the First Ten Books of Titus Livius*. Trans. Christian E. Detmold. 1882. https://www.marxists.org/reference/archive/machiavelli/works/discourses/index.htm.

Mackenzie, Donald A. *Crete & Pre-Hellenic*. London: Random House, 1996.

Malley, Robert. "15 Years of Tracking Conflict Worldwide." International Crisis Group. September 3, 2018. https://www.crisisgroup.org/content/15-years-tracking-conflict-worldwide.

Mann, Thomas. *Three Essays*. Trans. H.T. Lowe-Porter. New York: Alfred A. Knopf, 1929.

Marat, Jean-Paul. *Encyclopedia Britannica*. s.v. "Jean-Paul Marat." Accessed October 25, 2022. https://www.britannica.com/biography/Jean-Paul-Marat.

"Marat/Sade." Wikipedia Foundation. Last modified June 2, 2022. https://en.wikipedia.org/wiki/Marat/Sade.

Martin Luther Quotes." BrainyQuote online. Accessed November 16, 2022. https://www.brainyquote.com/authors/martin-luther-quotes.

Martin, Will. "The 28 Most Dangerous Countries in the World." Business Insider online. June 29, 2018. https://www.businessinsider.com/most-dangerous-countries-in-the-world-global-peace-index-2018-6.

Marx, Karl and Friedrich Engels. *The Communist Manifesto*. London: Workers Educational Association, 1848.

Marx, Karl. "A Contribution to the Critique of Hegel's Philosophy of Right." In *Works of Karl Marx*. https://www.marxists.org/archive/marx/works/1843/critique-hpr/intro.htm, 1843-44.

Marx, Karl. "The Victory of the Counter-Revolution in Vienna." In *Marx & Engels Collected Works*, Vol. 7. London: Lawrence & Wishart, 2010.

"Marxism and Religion." In Defense of Marxism. Accessed July 1, 2023. https://www.marxist.com/theory-marxism-and-religion.htm.

Maser, Werner. *Hitler: Legend, Myth & Reality*. New York: Harper & Row, 1971.

"Mass Shootings and Religion: A Hard Look at the Numbers." National Gun Network. Accessed May 30, 2018. https://www.nationalgunnetwork.com/mass-shootings-and-religion-a-hard-look-at-the-numbers.

Mayhall, C. Wayne. "Sigmund Freud and the Problem of Guilt." Accessed July 1, 2023. www.academia.edu/11346859/On_Sigmund_Freud_and_Guilt.

McDowell, Crystal. "7 Different Ways Jesus Showed Love." Telling Ministries, LLC. Accessed October 21, 2022. https://www.whatchristianswanttoknow.com/7-attributes-of-god-you-may-not-know.

McFarland, Willi, ed. "HIV/AIDS Programs & Research." Department of Public Health | HIV Epidemiology Section. Accessed October 24, 2022. https://www.sfdph.org/dph/files/reports/RptsHIVAIDS/HIVAIDSAtlas1981-2000.pdf.

Mcginnus, Barbara Callie. "African Tribalism." Penn State University. April 19, 2017. https://sites.psu.edu/global/2017/04/19/african-tribalism.

McLean, John. "History of Western Civilization II." ER Services. Accessed October 27, 2022. https://courses.lumenlearning.com/suny-hccc-worldhistory2/chapter/casualties-of-world-war-ii.

Mead, G.R.S. *Pistis Sophia.* London: The Theosophical Publishing Society, 1896.

Mental Health Disparities: Diverse Populations." Psychiatry.org. Accessed October 14, 2017. https://www.psychiatry.org/psychiatrists/cultural-competency/education/mental-health-facts.

Mercatante, Anothony S. *Good and Evil: Mythology and Folklore.* New York: Barnes & Noble. 1978.

Meslier, Jean. *My Testament.* Bellingham, WA: University Press of the Pacific, 2004.

Millet, Kate. "Theory of Sexual Politics." In *American Values in Transition: A Reader.* San Diego: Harcourt Brace Jovanovich, 1972.

Mills, Kim I. "Gay Groups Try to Put Distance Between Themselves and Pedophile Group." AP NEWS online. February 13, 1994. https://apnews.com/c64e816cac5b0fa1194dd40f576813b2.

Misachi, John. "Worst Countries for Human Trafficking Today." World Atlas online. January 17, 2019. https://www.worldatlas.com/articles/worst-countries-for-human-trafficking-today.html.

Modernism." Enotes.com. Accessed October 30, 2022. https://www.enotes.com/homework-help/what-themes-characteristics-modernism-743192.

Moleiro, Carla. "Culture and Psychopathology: New Perspectives on Research, Practice and Clinical Training in a Globalized World." *Frontiers in Psychiatry* 10. No. 9. (2018). https://www.frontiersin.org/articles/10.3389/fpsyt.2018.00366/full.

Montaigne, Michel. *Montaigne Essays: "On Custom."* Bristol: Penguin Classics, 1970.

Moreau, Julie. "'Overwhelming Number of Lesbians, Bisexual Women Incarcerated.'" NBCNews online. March 3, 2017. https://www.nbcnews.com/feature/nbc-out/overwhelming-number-lesbians-bisexual-women-incarcerated-n728666.

Morna, Colleen Lowe. "One Party Rule Dominates in Africa. FOR THE GOOD OF THE PEOPLE? Many Africans say traditions and development needs make pluralism a costly luxury." *The Christian Science Monitor online.* March 29, 1989. https://www.csmonitor.com/1989/0329/cone.html.

Muller, Herbert J. "Freedom and Justice in History." In *Freedom: Its History, Nature, and Varieties.* By James A. Gould and Robert E. Dewey. London: MacMillan, 1970.

Müller, Max. "Maitrâyana-Brâhmana-Upanishad: FIRST PRAPÂTHAKA." In *The Upanishads, Part 2,* 1879. https://www.sacred-texts.com/hin/sbe15/sbe15112.htm.

"National Intimate Partner and Sexual Violence Survey (NISVS), The." CDC. gov. Accessed June 30, 2023. https://www.cdc.gov/violenceprevention/datasources/nisvs/index.html.

"National Statistics." National Human Trafficking Hotline. Accessed October 22, 2022. https://humantraffickinghotline.org/en/statistics.

"Nazi Persecution of the Catholic Church in Germany." Wikipedia Foundation. August 26, 2022. https://en.wikipedia.org/wiki/Nazi_persecution_of_the_Catholic_Church_in_Germany.

Newport, Frank. "Continuing Change in U.S. Views on Sex and Marriage." Gallup online. June 18, 2021. https://news.gallup.com/opinion/polling-matters/351326/continuing-change-views-sex-marriage.aspx.

Nicolosi, Joseph. "An Open Secret: The Truth about Gay Male Couples." Reparative Therapy. April 26, 2017. https://www.josephnicolosi.com/collection/2015/5/28/an-open-secret-the-truth-about-gay-male-couples.

Niebuhr, Reinhold. *Moral Man and Immoral Society.* New York: Charles Scribner's sons, 1960.

Nietzsche, Friedrich. *The Joyful Wisdom.* Ed. Oscar Levy. Translated by Paul Cohn, Thomas Common, and Maude Petre. London: Project Gutenberg, 2016. https://www.gutenberg.org/ebooks/52124.

"Nihilism." Wikipedia Foundation. Accessed October 24, 2022. https://www.google.com/search?q=how+to+cite+wikipedia+in+chicago&rlz=1C1VDKB_enUS1011US1011&oq=how+to+cite+wikipe&aqs=chrome.1.0i512j0i20i263i512j69i57j0i512j0i20i263i512j0i512l5.4907j0j9&sourceid=chrome&ie=UTF-8.

"Number of Sex Scenes on TV Nearly Double Since 1998." Kaiser Family Foundation online. October 30, 2005. https://www.kff.org/other/event/sex-on-tv-4.

O'Brien, Barbara. "The First Buddhist Monks." Learn Religions. April 30, 2019. https://www.learnreligions.com/the-first-buddhist-monks-450082.

O'Brien, Barbara. "What Are the Four Noble Truths of Buddhism?" Learn Religions. April 23, 2019. https://www.learnreligions.com/the-four-noble-truths-450095.

O'Loughlin, Michael J. "'More Chinese at Church on a Sunday Than in the Whole of Europe.'" America Magazine online. September 14, 2011. https://www.americamagazine.org/content/all-things/more-chinese-church-sunday-whole-europe-0.

Official: More than 1M Child Prostitutes in India." CNN online. Accessed October 22, 2022. https://www.cnn.com/2009/WORLD/asiapcf/05/11/india.prostitution.children/index.html.

Oldfield, John. "Abolition of the slave trade and slavery in Britain." British Library online. February 4, 2021. https://www.bl.uk/restoration-18th-century-literature/articles/abolition-of-the-slave-trade-and-slavery-in-britain#:~:text=This%20occurred%20first%20through%20the,trade%20once%20and%20for%20all.

Paganism." Wikipedia Foundation. Last modified December 25, 2022. https://en.wikipedia.org/wiki/Paganism.

Palmer, Ron. "Fatherless Single Mother Home Statistics." Fix Family Courts. 2017. https://www.fixfamilycourts.com/single-mother-home-statistics.

"Paul Tillich." Wikipedia Foundation. Last updated June 15, 2023. https://en.wikipedia.org/wiki/Paul_Tillich.

Pavao, Paul. "Pliny the Younger: Letter to Trajan." *Christian History for Everyman*. Accessed January 4, 2023. https://www.christian-history.org/pliny-the-younger.html.

Perry, Mark J. "Quotation of the Day on Marxism . . . " American Enterprise Institute. Accessed October 27, 2022. https://www.aei.org/carpe-diem/quotation-of-the-day-on-marxism.

"Persecution of Christians in the Soviet Union." Wikipedia Foundation. Last edited on November 2, 2022. https://en.wikipedia.org/wiki/Persecution_of_Christians_in_the_Soviet_Union.

Petrarch, Francesco. "I desire that death . . . " QuoteFancy.com. https://quotefancy.com/quote/1365100/Petrarch-I-desire-that-death-find-me-ready-and-writing-or-if-it-please-Christ-praying-and.

Piedra, Alberto M. "The Dechristianization of France during the French Revolution." The Institute of World Politics. January 12, 2018. https://www.iwp.edu/articles/2018/01/12/the-dechristianization-of-france-during-during-the-french-revolution.

Prigg, Mark. "US Military Reveals $65m Funding for 'Matrix' Projects to Plug Human Brains Directly Into a Computer." Daily Mail Online. July 10, 2017. https://www.dailymail.co.uk/sciencetech/article-4683264/US-military-reveals-funding-Matrix-projects.html.

Pronechen, Joseph. "Archbishop Sheen's Warning of a Crisis in Christendom." National Catholic Register. Accessed October 30, 2022. https://www.ncregister.com/blog/archbishop-sheen-s-warning-of-a-crisis-in-christendom.

"Prostitution Is Legal in Countries across Europe, but It's Nothing like What You Think." Business Insider online. March 13, 2019. https://www.businessinsider.in/miscellaneous/prostitution-is-legal-in-countries-across-europe-but-its-nothing-like-what-you-think/slidelist/68397375.cms.

Psychological Analysis of Adolph Hitler His life and Legend-Psychological Analysis and Reconstruction, A." Jewish Virtual Library. Accessed October 27, 2022, https://www.jewishvirtuallibrary.org/a-psychological-analysis-of-adolph-hitler-his-life-and-legend-psychological-analysis-and-reconstruction.

PTI. "Handling of Human Trafficking Cases in India 'Disproportionately Low': US Report." Deccan Chronicle. June 29, 2018. https://www.deccanchronicle.com/world/america/290618/handling-of-human-trafficking-cases-in-india-disproportionately-low.html.

PTI. "Human Trafficking Takes 'Horrific Dimensions' in Europe: UN." The Hindu BusinessLine online. January 8, 2019. https://www.thehindubusinessline.com/news/variety/human-trafficking-takes-horrific-dimensions-in-europe-un/article25942442.ece.

Reardon, Sara. "Massive Study Finds No Single Genetic Cause of Same-Sex Sexual Behavior." Scientific American online. August 29, 2019. https://www.scientificamerican.com/article/massive-study-finds-no-single-genetic-cause-of-same-sex-sexual-behavior.

Rees, Christine and Neil Fauerso. "The Occult Is So Hot Right Now!" Glasstire. June 29, 2019. https://glasstire.com/2019/06/29/the-occult-is-so-hot-right-now.

Reid, John. *The Law of Blood: The Primitive Law of the Cherokee Nation.* Northern Illinois University Press, 2006.

Reinberg, Steven. "1 In 5 People Living in Conflict Areas Has a Mental Health Problem." HealthDay.com. June, 12, 2019. https://consumer.healthday.com/public-health-information-30/war-health-news-788/1-in-5-people-living-in-conflict-areas-has-a-mental-health-problem-747297.html.

"Religions." Pew Research online. Accessed December 29, 2022, https://www.pewresearch.org/religion/religious-landscape-study.

"Religious Views of Adolf Hitler." Wikipedia Foundation. Last edited January 3, 2023. https://en.wikipedia.org/wiki/Religious_views_of_Adolf_Hitler.

Revel, Jean-François and J. F. Bernard. *Without **Marx** or Jesus: The New American Revolution Has Begun.* Garden City: Doubleday, 1971.

Richter, Jean-Paul. *The Notebooks of Leonardo Davinci, Vol. 2.* Mineola, New York: Dover Publications, 2016.

Robinson, Howard. *Bayle the Sceptic.* New York: Columbia University Press, 2020.

Rodriguez, Cecilia. "Euthanasia Tourism: Is the E.U. Encouraging Its Growth?" Forbes online. March 17, 2019. https://www.forbes.com/sites/ceciliarodriguez/2019/03/17/euthanasia-tourism-is-the-e-u-encouraging-its-growth.

Rohwerder, Brigitte. "Conflict Analysis of Kenya." University of Birmingham online. May, 2015. https://gsdrc.org/publications/conflict-analysis-of-kenya.

Romey, Kristin. "Exclusive: Ancient Mass Child Sacrifice in Peru May Be World's Largest." National Geographic online. April 26, 2018. https://www.nationalgeographic.com/science/article/mass-child-human-animal-sacrifice-peru-chimu-science.

Rothman, Stanley, S. Robert Lichter, Neil Nevitter. "Politics and Professional Advancement Among College Faculty." *The Forum* 3. No. 1. Toronto: University of Toronto, 2005. https://studentsforacademicfreedom.org/wp-content/uploads/2020/05/Politics_Faculty.pdf.

Rousseau, Jean Jacques. *The Social Contract.* Vol. 4. No. 8. Transl. H.J. Tozer. London: Swan Sonnenschein, 1895.

Rubin, Jerry. *Do It: Scenarios of the Revolution.* New York: Simon & Schuster, 1970.

Russell, Bertrand. *History of Western Philosophy, The.* New York: Simon & Schuster, 1972.

Russell, Bertrand. *In Praise of Idleness and Other Essays.* London: Allen and Unwin, 1976.

Saad, Lydia. "Do American Believe in UFOs?" Gallup, Inc. August 20, 2021. https://news.gallup.com/poll/350096/americans-believe-ufos.aspx.

Saffy, Jacqueline. "Child Sexual Abuse as a Precursor to Prostitution." *Social Work* 39. No. 2. (August 2014). https://www.researchgate.net/publication/276320820_Child_sexual_abuse_as_a_precursor_to_prostitution.

Salvo, Victor. "Carl Wittman – Nominee." The Legacy Project. Accessed October 30, 2022. https://legacyprojectchicago.org/person/carl-wittman.

Schenoni, Luis and Scott Mainwaring. "Democracy is in crisis in Latin America. Brazil may be the next trouble spot." The Washington Post online. October 22, 2018. https://www.washingtonpost.com/news/monkey-cage/wp/2018/10/22/democracy-is-in-crisis-in-latin-america-brazil-may-be-the-next-trouble-spot.

Schiller, Friedrich. *Correspondence Between Schiller and Goethe from 1794 to 1805.* New York: Wiley and Putnam, 1845. https://archive.org/details/correspondencebe01schi/page/n9/mode/2up.

Seeskin, Kenneth. s.v. "Maimonides." In *Stanford Encyclopedia of Philosophy.* February 4, 2021. https://plato.stanford.edu/entries/maimonides.

Seng, MJ. "Child Sexual Abuse and Adolescent Prostitution: A Comparative Analysis." *Adolescence* 24. No. 95. 1989: 665-75. https://pubmed.ncbi.nlm.nih.gov/2801287.

"Share of Households Donating to Charity Drops to Lowest Level in Nearly 20 Years." *The Chronicle of Philanthropy.* July 27, 2021. https://www.philanthropy.com/newsletter/philanthrophy-today/2021-07-27.

Sharkey, Joe. "Word for Word/the Case Against the Nazis; How Hitler's Forces Planned to Destroy German Christianity." The New York Times online. January 13, 2002. https://www.nytimes.com/2002/01/13/weekinreview/word-for-word-case-against-nazis-hitler-s-forces-planned-destroy-german.html.

Shelley, Percy. *Vindication of a Natural Diet. Prose Works of the Romantic Period.* London: Penguin, 1956.

Shin, Sunny Hyucksun. "Childhood Sexual Abuse and Adolescent Substance Use: A Latent Class Analysis." Drug Alcohol Depend 109. Nos. 1-3. June 2010: 226-35. https://pubmed.ncbi.nlm.nih.gov/20197217.

Showalter, Brandon. "Witches Outnumber Presbyterians in the US; Wicca, Paganism Growing 'Astronomically.'" *The Christian Post.* October 10, 2018. https://www.christianpost.com/news/witches-outnumber-presbyterians-in-the-us-wicca-paganism-growing-astronomically.html.

Showalter, Monica. "Six Principles of Propaganda Lenin Used to Consolidate Power." Investor's Business Daily online. September 20, 2013. https://www.investors.com/politics/commentary/lenin-used-six-principles-of-propaganda-to-consolidate-control.

Shwayder, Maya. "A Same-Sex Domestic Violence Epidemic Is Silent." Atlantic Media Company. November 5, 2013. https://www.theatlantic.com/health/archive/2013/11/a-same-sex-domestic-violence-epidemic-is-silent/281131.

Sickinger, Raymond L. "Hitler and the Occult: The Magical Thinking of Adolf Hitler." *The Journal of Popular Culture* 34. No. 2. March, 2004: 107-225. https://www.researchgate.net/publication/229795572_Hitler_and_the_Occult_The_Magical_Thinking_of_Adolf_Hitler.

Silbert, MH. "Substance Abuse and Prostitution." *Psychoactive Drugs* 14. No. 3. (July 1982): 193-7. https://pubmed.ncbi.nlm.nih.gov/7143150.

Smith, Tom W. "Public Attitudes toward Homosexuality." NORC/University of Chicago. September 2011. https://www.norc.org/PDFs/2011%20GSS%20Reports/GSS_Public%20Attitudes%20Toward%20Homosexuality_Sept2011.pdf.

Smith, Tom. "Attitudes Towards Sexual Permissiveness: Trends, Correlates, and Behavioral Connections." University of Chicago. January 1994. https://www.researchgate.net/publication/237440754.

Sociology of Religion. Vol. 70. No. 3. *JSTOR.* Oxford: Oxford University Press, 2009. https://www.jstor.org/stable/i40016531.

Soto, Onell R. "'FBI Targets Pedophila Advocates.'" The San Diego Union-Tribune online. 2005. https://www.sandiegouniontribune.com.

Speer, Albert. "Religious Views of Adolf Hitler." Wikipedia Foundation. Accessed June 18, 2023. https://en.wikipedia.org/wiki/Religious_views_of_Adolf_Hitler.

Spencer, Nick. "Darwin's Complex Loss of Faith." The Guardian online. September 17, 2009. https://www.theguardian.com/commentisfree/belief/2009/sep/17/darwin-evolution-religion.

St. Augustine. *The City of God, The.* Garden City, NY: Doubleday, 1958.

St. Augustine. *Confessions.* London: Everyman's Library, 1975.

St. Augustine. *Confessions: Book XII.* New York: J.M. Dent & Sons, 1975.

St. Irenaeus. *Detection and Overthrow of the Gnosis Falsely So Called.* Collegeville: The Liturgical Press, 1970.

Stanford Encyclopedia of Philosophy. s.v. "Johann Gottfried von Herder." October 23, 2001. https://plato.stanford.edu/entries/herder.

Stoll, Julia. "Opinion on sex in TV shows in the U.S. 2019." January 13, 2021. Statista.com. https://www.statista.com/statistics/990852/sex-tv-shows-us.

Strmiska, Michael F., ed. *Modern Paganism in World Cultures: Comparative Perspectives.* Oxford: ABC-Clio, 2005.

Suicide Worldwide in 2019." World Health Organization. June 16, 2021. https://www.who.int/publications-detail-redirect/9789240026643.

Syphilis Statistics." Centers for Disease Control and Prevention. April 11, 2023. https://www.cdc.gov/std/syphilis/stats.htm.

Tatara, Christopher. "Hitler, Himmler, and Christianity in the Early Third Reich." *Constructing the Past* 14. No. 1. (April 2013). https://digitalcommons.iwu.edu/cgi/viewcontent.cgi?article=&context=constructing.

Taylor, Angus. "The Significance of Darwinian Theory for Marx and Engels." *Philosophy of the Social Sciences* 19. No. 4 (1989): https://doi.org/10.1177/004839318901900401.

Terry, Karen J. and Joshua D. Freilich. "Understanding Child Sexual Abuse by Catholic Priests From a Situational Perspective." *Journal of Child Sexual Abuse* 21. No. 4. (July 2012): 437-55. DOI: 10.1080/10538712.2012.693579.

Tertullian. *Apology, Faith of the Early Fathers.* Vol. 1. Ed. William A. Jurgens. Collegeville, MN: The Liturgical Press, 1070.

Thiery, Paul-Henry and Baron D'Holbach. "Nature and her Laws." In *The System of Nature.* Translated by Samuel Wilkinson. https://www.informationphilosopher.com/solutions/philosophers/dholbach/System_of_Nature.html#link2H_4_0008.

Thijssen, Hans. *Stanford Encyclopedia of Philosophy.* s.v "Condemnation of 1277." January 30, 2003. https://plato.stanford.edu/entries/condemnation.

Tillich, Paul. *The Protestant Era.* Chicago: The University of Chicago Press, 1966.

Tsanoff, Radoslav Andrea. "Goethe and philosophy." *Rice Institute Pamphlet—Rice University Studies* 19. No. 2. 1932. https://hdl.handle.net/1911/8553.

U.N. Suspends Group in Dispute Over Pedophilia." The New York Times online. September 18, 1994. https://www.nytimes.com/1994/09/18/world/un-suspends-group-in-dispute-over-pedophilia.html.

United States Congress House on Committee on Un-American Activities. *Facts on Communism: the Soviet Union, from Lenin to Khrushchev.* Vol. 1. Washington, D.C.: U.S. G.P.O., 1961.

VerBruggen, Robert. "Is Monagamy Unnatural?" Institute of Family Studies. March 29, 2016. https://ifstudies.org/blog/is-monogamy-unnatural.

Villa, Virginia. "Four-in-Ten Countries and Territories Worldwide Had Blasphemy Laws in 2019." Pew Research Center. Accessed January 25, 2022. https://www.pewresearch.org/fact-tank/2022/01/25/four-in-ten-countries-and-territories-worldwide-had-blasphemy-laws-in-2019-2.

"Violence against Women." World Health Organization. Accessed August 31, 2022. https://www.who.int/news-room/fact-sheets/detail/violence-against-women.

Von Hagen, Victor Wolfgang. *Encyclopedia Britannica.* s.v. "Inca Religion." Accessed October 18, 2022. https://www.britannica.com/topic/Inca-religion.

Von Holbach, Baron. "Priest." In *Good Sense Without God.* London: W. Stewart & Co, 1772.

Walker, Williston. *A History of The Christian Church.* New York: Charles Scribner's Son, 1970.

"What Is Human Trafficking?" DHS.gov. Accessed October 22, 2022. https://www.dhs.gov/blue-campaign/what-human-trafficking.

Whelchel, Hugh. "How the Reformation Changed Education Forever." Institute For Faith, Work & Economics. June 26, 2017. https://tifwe.org/how-the-reformation-changed-education-forever/.

"Why Americans Go (and Don't Go) to Religious Services." Pew Research Center's Religion & Public Life Project. Pew Research Center. August 1, 2018. https://www.pewresearch.org.

Wildsmith, Elizabeth, Jennifer Manlove, and Elizabeth Cook. "Dramatic Increase in the Proportion of Births Outside of Marriage in the United States from 1990 to 2016." Child Trends. August 8, 2018. https://www.childtrends.org/publications/dramatic-increase-in-percentage-of-births-outside-marriage-among-whites-hispanics-and-women-with-higher-education-levels.

Wootton, David. "Helvetius: From Enlightenment to Revolution." *Political Theory* 28. No. 3. June 2000: 307-336. https://www.jstor.org/stable/192208.

"Worst Decades for Crime, The." World Atlas online. Accessed July 9, 2017. https://www.worldatlas.com/articles/which-decade-had-the-most-crime.html.

Wright, Chrysalis L. and M. Craske. "Music's Influence on Risky Sexual Behavior: Examining the Cultivation Theory." *Media Psychology Review* 9. No. 1. (2015). https://mprcenter.org/review/musics-influence-on-risky-sexual-behaviors-examining-the-cultivation-theory.

Wright, Paul J. and Edward I. Donnerstein. "Sex Online: Pornography, Sexual Solicitation, and Sexting." *Adolescent Medicine State of the Art Reviews* 25. No. 3. December 2014: 574-89. https://experts.arizona.edu/en/publications/sex-online-pornography-sexual-solicitation-and-sexting.

Ybarra, Michele L. "Sexual Media Exposure, Sexual Behavior, and Sexual Violence Victimization in Adolescence." *Clinical Pediatrics* 53. No. 15. (November 2014): 1239-47. https://pubmed.ncbi.nlm.nih.gov/24928575.

Yennah, Robert. "Nature, Nurture, and the Mathematics of Culture in the Light of Selected Works of Voltaire and Rousseau." *Logon Journal of the Humanities*. Vol. 19. https://www.ajol.info/index.php/ljh/article/view/121519.

Zepp-LaRouche, Helga. *The Hitler Book*. New York: New Benjamin Franklin House, 1984.

Zinsmeister, Karl. "Less God, Less Giving?" *Philanthropy Roundtable*. Winter 2019. https://www.philanthropyroundtable.org/magazine/less-god-less-giving.

Zoba, Wendy Murray. "'Do You Believe in God?" ChristianityToday online. October 4, 1999. https://www.christianitytoday.com/ct/1999/october4/columbine-shooting-do-you-believe-in-god.html.

Zurlo, Dr. Gina A. "Who Owns Global Christianity?" Gordon Conwell Theological Seminary. September 27, 2019. https://www.gordonconwell.edu/blog/who-owns-global-christianity.

INDEX

B

DISCOGRAPHY

Dylan, Bob, "Gotta Serve Somebody." 1 1072. *Gotta Serve Somebody.* Columbia Records, 1979.

For more information about

William D. Howard
and
American Crisis
please visit:

www.williamdhowardauthor.com

For more information about
AMBASSADOR INTERNATIONAL
please visit:

www.ambassador-international.com
@AmbassadorIntl
www.facebook.com/AmbassadorIntl

Thank you for reading this book!

You make it possible for us to fulfill our mission, and we are grateful for your partnership.

To help further our mission, please consider leaving us a review on your social media, favorite retailer's website, Goodreads or Bookbub, or our website, and check out some of the books on the following page!

MORE FROM AMBASSADOR INTERNATIONAL

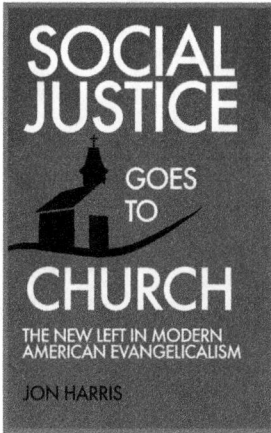

SOCIAL JUSTICE GOES TO CHURCH

THE NEW LEFT IN MODERN AMERICAN EVANGELICALISM

JON HARRIS

As pro-life evangelicals rush to support movements like #BlackLivesMatter and #MeToo, it is important to realize they are walking in footprints already laid down. Their mission may be more successful, but it is not new. To understand where the evangelical social justice movement is heading, it is vital to understand the origins of the movement.

Social Justice Goes to Church: The New Left in Modern American Evangelicalism answers, from a historical perspective, the vital question, "Why are American evangelicals moving Left?"

In *Political Correctness Does More Harm Than Good*, Douglas Kruger looks at each of the most popular arguments—their origins, their purpose, and their lies—and helps the reader fight back with the truth. In a politically correct world, Douglas Kruger helps the reader to see that being politically correct isn't creating peace but instead is starting a war. And he gives us the tools we need to ready ourselves for the fight for right.

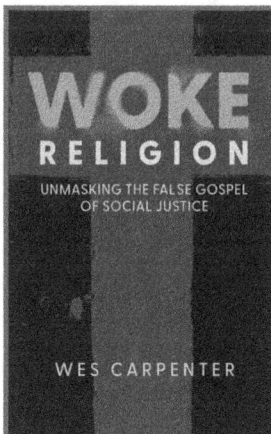

HOW TO
IDENTIFY, DEBUNK, AND DISMANTLE
DANGEROUS IDEAS

POLITICAL CORRECTNESS DOES MORE **HARM** THAN GOOD

DOUGLAS KRUGER

WOKE RELIGION

UNMASKING THE FALSE GOSPEL OF SOCIAL JUSTICE

WES CARPENTER

In today's society, everyone, including Christians, wants to be "woke." As woke critical theory seeps through the teachings of the Church, many Christians are being misled by their own spiritual leaders to take part in the newest attempt for their souls. Wes Carpenter unashamedly addresses these heretical teachings, calling on those in spiritual authority to deny woke philosophies and cling to the teachings of Scripture. Follow Wes as he takes the reader from the stirrings of woke critical theory in the early church to the teachings that are pervading the church today.

www.ingramcontent.com/pod-product-compliance
Lightning Source LLC
Chambersburg PA
CBHW050456270326
41927CB00009B/1769